On the cover: Residents inspect a police patrol van outside Sheka police station in the northern Nigerian city of Kano on 25 January 2012. The van was burned in bomb and shooting attacks on the police station the previous night by approximately 30 members of Boko Haram, wounding a policeman and killing a female visitor, according to residents. Photo used by permission of Newscom.

JOINT SPECIAL OPERATIONS

JSOU

UNIVERSITY

Confronting the Terrorism of Boko Haram in Nigeria

James J.F. Forest

JSOU Report 12-5
The JSOU Press
MacDill Air Force Base, Florida
2012

This monograph and other JSOU publications can be found at https://jsou.socom. mil. Click on Publications. Comments about this publication are invited and should be forwarded to Director, Strategic Studies Department, Joint Special Operations University, 7701 Tampa Point Blvd., MacDill AFB FL 33621.

****

The JSOU Strategic Studies Department is currently accepting written works relevant to special operations for potential publication. For more information please contact the JSOU Research Director at jsou_research@socom.mil. Thank you for your interest in the JSOU Press.

****

This work was cleared for public release; distribution is unlimited.

ISBN 978-1-933749-70-9

Recent Publications of the JSOU Press

Contents

Foreword

In this monograph counterterrorism expert James Forest assesses the threat Boko Haram poses to Nigeria and U.S. national security interests. As Dr. Forest notes, Boko Haram is largely a local phenomenon, though one with strategic implications, and must be understood and addressed within its local context and the long standing grievances that motivate terrorist activity. Dr. Forest deftly explores Nigeria's ethnic fissures and the role of unequal distribution of power in fueling terrorism. Indeed, these conditions, combined with the ready availability of weapons, contribute to Nigeria's other security challenges including militancy in the Niger Delta and organized crime around the economic center of the country, Lagos.

Born of colonial rule the modern state of Nigeria contains a multitude of ethno linguistic groups and tribes, religious traditions, and local histories. This complexity, spread out across diverse environments from the coastal southern lowlands to the dry and arid north, has long posed a daunting challenge to governance and stability. Nigeria has had 14 heads of state since independence in 1958—many of these have taken power by military coup, while only five, including the current president Goodluck Jonathan, have been elected. Approximately half of the population is Christian, the other half Muslim, adding a religious dimension to Nigeria's contested political life. Many groups feel economically and politically marginalized, a situation that increased following the discovery of significant oil reserves in the Niger Delta and offshore. Corruption is rife and state institutions are weak.

It is within this larger context that a group calling themselves Boko Haram, a Hausa term meaning "Western education is forbidden," appeared in 2009 and has attacked Nigeria, a key U.S. ally. Government entities, such as police stations and politicians (both Christian and Muslim), as well as others who they feel act in an 'un-Islamic' manner have been the primary focus of these attacks. The sect, which is loosely organized and contains numerous disagreeing factions, is centered in northeastern Nigeria. Most of its members are from the Kanuri tribe; it has little following among other ethnic groups in the region or other parts of Nigeria. Why then, do some find the group's violent ideology attractive?

To meet the security challenges posed by the Boko Haram and others, Dr. Forest advocates the use of intelligence-led policing and trust building between the government and citizenry. Nongovernmental organizations and community actors, which have legitimacy based on tribal or ethnic affiliations, should also play a key role in a broad spectrum approach that addresses both the terrorist threat of Boko Haram and the root grievances of the communities in which they operate.

Such an approach is in accordance with the whole-of-government or comprehensive approach that characterizes Special Operations Forces (SOF) missions and activities. Indeed, given Nigeria's role as a key U.S. strategic ally, the SOF community needs to acquire a nuanced understanding of its security challenges. We offer this monograph as a resource for anyone who wishes to learn more about this pivotal state, the challenges it faces, and possible means to address them.

Kenneth H. Poole, Ed.D.
Director, JSOU Strategic Studies Department

About the Author

James J.F. Forest, Ph.D. is an associate professor at the University of Massachusetts Lowell, where he teaches undergraduate and graduate courses on terrorism, weapons of mass destruction, and security studies. He is also a senior fellow with the Joint Special Operations University.

Dr. Forest is the former Director of Terrorism Studies at the United States Military Academy. During his tenure on the faculty (2001-2010) he taught courses in terrorism, counterterrorism, information warfare, international relations, comparative politics, and sub-Saharan Africa. He also directed a series of research initiatives and education programs for the Combating Terrorism Center at West Point, covering topics such as terrorist recruitment, training, and organizational knowledge transfer. Dr. Forest was selected by the Center for American Progress and Foreign Policy as one of "America's most esteemed terrorism and national security experts" and participated in their annual Terrorism Index studies (2006-2010). He has been interviewed by many newspaper, radio, and television journalists, and is regularly invited to give speeches and lectures in the U.S. and other countries. He has published 14 books and dozens of articles in journals such as Terrorism and Political Violence, Contemporary Security Policy, Crime and Delinquency, Perspectives on Terrorism, the Cambridge Review of International Affairs, the Georgetown Journal of International Affairs, the Journal of Political Science Education, and Democracy and Security. He has also served as an advisor to the Future of War panel for the Defense Science Board, and has testified before committees of the U.S. Senate.

His recent books include: *Weapons of Mass Destruction and Terrorism*, 2nd edition (McGraw-Hill, 2011, with Russell Howard); *Influence Warfare: How Terrorists and Governments Fight to Shape Perceptions in a War of Ideas* (Praeger, 2009); *Handbook of Defence Politics: International and Comparative Perspectives* (Routledge, 2008, with Isaiah Wilson); *Countering Terrorism and Insurgency in the 21st Century* (3 volumes: Praeger, 2007); *Teaching Terror:*

Strategic and Tactical Learning in the Terrorist World (Rowman & Littlefield, 2006); *Homeland Security: Protecting America's Targets* (3 volumes: Praeger, 2006); *The Making of a Terrorist: Recruitment, Training and Root Causes* (3 volumes: Praeger, 2005).

Dr. Forest received his graduate degrees from Stanford University and Boston College, and undergraduate degrees from Georgetown University and De Anza College.

Preface

The Islamic sect Boko Haram has been a security challenge to Nigeria since at least 2009, but the group has recently expanded its terrorist attacks to include international targets such as the United Nations building in Abuja in August 2011. In November 2011, the U.S. Department of State issued an alert for all U.S. and Western citizens in Abuja to avoid major hotels and landmarks, based on information about a potential Boko Haram attack. Their attack capabilities have become more sophisticated, and there are indications that members of this group may have received training in bomb-making and other terrorist tactics from al-Qaeda-affiliated groups in the north and/or east of the continent. A spate of attacks against churches from December 2011 through February 2012 suggests a strategy of provocation, through which the group seeks to spark a large scale sectarian conflict that will destabilize the county. These are troubling developments in an already troubled region, and the international community is focusing an increasing amount of attention on the situation.

This monograph explores the origins and future trajectory of Boko Haram, and especially why its ideology of violence has found resonance among a small number of young Nigerians. It is organized in sequential layers of analysis, with chapters that examine the grievances that motivate members and sympathizers of Boko Haram, sociopolitical factors that sustain their ideological resonance and operational capabilities, and how the Nigerian government has responded to the threat of terrorism in recent years. Special attention is given to the role of nongovernmental entities in the fight against Boko Haram—community and religious entities that have considerable influence among potential recruits and supporters of this group. These entities can play an important role in countering the group's ideology and the socioeconomic and religious insecurities upon which its resonance is based. Based on this analysis, the monograph concludes by identifying ways in which Nigeria could respond more effectively to the threat posed by Boko Haram, and provides some thoughts for how the U.S., and particularly Special Operations Forces, may contribute to these efforts. The observations provided in this JSOU monograph are based on interviews conducted during a research trip to Nigeria and via email, as well as extensive analysis of academic publications and open source documents.

The security situation in northern Nigeria is very dynamic and constantly evolving, thus a list of resources is offered in Appendix B for those interested in additional information.

Acknowledgments

Producing this research monograph required assistance from a number of individuals. To begin with, I must extend my sincere thanks to Mukhtari Shitu, Ibaba Samuel Ibaba, Jennifer Giroux, Peter Nwilo, Freedom Onouha, Lieutenant Colonel Matt Sousa, and Thomas Maettig for their invaluable assistance in arranging local interviews in Nigeria, to include places that I most likely wouldn't have been able to visit otherwise. Of course, any errors of fact or interpretation in this monograph are entirely my own. Also, the professional and administrative staff at the Joint Special Operations University provided a broad range of critical logistics support for my research trips to West Africa, and I am very grateful for all their efforts and patience. Further gratitude is given to Dr. Kenneth Poole and his senior colleagues in the Strategic Studies Department of the university, who graciously allowed me the flexibility to adapt a previously envisioned (but ultimately untenable) research project on West Africa into this focused study of Boko Haram. Finally, I give thanks to my family—Alicia, Chloe, and Jackson—for their patience and support.

1. Introduction

Nigeria, a key strategic ally of the U.S., has come under attack by a radical Islamic sect known as Boko Haram (a Hausa term for "Western education is forbidden"). It officially calls itself "Jama'atul Alhul Sunnah Lidda'wati wal Jihad" which means "people committed to the propagation of the Prophet's teachings and jihad." As its name suggests, the group is adamantly opposed to what it sees as a Western-based incursion that threatens traditional values, beliefs, and customs among Muslim communities in northern Nigeria. In an audiotape posted on the Internet in January 2012, a spokesman for the group, Abubakar Shekau, even accused the U.S. of waging war on Islam.[1] As will be described in this monograph, the group is largely a product of widespread socioeconomic and religious insecurities, and its ideology resonates among certain communities because of both historical narratives and modern grievances.

Members of Boko Haram are drawn primarily from the Kanuri tribe (roughly 4 percent of the population), who are concentrated in the northeastern states of Nigeria like Bauchi and Borno, and the Hausa and Fulani (29 percent of the population) spread more generally throughout most of the northern states. Kanuri also inhabit regions across the northern border into Niger, and there is evidence to suggest that these tribal relationships facilitate weapons trafficking and other cross-border smuggling transactions, but this is the extent to which Boko Haram's activities go outside Nigeria. While it is very much a locally-oriented movement, the group has not yet attracted a significant following among Nigerians of other tribal or ethnic backgrounds. Further, it has thus far proven difficult for the group to find sympathizers or anyone who would help them facilitate attacks further south, thus the majority of attacks have taken place within the north (and primarily northeastern corner) of the country. Since 2009, the group has attacked police stations and patrols, politicians (including village chiefs and a member of parliament), religious leaders (both Christian and Muslim), and individuals whom they deem to be engaged in un-Islamic activities, like drinking beer. Boko Haram has also carried out several mass casualty attacks and is the first militant group in Nigeria to embrace the use of suicide bombings. A representative list of these attacks is provided in Appendix A of this monograph.

Within the last year, Boko Haram expanded its terrorist attacks in Nigeria to include international targets, such as the United Nations (UN) building in Abuja in August 2011. The group also made significant leaps in its operational capability,[2] and there are indications that members of the group have received weapons and training in bomb-making and other terrorist tactics from al-Qaeda affiliates in the north and/or east of the continent. In November 2011, the U.S. Department of State issued an alert for all U.S. and Western citizens in Abuja to avoid major hotels and landmarks, based on information about a potential Boko Haram attack. A recent report by the U.S. House of Representatives expressed concerns about Boko Haram attacks against the aviation and energy sectors as well.[3] However, the overwhelming majority of the group's attacks have been focused on local targets, which makes sense given the local orientation of their ideology and strategy. For example, a spate of attacks against churches from December 2011 through February 2012 are seen by many as but the latest attempt to provoke Christians into retaliatory attacks against Muslims, part of an overall effort to spark widespread sectarian conflict in order to destabilize the government. As the later chapters of this monograph will discuss, the strategy pursued by Boko Haram has found only limited success, and there is a strong likelihood that they will eventually fail. The question then becomes how Nigeria, perhaps with the assistance of the U.S. and other allies, can expedite the eventual demise of this group, and minimize the amount of death and destruction Boko Haram will cause before they follow the typical trajectory of most terrorist groups into the bins of history.

It is important to note that Boko Haram is not a unified, monolithic entity. There are separate factions within the movement who disagree about tactics and strategic direction; in some cases they compete against each other for attention and followers. A recent U.S. House of Representatives report suggested that one faction of the group may be focused on domestic issues and another on violent international extremism.[4] Another report published in November 2011 indicated that the group may have even split into three factions: one that remains moderate and welcomes an end to the violence; another that wants a peace agreement; and a third that refuses to negotiate and wants to implement strict Shariah law across Nigeria.[5] There is at the very least evidence of disagreements among some Boko Haram members. In July 2011, a group calling itself the Yusufiyya Islamic Movement distributed leaflets widely in Maiduguri denouncing other Boko Haram factions as "evil." The authors of the leaflet, asserting the legacy of founder Mohammed Yusuf, distanced themselves from attacks on civilians and on houses of worship.[6] Some local observers now discriminate between a Kogi Boko Haram, Kanuri Boko Haram, and Hausa Fulani Boko Haram. And there are also individuals or groups of armed thugs whose attacks on banks or other targets are blamed on Boko Haram; in some cases, the perpetrators will even claim they are members of Boko Haram, when in truth they are motivated more by criminal objectives than by Boko Haram's core ideological or religious objectives.

Helping Nigeria confront this complex, multifaceted terrorist threat is in the interests of the U.S. and the international community. In early 2012, Nigerian President Goodluck Jonathan declared a state of emergency in four states—Yobe, Borno, Plateau, and Niger—in concert with the deployment of armed forces, the temporary closing of international borders in the northern regions, and the establishment of a special counterterrorism force. Should the country's latest efforts to confront and defeat Boko Haram fail, the terrorist violence could worsen, undermining an already fragile regime and possibly spilling over into neighboring countries. As the region's largest oil supplier, the global economic impact of a prolonged campaign of terrorism could be severe. The human toll of the terrorist violence is also reaching very worrisome levels; several hundred Nigerians were killed or injured in Boko Haram attacks in just the first two months of 2012.

This study is offered as a resource for those engaged in policy or strategic deliberations about how to assist Nigeria in confronting the threat of Boko Haram. The observations provided here are based on interviews conducted during a research trip to Nigeria and via email, as well as extensive analysis of academic publications and open source documents. The monograph is especially intended as a useful background for members of U.S. Special Operations Forces (SOF) with interests (or mission assignments) in sub-Saharan Africa. Much of the analysis illustrates the complex and intersecting kinds of information needed to understand the phenomenon of modern religiously-inspired domestic terrorism, so it should hopefully be useful to the general counterterrorism practitioner as well. It seeks to address several basic questions, including: How did Boko Haram emerge? Is it different from other terrorist groups? What do SOF leaders need to know about Boko Haram, and what does it represent in terms of broader security challenges in Nigeria or West Africa? And finally, what might SOF—if called upon—want or need to do in response to the terrorist threat of Boko Haram? To begin the discussion, this introductory chapter reviews the main themes addressed in the monograph and explains how these relate to the research literature in the field of terrorism studies.

Conceptual Framework and Organization of the Monograph

Terrorism is a highly contextual phenomenon. Indeed, the old maxim that "all politics is local" holds true for political violence as well. We sometimes hear a lot of talk about terrorism as if it were a monolithic, easily understood term, but it is really the opposite. Terrorism is a complex issue that has been studied and debated for several decades. In fact, there are dozens of competing definitions of the term, not only among scholars but among policymakers and government agencies as well. But one thing holds constant—terrorist attacks do not occur in a vacuum, but are instead a product of complex interactions between individuals, organizations, and environments.[7] Further, there are many different kinds of terrorism, defined primarily by ideological orientations like ethno-nationalism, left-wing, religious, and so forth. And just like there are many different kinds of terrorism, there are many different kinds of contexts in which terrorism occurs.

Within each context, we find a variety of grievances that motivate the terrorist group and its supporters, along with things that facilitate terrorist activities. From decades of research on these grievances and facilitators, two primary themes appear most salient for this research monograph on Boko Haram: preconditions, or "things that exist," and triggers, or "things that happen."[8] Chapter 2 thus provides a brief examination of Nigeria's political history, with an emphasis on how the government has struggled to develop legitimacy among its citizens. Of particular note, as Alex Thurston recently observed, state legitimacy is at its weakest in the northeast.[9] Naturally, the early history of West Africa is also salient: centuries of slave traders robbed the continent of its most productive laborers, then came the era of colonization by Western European powers, followed by independence movements, civil wars, and military coups. However, due to space constraints, Chapter 2 does not delve much into this deeper history, and focuses just on the post-independence era of Nigeria.

This is followed in Chapter 3 with a discussion of key grievances that are shared by most Nigerians. Generally speaking, the research literature describes grievances as structural reasons for why the ideology resonates among a particular community, and can include a broad range of political issues like incompetent, authoritarian, or corrupt governments, as well as economic issues like widespread poverty, unemployment, or an overall lack of political or socioeconomic opportunities. Terrorism is most often fueled by individuals and groups who are very dissatisfied with the status quo, and have come to believe in the need to use violence because they see no other way to facilitate change. In essence, they draw on what Harvard psychologist John Mack described as a reservoir of misery, hurt, helplessness, and rage from which the foot soldiers of terrorism can be recruited."[10] Clearly, one can find such a reservoir in many parts of Nigeria, and indeed throughout much of sub-Saharan Africa.

Terrorism is also seen as a violent product of an unequal distribution of power on local, national, or global levels. The unequal distribution of power feeds a perception of "us versus them," a perception found in all ideologies associated with politically violent groups and movements. The hardships and challenges "we" face can be framed in terms of what "they" are or what "they" have done to us. From this perspective, "we" desire a redistribution of power in order to have more control over our destiny, and one could argue that many terrorist groups use violence as the way to bring this about. As Bruce Hoffman notes, terrorism is "the deliberate creation and exploitation of fear through violence or the threat of violence in the pursuit of political change . . . [and] to create power where there is none or to consolidate power where there is very little."[11] There are few places on earth where the unequal distribution of power is more common than in sub-Saharan Africa. And in Nigeria, ethnic fissures are politicized and negatively impact a person's overall quality of life and their relative power to bring about change. Further, Muslims in Northern Nigeria at one point in history enjoyed considerably more power relative to others in West Africa, but they have witnessed the fall of the Sokoto Caliphate, the rise of Western European colonization followed by successive military regimes, and now a secular democracy. Furthermore, unemployment and illiteracy are highest in the northern parts of Nigeria, where Muslims are predominant. In essence, power—or lack thereof—plays an important role in the narrative of Boko Haram.

Government corruption is also cited by many researchers as a frequent motivator behind collective political violence, and is highlighted in Chapter 3. In states where such corruption is endemic, resources, privileges, and advantages are reserved for a select group of the people or ruling elite. Corruption encumbers the fair distribution of social services and adds another layer to the resentment caused by the lack of political participation. The rest of society, because they have no voice, is ignored or placated. This corruption erodes the government's legitimacy in the eyes of its citizens.[12] In Nigeria, as in much of West Africa, a combination of statist economic policies (building on the early post-independence nationalization of former colonial private industries) combined with patronage systems to create an environment in which the state became seen as a means of access to wealth, rather than a means to serve the people.

When a government fails to adhere to the conventional social contract between government and the governed, its citizens become disenchanted and seek the power to force change. This, in turn, has resulted in a variety of revolutionary movements throughout history. Corrupt governments seek to maintain and increase their power over others and over resources by any means necessary, while the powerless see the corruption and look for ways to combat it—even through violent acts of terrorism, as that may be perceived as their only form of recourse. In the African context, corruption has indeed been a common underlying factor in various forms of political violence, and is cited often by Boko Haram as one of the motivating causes for their campaign of terror.

> *When a government fails to adhere to the conventional social contract between government and the governed, its citizens become disenchanted and seek the power to force change.*

Beyond grievances, the study of terrorism also looks at a range of facilitators, loosely defined as the structural or temporary conditions at the community or regional level that provide individuals and organizations with ample opportunities to engage in various forms of terrorist activity. Chapter 4 looks specifically at security challenges that have plagued Nigeria for many years, focusing on three hotspots in particular: militants in the Niger Delta (southeast), organized crime in Lagos (southwest), and Boko Haram, based mainly in Borno and Bauchi states (northeast). In all three cases, the rise of violence has been aided by the availability of small arms and light weapons.[13] Meanwhile, traffickers in drugs, humans, and weapons cohabit with the warlords, militia leaders, and political opportunists in an environment that precludes good governance and judicial oversight.[14] Countries like Nigeria with a robust "shadow economy"—economic activities that are underground, covert, or illegal—can provide an infrastructure for terrorist organizations to operate in, whereby financing becomes easier and detecting it becomes more difficult.[15]

Chapter 5 then turns to look at the organization of Boko Haram itself. Here, in addition to describing the group's formation and initial leadership, we also have to look at how potential triggers may contribute to the emergence of a religiously oriented terrorist group like this. While the preconditions for terrorism are aplenty in northern Nigeria, the tough questions to answer here include: What has led to the current outbreak of violence, predominately, but not exclusively, in the form of Boko Haram? Have conditions somehow worsened in recent years? Is the violence largely a result of a particularly popular radicalizing agent? Studies of terrorism have described "triggers" as specific actions, policies, and events that enhance the perceived need for action within a particular environment. These are very dynamic and time-relevant, and seized upon by the propagandists of terrorist organizations in their attempts to enhance the resonance of their ideology. A trigger for action can be any number of things: a change in government policy, like the suspension of civil liberties, a banning of political parties, or the introduction of new censorship and draconian antiterrorist laws; an erosion in the security environment (like a massive influx of refugees, or a natural disaster that diverts the government's attention away from monitoring the group); a widely-publicized incident of police brutality or invasive surveillance; and even a coup, assassination, or other sudden regime change.[16] In some instances, a trigger may occur in an entirely different country. For example, the invasion and subsequent occupation of Iraq by U.S.-led coalition forces has been linked to major terrorist attacks in Madrid (2004) and London (2005), as well as in Iraq itself.

A trigger does not necessarily need to be a relatively quick or contained event. For example, research by Paul Ehrlich and Jack Liu suggests that persistent demographic and socioeconomic factors can facilitate transnational terrorism and make it easier to recruit terrorists.[17] Specifically, they describe how increased birth rates and the age composition of populations in developing countries affects resource consumption, prices, government revenues and expenditures, demand for jobs, and labor wages. In essence, these demographic and socioeconomic conditions could lead to the emergence of more terrorism and terrorists for many decades to come. Similarly, the National Intelligence Council's 2025 Project report notes that pending "youth bulges" in many Arab states could contribute to a rise in political violence and civil conflict.[18] This is particularly salient with regard to Nigeria: nearly half the population is under the age of 19.

Any potential triggers are far more likely to enhance a terrorist organization's ideological resonance when the structural conditions described earlier are already a source of grievances. A trigger could also be an event that leads to new opportunities for terrorism. For example, a sudden regime change may create an anarchic environment in which groups find greater freedom to obtain weapons and conduct criminal and violent activity. Terrorist groups will usually seize any opportunity to capitalize on events from which they could benefit strategically, tactically, or operationally.

This leads us to the case of Boko Haram: What events or contextual changes might they be capitalizing on to support their ideological rationale for violent attacks? To begin, the president of the country, Goodluck Jonathan, is a Christian from the southeast of Nigeria. In his 2011 re-election, virtually the entire northern part of the country voted for the opposition candidate. Riots erupted in various cities when the election results were announced, despite the assurances of independent observers that the voting had involved the fewest "irregularities" in Nigeria's democratic history.

Meanwhile, a growing sense of economic malaise has been felt throughout the country for some time, and is most palpable in the north, which has roughly half the gross domestic product (GDP) per capita as the south. A longstanding history of corruption and patronage at the federal, state, and local levels of government is a source of widespread dissatisfaction toward politicians, the legal system, and law enforcement, and these sentiments may be found in greater depths and concentration in the north than elsewhere in the country. As will be explored later in this monograph, several political and socioeconomic changes over the past several years can be identified as potential triggers behind the recent and growing threat of violence inflicted by members of Boko Haram. But in addition to these, a useful dimension for analysis is the impact of the slow waning of power and influence among Muslim leaders in a democratic Nigeria.

Ideological and Religious Dimensions

A terrorist group's ideology plays a vital role in an individual's decision to engage in terrorist activity by sanctioning harmful conduct as honorable and righteous. An ideology is an articulation of the group's vision of the future, a vision which its adherents believe cannot be achieved without the use of violence. These ideologies typically articulate and explain a set of grievances including socioeconomic disadvantages and a lack of justice or political freedoms that are seen as legitimate among members of a target audience, along with strategies through which the use of violence is meant to address those grievances.[19] Usually, but not always, the strategies they put forward require joining or at least supporting the organization—thus, an ideology also provides a group identity and highlights the common characteristics of individuals who adhere to, or are potential adherents of, the ideology. According to Assaf Moghadam, "ideologies are links between thoughts, beliefs and myths on the one hand, and action on the other hand ... [providing] a 'cognitive map' that filters the way social realities are perceived, rendering that reality easier to grasp, more coherent, and thus more meaningful."[20]

Research by Andrew Kydd and Barbara Walter indicates that terrorist organizations are usually driven by political objectives, and in particular, "five have had enduring importance: regime change, territorial change, policy change, social control and status quo maintenance."[21] These objectives have led to terrorist groups forming in Northern Ireland, Italy, Egypt, Germany, Sri Lanka, Japan, Indonesia, the Philippines, the United States, and many other nations. The members of these groups have viewed terrorism as an effective vehicle for political change, often pointing to historical examples of terrorism driving the United States (and later Israel) out of Lebanon, and convincing the French to pull out of Algeria. Ethnic separatist groups like the Liberation Tigers of Tamil Eelam in Sri Lanka the Abu Sayyaf Group in the Philippines and the Euskadi Ta Askatasuna in Spain all want the power to form their own recognized, sovereign entity, carved out of an existing nation-state, and believe terrorist attacks can help them achieve this objective. Groups engaged in the Middle East intifada—like the Al-Aqsa Martyrs Brigade, Hamas, the Palestinian Islamic Jihad, and the Palestine Liberation Front—want the power to establish an Islamic Palestinian state. Other groups want the power to establish an Islamic state in their own region, including Ansar al-Islam in Iraq the Armed Islamic Group in Algeria Al-Gama 'a al-Islamiyya in Egypt the Islamic Movement of Uzbekistan in Central Asia[22] Jemaah Islamiyah in Southeast Asia and al-Qaeda. In all cases, these groups seek power to change the status quo, to forge a future that they do not believe will come about peacefully, and are determined to use terrorism as a means to achieve their objectives.

A terrorist group's ideology plays a central role in its survival. From political revolutionaries to religious militants, ideologies of violence and terrorism must have resonance; that is, an ideology has no motivating power unless it resonates within the social, political, and historical context of those whose support the organization requires. The resonance of an organization's ideology is largely based on a combination of persuasive communicators, the compelling nature of the grievances articulated, and the pervasiveness of local conditions that seem to justify an organization's rationale for the use of violence in order to mitigate those grievances. When an organization's ideology resonates among its target audience, it can influence an individual's perceptions and help determine the form of their "decision tree," a menu of potential options for future action that may include terrorism. Thus, this monograph will focus particular attention on the ideology that has been articulated by leaders and spokespeople of Boko Haram in recent years. At the same time, it is important to recognize that support for terrorism among community members can rise and fall over time and is influenced by the choices made by individuals within an organization about the kinds of terrorist activities they conduct. How organizations choreograph violence matters; in particular, terrorist groups must avoid counterproductive violence that can lead to a loss of support within the community. This challenge confronts the leaders of Boko Haram, and is explored later in this monograph as a potential vulnerability of the group.

Overall, successful terrorist organizations capitalize on an environment in which their ideology resonates and their grievances are considered legitimate by smart, competent individuals who are then motivated to act either with or on behalf of the organization. The likelihood of ideological resonance is greater when members of a community are desperate for justice, social agency, human dignity, a sense of belonging, or positive identity when surrounded by a variety of depressingly negative environmental conditions, and intense outrage, or hatred of a specific entity because of their actions (real or perceived). How a local environment sustains a terrorist organization depends largely on how individuals within the community view the opportunities for that organization's success. The past also matters: Is there a history of political violence either locally or within the surrounding region? Are there regional examples of successes or failures of terrorism? These and other questions, addressed later in this monograph, inform our understanding of how a terrorist group like Boko Haram has come to exist, and how it is attracting individuals to support their cause.

Finally, our analysis of Boko Haram must take into account research on why some individuals may choose direct involvement in actions that kill, while others choose to engage in activities like providing funding, safe havens, or ideological support for a terrorist group. A variety of factors influence a person's decision to engage in terrorist activity—from kinship and ideology to the availability of weapons and criminal network connections. Scholars have also cited the importance of a person's hatred of others, desire for power or revenge, despair, risk tolerance, unbreakable loyalty to friends or family who are already involved in a violent movement, prior participation in a radical political movement, thirst for excitement and adventure, and many other types of motivations.

Over the years, psychologists have sought to illuminate a unique set of attributes that contribute to terrorism. There is clearly a demand for this among policymakers and the general public who seek clarity in what is in fact a very complex problem.[23] However, the most common result of research in this area actually reveals a pattern of "normalcy"—that is, the absence of any unique attribute or identifier that would distinguish one individual from another. Andrew Silke recently observed how research on the mental state of terrorists has found that they are rarely mad, and very few suffer from personality disorders.[24] According to John Horgan, "Many of the personal traits or characteristics [identified in the research] as belonging to the terrorist are neither specific to the terrorist nor serve to distinguish one type of terrorist from another. . . There are no a-priori qualities [of an individual] that enable us to predict the likelihood of risk of involvement and engagement" in terrorism.[25] Likewise, Clark McCauley has observed that "30 years of research has found little evidence that terrorists are suffering from psychopathology,"[26] and Marc Sageman agrees, noting how "experts on terrorism have tried in vain for three decades to identify a common predisposition for terrorism."[27]

Overall, there is no single psychology of terrorism, no unified theory.[28] The broad diversity of personal motivations for becoming a terrorist undermines the possibility of a single, common "terrorist mindset." Thus, profiling individuals based on some type of perceived propensity to conduct terrorist attacks becomes extremely difficult, if not altogether impossible.[29] This is critical for the Nigerian authorities to understand about terrorism: should they make the false assumption (which many governments in other countries have made) that terrorists can be identified by some sort of profiling, their effort to defeat Boko Haram will be counterproductive, and possibly even exacerbate the current security challenge.

The research indicates that individuals from virtually any background can choose to engage in terrorist activity. Thus, an especially promising area of research on the individual risk of terrorist activity uses phrases and metaphors like "pathways to radicalization" and "staircase to terrorism" to describe a dynamic process of psychological development that leads an individual to participate in terrorist activity.[30] In one particularly noteworthy example, Max Taylor and John Horgan offer a framework for analyzing developmental processes—"a sequence of events involving steps or operations that are usefully ordered and/or interdependent"—through which an individual becomes involved with (and sometimes abandons) terrorist activity.[31] Their research highlights the importance of understanding the dynamic context that individuals operate in, and how the relationships between contexts, organizations, and individuals affect behavior.[32] This returns us to the initial discussion provided in this chapter: context is key. Each day, countless individuals grapple with situations and environmental conditions that may generate feelings of outrage and powerlessness, among many other potential motivators for becoming violent. But an individual's view of these situations and conditions—and how to respond appropriately to them—is clearly influenced by their family members, peers, and personal role models, educators, religious leaders, and others who help interpret and contextualize local and global conditions. Because these interpretive influences play such a key role in how an individual responds to the challenges of everyday life events and trends that generate political grievances among members of a particular community, we sometimes see a contagion effect, whereby an individual's likelihood of becoming involved in terrorism is increased because they know or respect others who have already done so. Further, as Taylor and Horgan note, "There is never one route to terrorism, but rather there are individual routes, and furthermore those routes and activities as experienced by the individual change over time."[33]

The dynamics of an individual's connections to others—including, for example, family, friends, small groups, clubs, gangs, and diasporas—also help an individual interpret the potential legitimacy of an organization that has adopted terrorism as a strategy. Individuals are often introduced to the fringes of violent extremist groups by friends, family members, and authority figures in their community, among others.[34] For example, psychologist Sageman has argued that social bonds play a central role in the emergence of the global Salafi jihad, the movement whose members comprise organizations like al-Qaeda and its affiliates in North Africa and Southeast Asia.[35] As described earlier, an organization that is perceived as legitimate is then able to exert influence on the individual's perceptions of environmental conditions and what to do about them. Thus, the religious dimension of Boko Haram's ideology—and its perceived capability of providing that critical legitimacy—must be taken into account.

For many contemporary terrorist groups, a compelling ideology plays a central role at the intersection of religious, political, and socioeconomic grievances, organizational attributes, and individual characteristics. Religion can be a powerful motivator for all kinds of human action, because as psychologist John Mack has noted, religion "deals with spiritual or ultimate human concerns, such as life or death, our highest values and selves, the roots of evil, the existence of God... Religious assumptions shape our minds from childhood, and for this reason religious systems and institutions have had, and continue to have, extraordinary power to affect the course of human history."[36] Like many religious terrorist groups around the world, Boko Haram's ideology portrays the world in terms of an epic struggle between good and evil, and they are convinced in their own revealed truth from God. Many religious terrorist groups share a common belief that they are following the will of God, and that only the true believers are guaranteed salvation and victory.

> Boko Haram's ideology portrays the world in terms of an epic struggle between good and evil...

At the individual level, Harvard researcher Jessica Stern describes how for religious extremists "there is no room for the other person's point of view. Because they believe their cause is just, and because the population they hope to protect is purportedly so deprived, abused, and helpless, they persuade themselves that any action—even a heinous crime—is justified. They believe that God is on their side."[37] For these individuals, religion has helped them simplify an otherwise complex life, and becoming part of a radical movement has given them support, a sense of purpose, an outlet in which to express their grievances (sometimes related to personal or social humiliation), and "new identities as martyrs on behalf of a purported spiritual cause."[38] In their eyes, the superiority of God's rules provides them with a feeling of justification for violating man-made rules against violent atrocities. Doing the bidding of a higher power demands sacrifice but also means fewer limits on violence. It's easier to kill if you think you're doing God's will; violence is seen as necessary in order to save oneself, one's family, or even the world.

In terms of environmental conditions and grievances, Boko Haram's ideology articulates a vision of social and political order that is more pure and religiously grounded. As Boko Haram's founding leader Yusuf preached, "Our land was an Islamic state before the colonial masters turned it to a kafir land. The current system is contrary to true Islamic beliefs."[39] Boko Haram's ideology describes how white European colonial powers drew lines on a map in a somewhat arbitrary and capricious plan to carve up the African continent, and in many cases empowered local tribes—frequently, many of which had embraced Christianity—to rule as proxy landlords until the end of WWII and a wave of independence movements that saw the end of colonial rule. But what came next has been even worse: rampant corruption among a political and wealthy elite that is heavily invested in the status quo; a huge gap between aspirations of Nigeria's youth and the opportunities provided by the system for achieving a better life; a lack of critical infrastructure and basic support services; a history with long periods of military dictatorship and political oppression; a swelling population amid economic despair; and a system in which entrenched ethnic identities are politicized and constrain opportunities for meritocratic advancement or for being able to worship one's faith in accordance with a strict interpretation of the Koran. The cumulative result of these things is an environment in which radical extremist ideologies can thrive among communities that see themselves as politically and economically disadvantaged and marginalized.

Throughout the Muslim communities of northern Nigeria today, there is a sense of unease and insecurity about the spiritual and moral future of their children, and concern about the fading influence of religious leaders like the Sultan of Sokoto.[40] In addition, there are also specific political and socioeconomic frustrations found predominantly in northern Nigeria— poverty, unemployment, and lack of education are much higher here than in the rest of the country. Boko Haram, like other religious terrorist groups throughout the world, thus capitalizes on local conditions by offering envisioned solutions to the grievances shared by the surrounding communities. They portray the situation in terms of a Muslim population oppressed by non-Muslim rulers, infidels, and apostates backed by sinister forces that intend to keep the local Muslim communities subservient. Its followers are reportedly influenced by the Koranic phrase: "Anyone who is not governed by what Allah has revealed is among the transgressors."[41] More on Boko Haram's ideology, and the underlying reasons why it resonates among particular communities in Nigeria, will be provided in Chapter 5.

The final two chapters of the monograph explore ways in which the response to Boko Haram can be made more effective. To begin, because of the group's ideology and attack patterns, they are clearly a Nigerian problem requiring a Nigerian solution. There have been no attacks attributed to Boko Haram outside Nigeria, and most of their attacks have occurred within their traditional area of operation within the northern states of Bauchi and Borno. Thus, this is clearly a domestic terrorist problem, one that most observers believe the Nigerian government can handle. However, the final chapter of the monograph offers some observations for what the U.S. and the international community might be able to offer Nigeria's government and nongovernmental entities to aid them in their fight against Boko Haram. Further, in the event that SOF personnel are called upon to help the Nigerian government in some capacity, this monograph examines some implications of this analysis that should be useful for a SOF readership.

Summary

To sum up, this study is organized around a sequence of conceptual building blocks. First, because history is such a vital dimension of anyone's perception about the world and their place within it, a brief political history of Nigeria is provided. The next two chapters examine grievances that negatively impact the relationship between citizens and the state, and security challenges that stem from these grievances. The monograph then explores the origins and future trajectory of Boko Haram, and especially why its ideology of violence has found resonance among a small number of young Nigerians. And the final two chapters explore suggestions for responding to the terrorist threat with increasing effectiveness.

Clearly, no terrorist group has ever emerged in a vacuum; there are dynamic contexts—political, social, economic, temporal, spatial, even spiritual—that must be taken into account. Thus, a considerable amount of emphasis is placed throughout the monograph on identifying the array of environmental conditions and grievances among members of the local population that facilitate opportunities for Boko Haram to muster support and orchestrate acts of political violence. The government of Nigeria has struggled to deal effectively with these grievances and sources of tension throughout the country, and there is a pervasive belief particularly among northern Nigerians that the government continually fails to address critical needs of those who aspire for a better future. While resources are surely constrained, it is the inequitable distribution of those resources, and the widely acknowledged levels of corruption among elites, that detract from the government's effectiveness. In turn, patronage and corruption fuels a general perception that government officials (to include law enforcement) cannot be trusted, and this further undermines the government's ability to influence the behavior of local community members in positive directions, away from the lure of radical extremist ideologies like that of Boko Haram.

From this analysis, it is clear that the security challenge posed by Boko Haram is squarely framed by the Nigerian context, with only limited implications for countries outside Nigeria. Further, it is a challenge that the people of Nigeria can deal with effectively. Outside entities, like the U.S., may be of some assistance, but the thrust of any successful effort to defeat this terrorist group will come from both the Nigerian government and an array of nongovernmental entities. A purely state-centric approach is insufficient for combating non-state security threats like religious terrorist groups. Thus, the discussion in the later chapters of this monograph will emphasize the role of mass persuasion tools and efforts to mitigate underlying conditions that enable terrorist activity, as opposed to focusing on the application of kinetic force to combat a terrorist group.

However, organizing and implementing a comprehensive counterterrorism strategy employing both hard power and soft power takes time and considerable patience, and this is anathema to the more visceral, kinetic reaction that a government and its citizens have when being attacked by a terrorist group like Boko Haram. Thus, President Jonathan's current response to the terrorist threat, with its emphasis on a large security force presence in the northern states (a full 20 percent of the country's budget has now been dedicated to the defense sector) is understandable, but is unlikely to completely quell the violence. What is needed instead is the kind of intelligence-led policing that builds trust between citizens and a government that is perceived as legitimate, just, and effectively moving the country toward a better future. Further, given the strong influence of tribal, clan, and ethnic groups on security and stability in Nigeria, the discussion also describes ways in which nongovernmental entities—religious leaders, tribal elders, and civil society organizations—can play a critical role in diminishing the resonance of Boko Haram's ideology. In both arenas—government and nongovernment—the U.S. and our allies can find useful ways to contribute toward the eventual defeat of Boko Haram.

2. A Brief Political History of Nigeria

The Federal Republic of Nigeria became independent on 1 October 1960 mainly as a federation of three regions, corresponding roughly to the three largest ethnic identities of the country: the Hausa and Fulani (29 percent of the population), concentrated in the far north and neighboring country of Niger; the Yoruba (21 percent) of southwestern Nigeria; and the Igbo (18 percent) in the southeastern portion of the country.[42] Under the founding constitution, each of the three regions retained a substantial measure of self-government, while the federal government was given exclusive powers in defense and security, foreign relations, and commercial and fiscal policies. It is important to recognize, however, that in addition to the three main ethnic identities mentioned above, there are hundreds of ethnolinguistic entities throughout Nigeria[43]—including Ijaw (10 percent of the population), Kanuri (4 percent), Ibibio (4 percent) and Tiv (2 percent)—who have at times been historically marginalized and underrepresented among the political and economic elite. Roughly two-thirds of these "minority" ethnic groups are located in the northern states, but several are also prominent in the central states (such as the Tiv) and in the coastal Niger Delta region (such as the Ijaw and Ogoni).[44] Despite this cultural diversity, according to Abdul Raufu Mustapha, "the tendency of many minority groups to cluster—politically, linguistically and culturally—round the big three has given Nigeria a tripolar ethnic structure which forms the main context for ethnic mobilization and contestation."[45] Finally, approximately half the population is Muslim, and most of the other half is Christian, contributing a powerful religious dimension to Nigeria's tremendous ethnic and social diversity.[46] As described in later chapters of this monograph, the fact that northerners are mostly Muslim and southerners are mostly Christian contributes to our understanding of Nigeria's security challenges.

In 1958, significant oil reserves were discovered in Nigeria, and this had an enormous impact on the economic, social, and political life of the country. Prior to this, the Nigerian economy had been largely based on cash crop exports: cotton in the north, rubber in the south, palm oil in the southeast, and cocoa in the west of the country. It is important to note that most of the oil resources of Nigeria are located in just one region in the southeast, known as the Niger Delta, where the Igbo are the largest ethnic group. Other significant oil resources are found further south, offshore in the Gulf of Guinea. This has implications for where the oil extraction activities (and environmental impacts) are concentrated, as well as for resource distribution and a host of other issues that will be discussed later in this study.

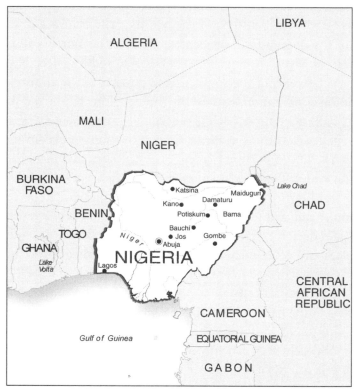

Figure 1. Map of Nigeria. Map courtesy U.S. Special Operations Command Graphics.

Today Nigeria has a population of over 155 million, 41 percent of whom are under the age of 15.[47] It has the largest military and the largest economy in West Africa. Geographically, the size of Nigeria is a little more than twice that of California, but its political system includes 36 state governments, 774 local governments, and over 200 ethnic groups, each with its own layers of authority and loyalty structures. By all measures, Nigeria is a dominant force in West Africa, and yet there is a notably fragile relationship between the state and its citizens. For decades, its massive oil resources have been plundered by various kleptocratic leaders, and corruption is endemic throughout the political and economic system. The average Nigerian can expect to die before they reach the age of 48, with major infectious diseases and Malaria causing many deaths in the country each year. Roughly 70 percent of the population lives on less than $2 a day.[48] Overwhelmingly negative views toward the government are common among ordinary Nigerians, and widespread grievances fuel conflict and violence that further exacerbate the challenges faced by the government. Before exploring these grievances (the focus of the next chapter in this monograph), it is first important to recognize the historical dimensions to Nigeria's contemporary security challenges.

Nigeria's Post-Colonial History

The modern history of Nigeria is far too deep and complex to provide a comprehensive summary here. For the purposes of this monograph, only a brief post-colonial history of Nigerian politics and political violence will be reviewed here, emphasizing events which contribute to the fragile contemporary relationship between Nigeria's citizens and its government.[49] When describing this relationship, an important point to make at the outset is that the country has experienced an exceptionally high number of military coups and a civil war.[50] Despite achieving independence over 50 years ago, peaceful democratic transfers of power are a very recent phenomenon in Nigeria (see Figure 5 at the end of this chapter).

During the first years of independence in the early 1960s, regional tensions escalated between ethnic nationalities based largely on issues of political representation. Prime Minister Tafawa Balewa (1960-66) routinely imprisoned leading opposition politicians, adding fuel to the already deteriorating political situation. Violence marred the Nigerian elections of 1964, and on 15 January 1966 a small group of army officers—mostly southeastern Igbos led by Major General Johnson Aguiyi-Ironsi—overthrew the government and assassinated Prime Minister Balewa and the premiers of the northern and western regions. The military government that assumed power was unable to quiet ethnic tensions or produce a federal constitution acceptable to all sections of the country. On 29 July of that year, a group of northern Hausa-backed army officers staged another coup, killing Ironsi and replacing him with Lieutenant Colonel Yakubu Gowon. The coup was followed by a massacre of thousands of Igbo in the northern territories, who fled to their homelands in the southeast. These events contributed to an increasingly strong Igbo secessionist movement.

In May 1967, Gowon's administration unveiled a plan to create a new 12-state structure for Nigeria. Among the most significant changes was that the eastern region would be divided into three states, two of them dominated by non-Igbo groups, ensuring that the Igbo would not dominate the oil-rich Niger Delta region. The Igbo rejected these proposed constitutional revisions and insisted on full autonomy for the east. Then on 27 May 1967, Lieutenant Colonel Emeka Ojukwu—the military governor of the eastern region and a leader of the Igbo secessionist movement—declared the independence of the region, which adopted as its new name the "Republic of Biafra," and a violent civil war ensued. Biafran forces crossed the Niger River, moving west in an effort to capture Lagos, the capital of Nigeria at the time. Gowon's military drove them back, imposed a naval blockade, and launched its own invasion of northern Biafra. Although France granted formal recognition to the independent Republic of Biafra and provided military support to the rebels, the United Kingdom backed the Nigerian federal government, and by January 1970 the Biafran revolt had been crushed and Nigerian forces declared victory in the civil war.

More than 2 million Nigerians died in the conflict, which formally ended on 12 January 1970 with a declaration of surrender over Biafran radio by Major General Philip Effiong. Nigerian President Gowon announced he would remain in power for six more years to ensure a peaceful transition to democracy. However, in 1974 Gowon announced that the return to civilian rule would be postponed indefinitely. His timing was poor: high prices, chronic shortages of food and necessities, growing corruption, and the failure of the government to address several regional issues had already created a restless mood.

As a result, on 29 July 1975, Brigadier Murtala Ramat Muhammed overthrew Gowon in a bloodless coup. Muhammed moved quickly to address issues that Gowon had avoided. He replaced corrupt state governors, purged incompetent and corrupt members of the public services, and instigated a plan to move the national capital from industrial, coastal Lagos to neglected, interior Abuja. Civilian rule, he declared, would be restored by 1979, and he began a five-stage process of transition. However, subsequent political and economic reforms made Muhammed extremely unpopular with many Nigerians, and on 13 February 1976, he was assassinated in a coup attempt, although his administration remained in power. His successor, Lieutenant General Olusegun Obasanjo, continued Muhammed's reforms, including the move toward civilian rule. Obasanjo also created seven new states to help redistribute wealth and began a massive reform of local government. In 1977, he convened a constitutional assembly, which recommended replacing the British-style parliamentary system with an American-style presidential system of separate executive and legislative branches. To ensure that candidates would appeal to ethnic groups beyond their own, the president and vice president were required to win at least 25 percent of the vote in at least two-thirds of the 19 states. The new constitution took effect in 1979. The restructured administration was called Nigeria's Second Republic, and a subsequent presidential election that year was won by Shehu Shagari. For his part, Obasanjo won considerable acclaim when he became Nigeria's first military leader to voluntarily surrender power to a civilian administration in 1979.

Unfortunately, a few years later Nigeria experienced yet another military coup. The collapse of the world oil market left Nigeria unable to pay its short-term debts, much less finance the projects to which it was committed. Eventually, the country was also unable to import essential goods. In January 1983, the government ordered the expulsion of all unskilled foreigners, claiming that immigrants who had overstayed their visas were heavily involved in crime and were taking jobs from Nigerians. In the elections of 1983, the ruling party claimed a decisive victory over several opposition parties, while observers cited widespread instances of fraud and intimidation. Finally, on New Year's Eve 1983, army officers led by Major General Muhammadu Buhari overthrew the Shagari government in a bloodless coup. Buhari's government enjoyed widespread public support for its condemnation of economic mismanagement, of government corruption, and of the rigged 1983 elections. This support waned, however, as the government adopted a rigid program of economic austerity and instituted repressive policies that included a sweeping campaign against "indiscipline," a prohibition against discussing the country's political future, and the detention of journalists and others critical of the government.

Buhari's support withered and in August 1985, Major General Ibrahim Babangida overthrew him, rescinded several of Buhari's most unpopular decrees, initiated a public debate on the state of the economy, and eased controls over business. These actions set the stage for negotiations with the International Monetary Fund (IMF) for aid, a new round of austerity measures, and better relations with the country's creditors. For a time,

Figure 2. File photo dated 1996 shows Nigerian President General Sani Abacha at the airport of Abuja. Photo used by permission of Newscom.

Nigeria achieved a measure of economic recovery, although with the implementation of the structural adjustment program required by the IMF and World Bank, prices of goods and services skyrocketed.[51] Babangida also maintained a firm grip on power, shuffling key officers from position to position to ensure they would not become too strong, and forbidding political parties. Many Nigerians were disturbed by the general's favoring of northern (Hausa) elite interests, and Babangida faced and suppressed coup attempts in 1986 and 1990. Other tensions escalated, particularly religious strife between Christians and Muslims; several states, including Kaduna, Katsina, and Kano, had severe religious riots in the early 1990s.

Then the parade of coups and military rulers took a turn for the worse. In 1993, Babangida allowed for an open presidential election—the first since 1983. Moshood Abiola, a wealthy Yoruba publisher from the south, was widely believed to have won the election by a large majority, but the northern Hausa-supported military leader Babangida annulled the vote, and the country was plunged into political turmoil. In November 1993, General Sani Abacha—the powerful secretary of defense—seized power and outlawed political activity. Abiola was later imprisoned after attempting to claim the presidency and died in prison in July 1998.

The Nigerian Labor Congress, which had already held a general strike to protest the annulled election of Abiola, organized another general strike to protest Abacha's coup. Political pressure groups such as the Campaign for Democracy also stepped up protests against Abacha. In May 1994, the government announced plans for political reform and held elections for local governments and delegates for yet another constitutional conference. In October 1995, Abacha lifted the ban on political activity, promised a transfer to civilian power in 1998, and later allowed five parties to operate.

However, he continued his repression of dissidents, the most notorious instance of which was the hanging of several political activists in November 1995. During the early 1990s, playwright and prominent environmental activist (and eventual Nobel prize nominee) Ken Saro-Wiwa led a series of protests against the Western oil operations in the Niger Delta region of Nigeria, highlighting the fact that while his tribal lands were being destroyed, the revenues from these operations were not being used to improve public services. He also founded a more radical youth movement, which reportedly engaged in sabotage against the Shell Petroleum Development Company of Nigeria (the Nigerian subsidiary of Royal Dutch/Shell, and the largest oil producer in the region). In his writings, Saro-Wiwa criticized corruption and condemned both Shell and British Petroleum.

Although Shell decided to cease operations in Ogoniland in 1993, the Nigerian government decided to arrest Saro-Wiwa and a number of his supporters in 1995. He continued writing letters from prison, some of which were published in newspapers like the *Mail* and *Guardian*, in which he wrote "The most important thing for me is that I've used my talents as a writer to enable the Ogoni people to confront their tormentors. I was not able to do it as a politician or a businessman. My writing did it… I'm mentally prepared for the worst, but hopeful for the best. I think I have the moral victory." Following a brief trial—at which he was accused of murdering government supporters—Saro-Wiwa was executed along with eight other Ogoni leaders, and his body was buried in an unmarked, common grave in the eastern city of Port Harcourt. The international condemnation that followed did little harm to the government, and the foreign oil companies continued their work with little disruption. Indeed, in November 1995 Shell announced a new $3 billion investment in Nigeria just a week after the execution of the Ogoni leaders.[52]

The Abacha government imprisoned many people, among the most prominent being former president Olusegun Obasanjo and former vice president Shehu Musa Yar'Adua (who died in prison in December 1997), while other prominent Nigerians, including Nobel laureate Wole Soyinka, fled into exile. The execution and imprisonment of opponents and other violations of human rights intensified international pressure on Abacha and resulted in Nigeria's suspension from the British Commonwealth of Nations from 1995 to 1999. Meanwhile, the number and violent ferocity of militants in the Niger Delta began to swell, a trend that would continue for the next 10 years resulting in many attacks against Nigeria's oil producing infrastructure. When Abacha died unexpectedly in 1998, the country began a rapid march toward civilian rule. His deputy, General Abdusalam Abubakar, provided interim leadership during which an open presidential election was held and won in 1999 by retired general and former president Olusegun Obasanjo.

Figure 3. Nigerian President Olusegun Obasanjo, 10 June 2005. Photo used by permission of Newscom.

Under the leadership of Obasanjo, Nigeria began to emerge from the tyranny and corruption of the past, though the historical concentration of national power in the office of the presidency remained unchanged. He was re-elected in 2003 with over 60 percent of the vote, although "irregularities" were reported among the voting in various parts of the country. In April 2004, a plot to overthrow his government was discovered and prevented. Four military officers, led by Major Hamza al-Mustapha—the former security chief of the late military dictator Sani Abacha—and a civilian were charged with planning to assassinate President Obasanjo. Most of the officers were Hausa, a majority of whom had supported the opposition party during the 2003 elections in which Obasanjo won a second term.[53] According to the charges read in court, the group had been actively seeking to purchase a Stinger surface-to-air missile to be used in shooting down President Obasanjo's helicopter. One member of the group had already prepared a draft of a speech outlining the new regime that would replace Obasanjo's elected government.[54]

Overall, Obasanjo's two terms in office are seen by many as a positive turning point in the country's history.[55] His successor, Umaru Musa Yar'Adua—a Hausa from the northern part of the country who was elected in 2008—continued many of Obasanjo's policies, and was lauded for establishing an amnesty program as an attempt to encourage militants in the

Niger Delta to hand in their weapons and enter a dialogue meant to resolve the longstanding conflict in that region. Unfortunately, Yar'Adua became ill during the second year of his term, and passed away on 5 May 2010. His vice president, Goodluck Jonathan—an Ijaw from the southeast of the country—was sworn in as president, and continued many policies of his predecessor.

A year later, a national election for president—which independent observers declared was the most fair and honest in Nigeria's history—was won by Jonathan, whose inauguration on 29 May 2011 marked the beginning of his first full term as president. However, he had a serious challenge rallying all Nigerians around a common national vision: roughly half the country did not vote for him. As noted in Chapter 1, states north of the capital Abuja voted against him, and all but one state south of it voted for him.[56] The distinctions between north and south run deeper than the ethno-religious distinctions described earlier. As examined later in this monograph, the north has higher rates of poverty and illiteracy; the northeast, where Boko Haram and other Islamist extremist groups have taken root, is the poorest in Nigeria. Several states there are governed by the opposition All Nigeria People's Party. The region yields little national political power and has never produced a head of state. In essence, as Alex Thurston recently observed, state legitimacy is at its weakest in the northeast.[57]

From this perspective, few observers were surprised when immediately following the election there were spurts of violence in several northern communities that had supported Muhammadu Buhari (a Muslim from the north who had briefly served as president in the mid-1980s). When the presidential results first started to leak, pro-Buhari protestors in several northern cities attacked supporters and officials of Jonathan's ruling People's Democratic Party.[58] At the core of the unrest were grievances about power, as so often is the case with all kinds of political violence. After two terms of a southerner as president (Obasanjo), a northerner (Yar'Adua) had been elected, but because he died of ill health before completing his term, the northern elites felt it was still "their turn" to rule. In addition to various politicians and political offices, some protesters also targeted the traditional Muslim leadership—the Sultan of Sokoto, the Emir of Kano, and the Emir of Zaria—who were widely perceived as being on the People's Democratic Party's payroll.[59] Offices, shops, and homes were burned down, and Human Rights Watch estimates at least 800 people were killed and 65,000 displaced.[60] According

Figure 4. Goodluck Ebele Jonathan, president of the Federal Republic of Nigeria, speaks at the 66th United Nations General Assembly in the UN building in New York City on 21 September 2011. Photo used by permission of Newscom.

to a report by John Campbell, former U.S. ambassador to Nigeria, the security services responded violently against the protestors; some reports say they may have been responsible for many of the first deaths.[61] However, the violence soon acquired a religious and ethnic dimension, with churches and mosques set ablaze, prompting Muslims to attack Christians and vice versa in a downward cycle of revenge killings.[62] But the post-election bloodshed soon ended. One can only hope that a more peaceful and prosperous future for Nigerians is finally on the horizon.

Summary

Just a short while after independence the military intervened in the country's politics, and for the next three decades—with the exception of a brief four-year period (1979-1983)—the country was administered by the military. Nigeria experienced military coups in 1966 (twice), 1975, 1976, 1983, 1985, and 1993, as well as a bloody civil war from 1967 to 1970 (see Figure 5).[63] The civil war, in which rebels tried but eventually failed to establish an independent state of Biafra, was fought mainly over the oil-rich area dominated by Igbo and a handful of ethnic minorities in the Niger Delta, including Ijaws, the fourth largest ethnic group in Nigeria. Following the civil war, the government used money from the north to finance oil exploration in the south, and to invest in a robust infrastructure for exporting the oil to Western markets. These and other decisions made by the central government, including the collection and distribution of oil revenues, did nothing to foster national unity, and in fact resulted in sentiments to the contrary. As RAND researcher Peter Chalk recently observed, "The oil boom of the 1970s is often regarded as instrumental in driving the graft, cronyism, and social dysfunctionality that have been such an endemic feature of the contemporary Nigerian political scene."[64]

This long and tortured history derailed Nigeria from the path of liberal democracy, setting it back at least 30 years compared with other African countries that gained their independence around the same time. There remains widespread distrust among Nigerian citizens toward their government, particularly because of endemic corruption and this long history of military coups and abuses of power. The scars of military rule endure today—as one of the interviewees for this study noted, "A civilian government is always better, because you can criticize it without getting shot."[65] As described in the next chapter of this monograph, distrust of the government is reinforced by a system of ethnic politics, corruption, and cronyism, a widespread lack of services, low quality education, lack of reliable electricity, and a whole array of grievances that have been covered extensively in the media and which interviewees for this study emphasized on several

Years in Power	Name	Means of Taking Power
Oct. 1960 – Jan. 1966	Benjamin Nnamdi Azikiwe	Elected
Jan. 1966 – July 1966	Johnson Aguiyi Ironsi	Military Coup
Aug. 1966 – July 1975	Yakubu Gowon	Military Coup
July 1975 – Feb. 1976	Murtala Ramat Mohammed	Military Coup
Feb. 1976 – Oct. 1979	Olusegun Obasanjo	Military Coup
Oct. 1979 – Dec. 1983	Shehu Shagari	Elected
Dec. 1983 – Aug. 1985	Muhammadu Buhari	Military Coup
Aug. 1985 – Aug. 1993	Ibrahim Babangida	Military Coup
Aug. 1993 – Nov. 1993	Ernest Shonekan	Appointed (interim)
Nov. 1993 – Jun 1998	Sani Abacha	Military Coup
June 1998 – May 1999	Abdulsalam Abubakar	Appointed (interim)
May 1999 – May 2007	Olusegun Obasanjo	Elected
May 2007 – May 2010	Umaru Musa Yar`Adua	Elected
May 2010 – present	Goodluck Jonathan	Appointed (interim) May 2010 Elected May 2011

Figure 5. Nigeria's Heads of State since independence

occasions. These grievances, in turn, lead many Nigerians to put their faith in alternative governance and economic systems, or do what they can to get what they can from a system of central governance that they view as ineffective and untrustworthy.

3. Grievances of the Governed

There is of course no country in the world in which citizens do not have at least some form of complaints about their government. As noted in the introduction to this monograph, many kinds of grievances can lead to schisms between the state and its citizens, and sometimes these can result in various forms of political violence, including insurgency and terrorism. Throughout Africa, one of the most common areas of a population's animosity toward the state has involved bad governance. As William Reno notes, governance in Africa has often been based on very narrow, parochial interests—including tribal, clan, or family loyalties—to which collective interests of the general citizenry are subordinated.[66]

The political history of Nigeria provided in the previous chapter surely exemplifies the ways in which ruling elites have shown their disregard for the general citizenry. Further, their actions and policy decisions have contributed to a loss of legitimacy among ordinary Nigerians. Some no longer believe in the country's political, economic or legal institutions. The interviews and document analysis conducted for this monograph revealed that in Nigeria there is truly an abundance of problems that challenge most people's basic quality of life. None of these problems can be easily mitigated, and many of them are a result of policy decisions made by government leaders. For the purposes of this discussion, the most common and salient grievances include corruption among political and economic elites, economic disparity, barriers to social and educational opportunity, energy poverty, environmental destruction, human insecurity, and injustice. These topics were discussed by virtually every person interviewed for this research monograph, often in considerable detail, and are well-represented in the media and the scholarly literature on Nigeria. They are thus summarized here as a background that informs our understanding of the contemporary terrorist threat posed by Boko Haram.

Corruption

In Nigeria, as in many parts of sub-Saharan Africa, the blight of corruption greatly weakens the strands of trust between the state and the citizens it aims to govern. One interviewee used a medical analogy to describe how "there are so many symptoms of corruption... corruption is killing Nigeria, a slow, painful death."[67] Throughout the country, there are myriad examples of what John Alexander describes in his 2009 monograph as the "concentration of wealth and power in the hands of a very few, with nepotism and tribalism as key factors."[68] Income distribution in Nigeria is among the worst in the world, with most of the wealth going to a select few.[69]

Perceived authority to govern is based on power, and power in Nigeria is based on patronage. The country reflects quite well what Hisham Sharabi describes as *neopatriarchy*:

> Despite all ideological appearances, the individual's basic affiliation in "modernized," neopatriarchal society is to the family, the clan, the ethnic or religious group. For the common person in this society the concept of society or fatherland is an abstraction, which has meaning only when reduced to the primordial significations of kinship and religion... This practice strengthens both personal loyalty and dependence, cultivated early within the family, and bolsters them within the larger social whole in a system of patronage and the distribution of favor and protection.[70]

In Nigeria, the powerful make decisions based on what they believe is required for their political survival and the economic security of their family, clan, and close associates. They have often used illegal and extrajudicial means to coerce or eliminate those who might oppose them. Notably, the president of Nigeria has enormous power; there are very few constitutional constraints on the president.

During the 1990s in particular, the Sani Abacha regime set an awful standard for plundering a nation's resources. Money was stolen openly and with impunity (by some estimates, over $8 billion), and most of those responsible have never been held to account for their crimes. The system that enabled such thievery remains in place today, a system in which resources are channeled through state entities that control access to jobs and wealth. The easiest, and often the only way to make money is a position in the government. A university professor's salary is 400,000 naira (roughly $2,500) per month, while a local government chairman's salary is 1.2 million naira (over $7,500) per month. This creates an obvious incentive for medical doctors, scientists, and academics to leave their professions and go into politics just to make money. For example, as a May 2011 article in the *Economist* describes, "Three quarters of the government budget goes toward recurrent expenditure, including salaries. Parliamentarians are paid up to $2 million a year—legally. Very little is invested in infrastructure."[71]

Leaders in each of the 36 states of Nigeria receive up to 715 million naira ($4.5 million) per month as a "security fund," with much of it winding up in personal bank accounts. There are 774 Local Government Authorities (LGAs)—essentially government councils with 10-12 members on each council—in which loyalties are bought and sold far more often than real decisions are made. As Murray Last notes, the creation of these LGAs, "to whom huge sums are disbursed each month from the federal oil-revenue account in Abuja, has made access to LGA's funds of the utmost significance: any individual who can share in the control of his LGA has potentially untold riches coming to him personally."[72] According to Philip Ostien:

> The resources to which access is gained by control of LGAs include land, a lot of money, a lot of jobs, admissions and scholarships to schools and universities, health care, and more. Large sums of money are misappropriated by those holding office and those with whom they do business, including people in the state and federal governments. What is not misappropriated is spent on projects benefiting only certain groups.[73]

Because of this system of patronage and personal largesse, a political culture has developed in which the government is not seen as a means to serve the people and the state, but rather, the means to wealth. Any member of a family or clan who can get a government job becomes the centerpiece of an extended support system, a type of relational social security built exclusively on who you know or who knows you. It is a system in which anyone who holds a position within the government—even at the lowest levels of authority—is expected by their family and friends to supplement their meager income with alternative sources, stealing money, and sharing the wealth. Worse, as a recent Human Rights Watch report notes, "corruption is so pervasive that is has turned public service for many into a kind of criminal enterprise."[74] In essence, a vicious cycle is perpetuated in which individuals with even the very best intentions find it in their best interests to keep the status quo instead of trying to combat corruption. It is the kind of environment in which money transforms a student protest leader overnight into a quiet passivist or even a regime supporter; in some cases, charismatic individuals will pursue a vocal protest strategy simply because he is seeking a personal government payout.

Granted, over the past decade there has been a greater effort to try and reign in the country's endemic corruption among the elite. For example, in May 2011 the speaker of the lower house of parliament was investigated for "misappropriating" $140 million.[75] However, attempts by the government to tackle corruption have frequently deteriorated into attacks against opposition politicians, ensuring that those in power will remain in power. Further, there is an unspoken alliance between the country's wealthy elites and its government which is meant to preserve the system and the economic conditions under which they survive.[76] While labor-intensive industries such as mining collapsed years ago, some sectors of the economy have made a few Nigerians very wealthy. When Nigeria privatized during the early part of the 1990s, scores of industries went to friends and associates of President Obasanjo, especially the capital-intensive ones like telecommunications and banking. Today, in places like Lagos and Onitsha, the concentration of wealth and power gives significant influence to individuals who benefit from the status quo.[77]

One interviewee for this study noted, "the problem is not resources, but the inability of those with responsibilities for the deployment of resources."[78] For example, he described how during 2009-2010, oil prices had risen to an average of $70 per barrel (bbl). However, the government had projected its budget based on a price of $55/bbl. Further, the budget estimated a production rate of one million bbl but was producing 40-50 percent more each day. The result was an excess of 400,000-500,000 bbl/day and an excess $15/bbl for the entire amount produced. Yet, at the time of my interview with this well-known Nigerian academic in mid-November 2010, 30 percent of Nigeria's budget was not funded, leading to wild speculation and accusations about looting and corruption throughout the government. According to another local interviewee, there is so much thievery that a $10 project will need a budget of $100 in order to cover all the additional costs of corrupt officials.[79] Further, ordinary items cost more—for example, the price of a 50 kilogram bag of cement is about three times higher than in neighboring countries.[80]

According to one interviewee, this system of patronage politics and resource-based power, fed by oil revenues and endemic corruption, is actually keeping the system from imploding altogether; it has become an essential mechanism for Nigeria's survival.[81] Most of the corruption takes place with impunity, but it is a system that works for people in power, not for people out of power. This naturally leads to tremendous resistance to change among elites, and tremendous animosity among the rest of the population. Government officials are widely seen as accountable to foreign oil companies and wealthy elites, not to the general public, and many Nigerians feel powerless to bring about positive change. Comments from interviews that exemplify this sentiment include: "We are resigned to our fate; there is no sense of hope,"[82] and "When this generation is no longer in power, it's going to explode here."[83]

Lack of Infrastructure, Basic Services and Equality

In concert with massive corruption, there is high unemployment and unequal provision of basic services (like clean drinking water). According to one report, Nigeria has the worst income disparities in all of West Africa, with only 1 percent of the elites controlling 80 percent of the accrued oil wealth, almost 70 percent of which is held in foreign banks.[84] Further, an overwhelming majority of Nigerians live below the UN-designated poverty threshold, with no access to jobs or a decent education, and a minimum wage in some parts of the country at $50/month or less.[85] Despite having Africa's second largest economy, the level of absolute poverty in Nigeria was 60.9 percent of the population in 2010, an increase from 54.7 percent in 2004, according to the National Bureau of Statistics.[86] In this environment, many view thievery and corruption as a normal part of making ends meet, a sort of accepted "social contract." The private sector is anemic and dependent upon government connections (and the system of corruption) for all kinds of permits to do business. In addition, there is also a widely-held perception of 'favored justice' in which some individuals allegedly receive better treatment in the courts than other Nigerians because of their wealth, ethnicity, kinship, or other ties to powerful elites.

In other words, the pain in Nigeria is certainly not shared equally. Some of it is due to the aforementioned corruption, which has produced a tiny English-speaking elite who prominently display their massive wealth through their cars, houses, clothing, and elaborate parties. They are concentrated in just a few places, mainly Lagos, Onitsha, and Abuja. But much of the economic inequality is structural. Incomes in the (primarily Muslim) north are 50 percent lower than in the south. Literacy rates in the northeast are two-thirds lower than in Lagos.[87] Disenchantment with government is expectedly stronger in parts of the country where living is hardest. As will be discussed in the next chapter, these are also parts of the country in which political violence has recently become the most pronounced.

Beyond pervasive inequalities, there is also a wide gap between expectations for a better life and daily reality. Unfortunately, what has been called the "curse of oil" plays a role here. The massive oil revenues generated from the Niger Delta have, over time, disincentivized initiative at the local or personal level for many Nigerians. As noted earlier, local indigenous economic activities were allowed to atrophy as oil extraction became the country's primary source of revenue. As an industry that employs very few Nigerians, the country's economy in essence replaced its most important resource—its people—with one that is dependent on global market prices to bring in revenue that its people did not have to work for. Further, the government has not invested in economic development beyond the Niger Delta's oil infrastructure.

Beyond pervasive inequalities, there is also a wide gap between expectations for a better life and daily reality.

With no income taxes or social security, the economic system results in ordinary Nigerians having less interest in fulfilling their obligations in a participatory democracy—like holding their government officials accountable. Further, according to one interviewee, being Africa's largest oil producer and exporter means that many Nigerians have "expectations that things should be better, but instead things have gotten worse."[88] Despite billions spent over the last decade, Nigeria's roads are in disrepair, its water, energy, health, and education systems are in crisis, and basic necessities like jobs or credit from banks are in short supply.

Nigeria's large and growing population of youth (roughly half of the population is under the age of 19) see only limited opportunities to achieve a better future for themselves, their families, or their country. The structural obstacles to such aspirations are many. Despite an officially declared commitment of 6 percent to 8 percent of Nigeria's budget, the education system is widely considered sub-standard at best. Across Nigeria at any given time, one finds students not going to school and university staff on strike for several months at a time, demanding reforms or simply to receive their paychecks. Nigeria has over 100 universities, many of them funded by federal and state governments. Each year more than 500,000 young men and women (ages 16-25) apply to one or more of these institutions, but because of intake capacity only 150,000 of them are admitted.[89] Unlike the U.S. and other industrialized countries, there are very few opportunities for higher education outside the university system—no community college system, no reputable online degree programs, or other postsecondary programs that contribute to individual advancement or to the country's human capital.

Further, there is no social safety net, nor a functioning insurance system in the country. As one interviewee recounted, "You can purchase medical, health, life, automobile or other kinds of insurance policies, but if something happens like theft or an accident, you will never see a payment from the insurance company." Poor medical services are another source of grievances—patients seeking treatment for malaria routinely travel to other countries; thousands have died from cholera, hepatitis, typhoid fever, meningitis, and other such diseases in recent years. Worse yet, there is a vibrant trade in cheap, counterfeit drugs falsely marketed as effective for treating malaria and other diseases. Infant mortality in Nigeria is tenth highest in the world, average life expectancy is less than 48 years, and overall deaths—16 per 1,000 in 2010—was fourth highest in the world, behind Angola, Afghanistan, and South Africa.[90] Further, Nigeria is second only to South Africa in the number of deaths each year related to HIV/AIDS.

Another basic service that is sorely lacking in Nigeria is electricity. A recent *Economist* article described it best: "Nigeria is the seventh most populated country in the world, and its seventh biggest oil exporter, but it has as much grid power as Bradford, a post-industrial town in the north of England."[91] Over $30 billion has been spent on improving the energy sector in recent years, yet Nigeria is the world leader in private demand for generators.[92] A lack of electricity is, by one account, the Nigerian economy's "single biggest bottleneck."[93] It is somewhat ironic that the country with Africa's largest energy resources would be so energy poor, but large regions of Nigeria are without any electricity whatsoever, while those who live in the larger cities that are connected to the nation's power grid experience daily blackouts of 12-16 hours. The lack of access to reliable electricity affects everyone from the barber to the grocery store owner to the factory worker.

Private telecommunication companies have installed generators and guards at signal towers in order to help ensure reliable service.[94]

Meanwhile, the widespread reliance on personal generators is intertwined with the corruption challenges noted above. For example, millions of Nigerians make a meager living through a vibrant black market for fuel to power these generators. Often, this fuel is stolen—or more precisely, allowed by government operators to be stolen in return for a percentage of the profits generated. At the same time, the government spends billions subsidizing fuel, which would otherwise not be affordable for the vast majority of Nigerians. As noted earlier, the country is Africa's largest oil exporter, but its four refineries are nearly broken and produce only 15 percent of their intended capacity.[95] So, the government pays enormous sums each year to import tons of fuel, and then provides a subsidy to lower the price at which it is made available to the country's citizens. This system, in turn, allows for huge amounts of corruption. According to a January 2012 news report, a Nigerian legislative committee discovered a scandal involving roughly $4 billion annually, in which fuel importers delivered and were paid by the government for significantly more fuel than the country consumed, with the remaining millions of liters made available for smugglers to export, sometimes to buyers in neighboring countries.[96]

As Abdel-Fatau Musah recently observed, Nigeria has an uncanny habit of exporting what is in scarce supply in the country (electricity to Benin and Togo, conflict resolution, and democracy to Liberia and Togo) while importing what it has in abundance, such as petroleum products.[97] Further, instead of investing in the development of their country and its future, Nigeria's leaders have left a legacy of enriching only their families and close associates. As a result, ordinary Nigerians are not only disappointed with the ongoing lack of services or infrastructure, they are disenchanted, if not furious with their government. This fury was manifested in the street protests at the beginning of 2012 when the government abruptly cancelled the fuel subsidy—by most observers, a sound and necessary policy decision as part of an ambitious economic restructuring plan. But protestors argued that the money the government saves by canceling the subsidy would just go toward other forms of corruption rather than to benefit the needs of ordinary Nigerians. Notably, the government reinstated the subsidy, or at least part of it, and the protests subsided. One could argue that the government first needs to provide reliable electricity throughout the country before this subsidy can be withdrawn without adversely affecting the majority of Nigerians.

Another source of anger toward the government stems from years of environmental destruction and neglect. In the Niger Delta, the oil extraction industry has destroyed once-fertile farmland and fishing waters. Laws about protecting the environment were never enforced, allowing oil companies to pollute rivers and waterways throughout the region at will, and by extension destroying the livelihoods of countless fishermen and farmers.[98] Oil spills from 30 years ago are still not cleaned up. According to a recent UN Environmental Program report, decades of oil pollution in the Ogoniland region has created such a catastrophe it could take 25 to 30 years to completely clean up; "floating layers of oil vary from thick black oil to thin sheens… In at least 10 Ogoni communities where drinking water is contaminated with high levels of hydrocarbons, public health is seriously threatened… At some sites, a crust of ash and tar has been in place for several decades."[99]

During the 1980s, as pipelines laid 20 years earlier began to age and burst open, oil companies paid damages to local chiefs, who did not distribute the wealth locally nor fix the damaged areas, but instead used the influx of cash to perpetuate longstanding systems of patronage and exclusion. In several cases, this practice created an incentive to intentionally cause oil spills in order to get money for compensation; some entrepreneurs even viewed this phenomenon as a new source of consulting for oil damage cases. Environmental destruction was the grievance that animated Ken Saro-Wiwa, the environmental activist from the Ogoniland region and eventual Nobel prize nominee described earlier in this section who was executed by Sani Abacha's regime during the 1990s.

The cumulative effect of this toxic brew of grievances is dejection and marginalization. With the combination of bad governance, centralization of power and wealth, political intrigue, crumbling (or nonexistent) infrastructure, regional disparities and many more problems that cannot be addressed here due to space limitations, it is no wonder that many observers have argued that Nigeria offers the kinds of conditions in which revolutionaries and extremists have found fertile ground for recruiting and launching violent movements. But exacerbating these conditions even further is the prominent role that the system of institutionalized ethnic identity—a key factor in many instances of political violence worldwide—plays in the political and social lives of Nigerians.

The Exacerbating Role of Ethnic Identity Politics

As noted earlier, Nigeria has hundreds of ethnic groups, three of which dominate specific "zones" of the country: Hausa-Fulani in the northwest and northeast, Igbo in the southeast and south central, and Yoruba in the north central and southwest. Ethnicity in Nigeria has a significant impact on a person's experiences, perceptions of injustice, social and educational opportunities, and much more. For example, the most prosperous parts of the country—including the major cities of Lagos, Onitsha, and Abuja—are all located in Yoruba-dominated territory, thus Yoruba are more represented among the wealthy and powerful of Nigeria than members of other ethnic groups.

Nigerians in general are acutely aware of—some might say obsessed with—a person's ethnic identity. Interviewees for this report claimed that most Nigerians can tell a person's background just from looking at or listening to them. Igbo are said to have lighter complexion compared to Yoruba; Hausa are characterized as tall and slim, prone to wearing traditional dress and hats. According to Nigerian scholar Samuel Ibaba, a "politicization of ethnic consciousness" emerged under colonial rule, which "resulted in ethnicity-based political competition after independence in 1960. Ethnic groups engaged in competition for power to advance their group and parochial interests as against the national interest or public good. State laws and policies thus reflected ethnic interest."[100]

Indeed, ethnic identity impacts daily life throughout the country. All official papers and documents identify a person's place of birth. Any forms that a person needs to fill out (e.g., applying for a driver's permit or university admission, opening a bank account, leasing a home, et cetera) requires them to indicate their place of birth, not where they currently live, regardless of how long they have lived there. From the person's birthplace information, assumptions are made about that person's ethnicity, which then directly impacts their quality of life. Preferential treatment in all aspects of daily life including access to jobs, education, housing, and public services is given to individuals whose ethnicity is indigenous to the local area.[101] For example, if you were born in Rivers state, it will be much more difficult to find work in Bayelsa state. Locals will always prefer to rent or sell their homes to others indigenous to the area. One interviewee noted that he had lived in the southwest of the country for 30 years, but because he was born in the southeast he was still considered an "outsider" or "visitor" and had to deal with various forms of discrimination that come with that distinction. As Philip Ostien notes, the distribution of resources is controlled,

> ...by a system of "indigene certificates" issued by local governments. Access to indigene certificates and the resources depending on them is directed primarily towards members of the ethnic or subethnic group controlling the LGA. Other groups living there, even groups settled there for scores or hundreds of years, are excluded. They are told to "go back where you came from" if they want the benefits of indigeneship.[102]

While ethnicity and religion amplify some of the structural disadvantages described above, the difference between indigenous and non-indigenous settlers contributes greatly to underlying conflicts and grievances throughout Nigeria. Consider the case of Plateau: there are 15 ethnicities considered indigenous, and all others are settlers. The government will not issue official birth certificates to children of settlers, so they are forced to return to their parents' place of origin in order to acquire official papers. Hausa-Fulani children born in the northern city of Jos are not issued indigenous birth certificates or any documentation recognizing them as an indigene of the city, but rather are identified as foreigners regardless of how long the family may have lived there. The fact that these non-indigenous people are predominately Hausa and Muslim exacerbates the ethnic discrimination problems already discussed. Christians from southern regions of the country who migrate north are also discriminated against in the same way.

The relationship between preferential treatment and place of birth has grown much weaker in the major cities like Abuja and Lagos, but is a basic way of life throughout the rest of the country. And yet, the Nigerian constitution prohibits discrimination based on place of birth. In fact, the Federal Character Principle mandates that any federally established committees, appointments, et cetera, must have representation from different ethnic groups. Further, every state must have a member in cabinet—an institutionalized effort to ensure at least some kind of ethnic representation in federal government leadership positions. During the immediate years prior to independence, the overriding principle in the composition of Nigerian cabinets was the equality of regions, each of which contributed three ministers apiece, but from 1960-1966, the North began to have a majority in the cabinet.[103] In 1966, General Yakubu Gowon—a Christian from the Hausa-dominated north—assumed power in a military coup and instigated political reforms that effectively increased ethnic minority representation in the federal government. Successive regimes have, at various times, attempted to address concerns raised by ethnic minorities, but historically the federal government, the military leadership, and the wealthy elite of the country have been dominated by Yoruba and Hausa-Fulani.

Nigerians' structural and sociopolitical emphasis on ethnic identity is a core challenge to the future security and prosperity of their country. In essence, local customs and government policies enforce and amplify ethnic divisions instead of national unity. A person's identity is first and foremost a Hausa, Igbo, Yoruba, Ijaw, et cetera—not a "Nigerian." There has been a failure to create a national consciousness, a universal patriotism across Nigeria. According to Abdul Mustapha:

> Since 1966, the efforts at reforming inter-ethnic relations in Nigeria have had only a limited success. . . It has been relatively easier to broaden ethnic representation in the executives and legislatures than to create genuine structures of social inclusion. Even in the context of increased ethnic representativeness, hegemonic impulses of particular ethnic groups are not totally suppressed. This problem is even more obvious in the organization of political parties, where efforts at wider representation remain subject to manipulation by the more powerful ethnic groups.[104]

Perhaps the pervasive nature of this problem is a reflection of a very young democracy. In fact, it was not long ago that southerners living in the north were killed *en masse* following a military coup led by northern officers in July 1966, and many Nigerians today have vivid memories of that tragic period. Likewise, the bloody civil war of 1967-1970, in which underlying ethnic tensions played a key role, is still prominent in the minds of the older generation of Nigerians.

Overall, the politics of ethno-centric identity undermine the strength of civil society and contribute to an unhealthy political culture, myopic mistrust across ethnic lines, corruption, and a whole host of other problems. Unless a new, more nationalist ethos is embraced throughout the county, Nigeria will not be able to meet anyone's expectations for a successful future—especially their own.

Summary

These are just some of the many grievances that Nigerians have expressed in interviews, books, articles, newspapers, and other sources. Daily life is difficult for a great many people, and more difficult for a large majority than for a tiny minority. Further, the difficulties of life in Nigeria are greater in the north, which has roughly half the GDP per capita as the south. A legacy of corruption, infrastructure neglect, social deprivation, and ethnic identity politics combine with modern trends in migration and urbanization to create new conflicts and rising perceptions of insecurity. As many scholars and observers are quick to point out, the lack of good governance is at the root of many challenges faced by Nigerians today. While bad policy choices have been made, not exclusively due to corruption, decades of autocratic rule have produced a political culture in which protests are seen as a subversion of authority. Investigating elites is difficult and dangerous, and in some cases elites sponsor sectarian conflicts in order to divert attention from their faults in a bid to remain in power.

Collectively, these are the kinds of grievances and tensions that contribute to an enabling environment for vigilante groups, criminal gangs, thugs, drug smugglers, and radical extremists. It is perhaps a modern miracle that the cauldron of Nigeria has not yet boiled over into mass atrocities and internecine bloodshed throughout the country. But as described in the next chapter, there are significant pockets of political violence and other security challenges, particularly in the north and south, in which armed groups feed off this kind of environment.

4. The Complex Security Environment of Nigeria

Terrorists and criminals thrive in a climate of sustained grievances. It is no coincidence that the worst forms of political violence in Nigeria today originate in the most socioeconomically disadvantaged parts of the country. In the north, where unemployment and poverty are the highest, radical Islamists and the imposition of Sharia law have challenged the authority of the state. In the southeast, where environmental destruction resulting from oil extraction in the Niger Delta has made local Nigerians' traditional fishing and agricultural efforts virtually impossible, a flurry of criminal groups and armed militant gangs often consisting of unemployed youth have engaged in kidnappings, extortion, car bombings, murder, and other forms of violent attacks against the government and the nation's critical oil infrastructure.

Over the last several years, there have been ample news reports and scholarly analyses of these security challenges, as well as the links between them and the many grievances described in the previous chapters. Scholars have also highlighted various enablers of insecurity throughout the region, including porous borders and the widespread availability of small arms and light weapons. An understanding of these and other complex dimensions of the Nigerian security environment is necessary for placing any analysis of Boko Haram and the government's response to it in the proper context. While entire books can be written about Nigeria's contemporary security challenges, this chapter of the monograph highlights the most pressing issues organized around three primary themes: political violence in the south, organized crime, and the rise of ethno-political and religious violence in the north.

Political Violence in the South

Nigeria's government has struggled for several decades with security challenges in the southeast of the country, particularly the Niger Delta. The civil war described in Chapter 2 of this monograph is one of the earliest examples of how violent unrest in this region has often been fueled by ethnic identity politics and inequities in the distribution of resources. Various groups operating in and around the region have challenged the authority of the state since 1966, when the Niger Delta Volunteer Service led by an Ijaw, Major

Isaac Adaka Boro, declared a newly independent "Niger Delta Republic" and took up arms against the Nigerian State. Their motivations for wanting to secede from the state included "development neglect arising from ethnicity-based political domination."[105] The revolt lasted less than a month; the rebels were captured by federal troops, prosecuted on charges of treasonable felony and sentenced to death, but were later pardoned and released from jail.[106] Some Ijaws consider this event an "unfinished revolution."

According to Samuel Ibaba, four interrelated factors have created conditions for the conflicts in this region:

> First, the Niger Delta is the hub of Nigeria's oil industry. Second, oil is the mainstay of the Nigerian economy and has generated huge revenues for the country; contributing 40 percent of GDP, about 90 percent of total earnings and about 80 percent of national gross income. Third, oil related environmental problems – such as oil spills and gas flares – have undermined environmental quality and the productivity of the local economies where oil is produced. Fourth, the Niger Delta is a strange paradox as it represents one of the extreme conditions of poverty and lack of development in the country, despite its oil and gas resources. These grievances have motivated conflicts against the Nigerian government, accused of development neglect and deprivation, and against the oil companies for neglecting corporate social responsibility. [107]

During the 1970s and 1980s, an array of activist groups formed in the region, including the Movement for the Survival of the Ogoni People (MOSOP), the Ijaw National Council, the Ijaw Youth Council, and the Movement for the Survival of the Ijaw Ethnic Nationality in the Niger Delta. These groups were animated by a combination of historical marginalization, the politics of resource control, and protests against the damage to the environment caused by the extraction of those resources. For example, as a recent United States Institute for Peace report about the region noted, "between 1976 and 2001 there were over 5,000 [oil] spills amounting to 2.5 million barrels, equivalent to ten Exxon Valdez disasters within a confined deltaic zone."[108]

International attention toward the plight of these Niger Delta communities was heightened in the early 1990s when the Sani Abacha regime executed MOSOP leader Ken Saro-Wiwa, and then again in 1998 when the government responded violently to the so-called Kaima Declaration—a document produced from a meeting held by political activist Ijaw youth groups in Kaima, Bayelsa state, organized to facilitate discussions on the survival of the Ijaw nation in Nigeria. The 10-point resolution that resulted from the meeting included the following passages:

"All land and natural resources (including mineral resources) within Ijaw territory belong to Ijaw communities and are the basis of our survival... we cease to recognize all undemocratic Decrees that rob our peoples/communities of the right to ownership and control of our lives and resources... we demand the immediate withdrawal from Ijaw land of all military forces of occupation and repression by the Nigerian State...we demand that all oil companies stop all exploration and exploitation activities in the Ijaw area."[109]

The Nigerian government responded to this perceived threat to its authority with considerable force, resulting in many violent confrontations between the youth and the security forces. In this setting, the political activist groups became transformed into armed militia organizations, who increasingly claimed that they needed to fight for the survival of their people. The armed groups active today in the Niger Delta can be loosely organized into three main categories, as illustrated in Figure 6.

Private Militia	Ethnic Militia	Pan-Ethnic Militia
Niger Delta People Volunteer Force (NDPVF)	The Meinbutus	Movement for the Emancipation of the Niger Delta (MEND)
Adaka Marines	Arugbo Freedom Fighters	
Martyrs Brigade	Iduwini Volunteer Force (IVF)	The Coalition for Militant Action in the Niger Delta (COMA)
Niger Delta Volunteers	Egbesu Boys of Africa	
Niger Delta Militant Force Squad (NDMFS)		The Niger Delta People Salvation Front
Niger Delta Coastal Guerillas (NDCGS)		

Figure 6: Categories of Militia Groups in the Niger Delta. Source: Ibaba and Ikelegbe, 2009.[110]

Most of the groups listed in the first two columns of Figure 6 are comprised of Ijaw youth, and while they pursued a common objective, each group acted on its own with no single command. This changed in 2006, when leaders of several militia groups in the region met to form an umbrella organization, called the Movement for the Emancipation of the Niger Delta (MEND), combining their efforts an in attempt to more effectively match the capabilities of the Nigerian armed forces. MEND has consistently claimed that it is fighting on behalf of those who have borne the brunt of the environmental destruction—the Igbo, Ogoni, Ijaw and other ethnicities—resulting from decades of oil extraction in the Niger Delta. On 18 February 2006, the military leader of MEND, Godswill Tamuno, declared a total war on all foreign oil companies and their employees. His declaration of war came as militants and the army exchanged fire after a government helicopter gunship attacked barges allegedly used by smugglers to transport stolen crude oil. On the same day, MEND kidnapped nine employees of the U.S. oil company Willbros and threatened to use them as human shields.[111]

The same year that MEND was established, a meeting was held between community leaders in the Niger Delta and the federal government in order to try to address the violence. Representatives from the Niger Delta demanded 50 percent of oil revenues, but the government agreed to provide only 10 percent. Locals then felt disrespected by the government, and many argued that there was a sinister ethnically-driven reason behind their plight: the government had purposefully neglected them, allowing the destruction of their livelihoods because of their status as ethnic minorities. This narrative resonated in the climate of ethnic identity politics described earlier in this monograph, and helps to explain why groups like MEND found tacit support among locals for their attacks against government and oil corporation targets. As one interviewee put it, these groups and their supporters "believe they are engaged in an armed struggle to get the government to do what it is supposed to do."[112]

During most of the last decade, MEND claimed responsibility for a variety of attacks against oil infrastructure facilities and equipment, including oil pipelines, flow stations, manifolds, and well heads.[113] They also engaged in kidnapping, at one point holding hostages until the successful prison release of Alhaji Asari Dokubo, the leader of the Niger Delta Peoples Volunteer Force. Collectively, these forms of violence had a negative impact on oil production in the region. Foreign oil companies closed down several facilities and sent personnel back home. The resulting decline in oil production was most significant in 2008, when Nigeria produced an average of 1.1 million bbl/day, less than 50 percent of its 2.6 million bbl/day capacity.[114]

Unfortunately, MEND and the other Niger Delta militant groups have not limited their violence to that which can be rationalized by a political ideology of defending ethnic communities and the environment. Several attacks have killed innocent civilians, like the

Figure 7. Cars are destroyed at a blast site in Abuja 1 October 2010. At least 14 were killed. MEND claimed responsibility for the twin car bomb blast. Photo used by permission of Newscom.

2006 car bombings in Port Harcourt and Warri, and the March 2010 car bombs in Warri. Most recently, MEND detonated a car bomb that killed 12 and injured 17 people in Abuja on 1 October 2010. This bombing had additional significance, as it took place near the Eagles Square where President Goodluck Jonathan and foreign friends of the country had gathered to celebrate the 50th anniversary of Nigeria's independence.

Beyond attacks of these kinds, militant groups in the Niger Delta have also become increasingly involved in extortion, oil bunkering, drug trafficking, and other kinds of criminal activity. Through such actions, MEND and other groups have eroded their own support among the local populations on whose behalf they originally claimed to be fighting. Despite their original intentions, many locals now tend to view these groups as just another kind of armed criminal thugs.

Organized Crime in Nigeria

According to the South Africa-based Institute for Security Studies, "Transnational criminality in West Africa is generally thought to consist of (i) drug and human trafficking; (ii) smuggling of various items, particularly arms; (iii) terrorism and violent crime; (iv) maritime piracy, particularly in the Gulf of Guinea; and (v) money laundering and currency counterfeiting."[115] The amount of drug trafficking in particular has increased dramatically over the past decade[116]—by some accounts, 50 percent of non-U.S.-bound cocaine now goes through West Africa.[117] Nigerian organized crime groups have been important players in the drug smuggling business since the 1970s, when they emerged as key suppliers of "mules" (human traffickers) for the illegal trade from South Asia to the United States.[118] Often they are credited with inventing the "swallow" method of drug smuggling in which couriers swallow drugs in condoms and transport them across borders in their bodies.[119] Recent reports by the United Nations Office on Drugs and Crime (UNODC) describe Nigeria as a transit point for drug trafficking organizations to smuggle large amounts of cocaine and marijuana from South America to markets in Europe and North America, as well as the trafficking of heroin and psychotropic substances.[120] From 2006 to 2007, over 30 percent of all cocaine traffickers arrested in France were Nigerian.[121]

Nigerian criminal elements are also engaged in various online fraud schemes and oil bunkering in the Niger Delta. UNODC estimates the annual volume of oil smuggling from Nigeria to be 55 million barrels, generating revenues of at least $1 billion per year.[122] Insurgent groups like MEND siphon off oil by attaching an unauthorized secondary pipeline to a company mainline by the techniques known as hot and cold tapping; in some cases, gangs have blown up a pipeline, putting it out of use long enough for them to attach a spur pipeline which then transports the oil to surface tanks or barges.[123] The oil is then sold to local crime syndicates who either distribute it for sale locally or transport it to world markets. Corrupt government officials and private corporation employees have also participated in oil bunkering through various schemes of embezzlement and bribery. In some cases, unauthorized vessels will be allowed to load oil directly from the terminal while a bribed employee looks the other way; in others, authorized vessels can be "topped"—filled with oil beyond their stated capacity—and the excess load sold for personal profit. Within Nigeria, hundreds of makeshift illegal refineries allow the oil to be converted to other petroleum products that are smuggled throughout West Africa. The increasing emphasis on oil bunkering profits has led to spates of violence between different groups over territorial control, money, and power—similar to the street fighting that takes place between drug gangs in Mexico.

Other criminal enterprises in West Africa include the smuggling of prohibited commodities (or the illegal marketing of legal ones), illegal logging and fishing, dumping of toxic waste, oil theft, and diversion of humanitarian aid.[124] A recent report by UNODC placed the annual value of the trade in fake and low-quality anti-malarial drugs at $438 million, while cigarette smuggling from the Gulf of Guinea to North Africa and Europe was estimated to net approximately $775 million per year.[125] In addition, small arms and light weapons from throughout sub-Saharan Africa have found their way to this volatile region, and armed robbery, carjacking, and kidnapping are on the rise.[126] And Nigeria is seen as a source, destination, and transit country for human trafficking. Mainly young women and girls are trafficked to Europe and other destinations, and there is growing evidence for the involvement of Nigerian criminal networks.[127] According to one UNODC report, "Since the 1980s, Nigerian women from around Benin City have had a presence in European prostitution markets, comprising a significant share of the sex workers detected by authorities in several countries. These women are often victims of exploitative debt bondage, and may work without pay for two to three years to settle the costs of their illegal importation."[128]

The security implications for the wide ranging activities of organized crime in Nigeria are fairly obvious. A shadow economy empowers the criminals and undermines the legitimate economy as well as the authority of the state. The drug trade is intensifying corruption, predatory behavior of political elites, political instability, and a basic weakening of law enforcement and rule of law. The desire to control the massive flows of drug trafficking and oil bunkering profits has led to several turf battles, particularly among Niger Delta militants. Turf battles are also common among armed gangs in northern Nigeria, including the Yan Tauri, Yan Daba, Yan Banga, and Yan Dauka Amarya. Some of these can be described, according to

> The drug trade is intensifying corruption, predatory behavior of political elites, political instability, and a basic weakening of law enforcement and rule of law.

Abimbola Adesoji, as economic opportunists and mercenaries who are prepared to offer their services to whomever hires them, and can be used by anybody to start a civil disturbance.[129]

Transnational traffickers are sometimes viewed locally as powerful and effective at getting things done, and as having significant resources. This translates for many into a belief that organized crime networks have good leadership, and they take care of their own and those who assist them—a belief that in turn helps the trafficking networks attract new recruits and secure local support or acquiescence of their illicit activities. Similarly, there have been several instances in which militants in the Niger Delta have provided social services, electricity, fees for students to pay for exams, micro-credit for local businesses, hospital supplies, subsidies for teacher's pay, and so forth.

In a country where access to resources is constrained by policy and socioeconomic factors, a shadow economy can also fuel military conflict and terrorist activity.[130] Certainly, the intersection of crime and terrorism in Nigeria is a key aspect to our understanding of the operating environment that sustains militant groups of many kinds, including Boko Haram. But while similar kinds of violence and lawlessness are found in both the Niger Delta and northern Nigeria, there are also additional factors that have enabled the rise of militant Islamist ideologies in the north.

Ethno-Political and Religious Violence in the North

While the violence in the south of Nigeria is mainly secular and driven by grievances associated with resources and environmental damage, the north has seen far more ethnic, tribal, and religious violence, often manipulated by politicians for political gain and profit—especially in areas where neither Muslims nor Christians are a clear majority.[131] Resource scarcity and ethnic identity politics play a prominent role in the conflicts of this region. For example, over the last decade an increasing number of the pastoralist Hausa-Fulani have migrated southward from the drought-ridden north, bringing with them cattle that are encroaching on more fertile lands historically owned by other ethnicities. The resulting conflicts have sometimes been portrayed in the media as being Muslim versus Christian, while in fact the violence has frequently been fueled by land use issues and indigenous versus settler rights.[132] For example, a major outbreak of violence in February 1992 in the town of Zango, Kaduna state between Hausa-Fulani and Kataf Christians was largely over land ownership and access to markets.[133] More recently, in late November 2011, what was initially described by Reuters as religious violence was actually a clash over the ownership of cattle and fertile farmland in Barkin Ladi—an area in the city of Jos, the capital of Plateau state—that left at least 10 people dead.[134]

In a 2009 case study of Jos, Philip Ostien explains how local conflicts have arisen "primarily out of ethnic differences, pitting Hausa 'settlers' against the Plateau 'indigene' tribes of Afizere, Anaguta and Berom."[135] The underlying problem, as he sees it, is "the alleged rights of indigenes… to control particular locations."[136] Further, Nigeria's 1979 constitution uses the phrase "belongs or belonged to a community indigenous to Nigeria" in its definition of citizenship, and a formal government agency—the Federal Character Commission established 1995—has the authority to "define an indigene of the state."[137] This constitutional entrenchment of distinctions based on ethnicity and place of origin has direct implications for who can be elected as an LGA councilor: as Murray Last notes, "a candidate who is not classified as 'indigenous' to the local government area can be debarred from being elected."[138] In the north of the country, this means that in some cases a non-indigenous Muslim would not be allowed to run for election, while an indigenous Christian would, potentially inflaming any pre-existing conflicts within a Muslim majority and Christian minority population.

It is also important to note that roughly two-thirds of Nigeria's "minority" ethnic groups (like the Kanuri, the tribe most strongly represented among members of Boko Haram) are located in the northern states, contributing to a shared sense of being marginalized or disadvantaged in terms of receiving a "fair share" of Nigeria's system of resource distribution. The combination of resource scarcity and ethnic identity politics is particularly volatile among marginalized communities during times of national elections. For example, as noted earlier, rioting in several northern cities after the 2011 presidential election (which was won by Goodluck Jonathan, a southern Christian) left more than 800 people dead.

In essence, the socioeconomic and political roots of the conflicts in northern Nigeria tend to run much deeper than the grievances that animate the violence in the south. However, this discussion of the secular dimensions of the conflicts in the north is not meant to diminish the importance of religiously-oriented violence. In truth, an understanding of the complex security environment in the north of Nigeria can only be gained through an appreciation of the history of Islamism in the region, and especially the ways in which several Muslim communities have responded to the declining influence of the Sokoto Caliphate and religious authority.

A Brief History of Radical Islamism in Northern Nigeria

One of the most significant developments in the history of modern Islam in Nigeria was the establishment of the Sokoto Caliphate.[139] During the early 1800s, a Fulani leader named Usman dan Fodio led a revolt against the Hausa kingdoms in the north and subsequently established a theocratic caliphate (a large Muslim empire), with its headquarters in the city of Sokoto.[140] A member of the Qadiriyyah order,[141] dan Fodio was highly critical of greed and violations of the standards of Sharia law among Hausa elites, and encouraged literacy and scholarship among his followers. Upon his death in 1817, his son Muhammad Bello followed him as "Sultan of Sokoto"—leader of the Sokoto Caliphate, which at that time had become a loose confederation of about 30 emirates stretching from modern-day Burkina Faso to Cameroon that recognized the leadership of Usman Dan Fodio as "Commander of the Faithful."[142]

Islam in Nigeria, and indeed throughout much of Africa, is of the Sufi tradition, which is moderate and relatively conservative. According to John Esposito, Sufis view themselves as "Muslims who take seriously God's call to perceive his presence both in the world and in the self... [and] stress inwardness over outwardness, contemplation over action, spiritual development over legalism, and cultivation of the soul over social interaction."[143] Jonathan Hill suggests that "it is this commitment to introspection and quiet meditation that has sustained descriptions of *Sufism* as being mystical and esoteric."[144] But the Sokoto caliphate provided a unifying structure for organization and leadership within the Sufi Muslim communities of West Africa, as well as an official language (Hausa). While military victories against other entities helped secure respect for the Sultan's authority, arguably the most important activity of the caliphate was the scholarship produced by its prolific leaders. For example, Usman dan Fodio and Muhammad Bello published a significant amount of poetry and texts on religion, politics, and history. These writings continue to influence the spiritual and intellectual lives of Nigerian Muslims even though the reign of the Sokoto caliphate ended in the early 20th century, when the British and French began colonizing West Africa.

Britain's colonization of Nigeria during the late 1800s began in Lagos and other points south before moving north and east. By 1903, they occupied the two major cities of the caliphate, Sokoto and Kano. However, colonial administrators decided to keep a weakened version of the Sokoto dynasty as part of their system of indirect rule, though they banned punishments associated with Shariah law, like amputation and stoning. During the last years of British colonial rule, Sheik Abubakar Mahmoud Gumi became one of the most influential and revered Nigerian Muslim leaders of the 20th century. A native of Sokoto, Gumi studied law, religion, and Arabic, and eventually became widely known among Nigerian Muslims for his translation of the Koran into Hausa. During the late 1980s, the elderly Gumi became an outspoken critic of the country's military rulers, but also preached peaceful coexistence, and refused to condone the outbreaks of religious violence. When he passed away in 1992, Gumi left an influential legacy that few other Nigerian Muslim leaders have been able to emulate.[145]

After independence in 1960, Nigeria's new secular constitution declared that criminal law was now a matter for the secular courts; Islamic courts were limited to family law.[146] The weakening of the central authority in Nigeria's Muslim community allowed for new political and spiritual movements, led by charismatic and influential leaders in places like Kano, Katsina, and Zaria.[147] Some of them were radical Islamist clerics (like Ibrahim Zakzaky, Yakubu Yahaya, and Mallam Yakubu) who refused to recognize the state of Nigeria because its laws are not Islamic, and at various times were responsible for inciting religious unrest in several northern regions, such as Bauchi, Kaduna, Kano, and Katsina.[148]

Implications: The Religious Dimensions of Violence in the North

Since Nigeria's independence, religious authorities have faced growing competition by secular forces for influence in Muslim communities. This, as Benjamin Barber has observed, is a common trend among traditional societies in many developing countries impacted by modernization, and by Western globalization in particular. In his analysis, a "tribalism and reactionary fundamentalism" produces militants "who detest modernity— the secular, scientific, rational and commercial civilization created by the Enlightenment as it is defined by both its virtues (freedom, democracy, tolerance, diversity) and its vices (inequality, hegemony, cultural imperialism, and materialism)."[149] This is in part an apt description of the motivations and ideology articulated by members of Boko Haram, as noted in the next chapter of this monograph.

Further, according to British anthropologist Murray Last, a driving force behind the rise of various militant Islamist groups in the north over the last few decades has been a growing sense of spiritual and economic insecurities.[150] Since 1960, the increasing corruption and disarray of post-colonial governance inspired a reactionary, conservative movement among the Muslim communities which called for the introduction of Sharia law among other things as a means for improving public order and moral discipline. But not many in these communities embraced this view, and violence ensued on several occasions across ethnic and religious lines. After years of ineffectively dealing with the communal violence, in 1999 the Nigerian central government allowed the country's states to adopt Sharia. This, in turn, created new tensions between Muslim and Christian communities which had for centuries coexisted peacefully. There are small communities of Muslims within Igbo society and elsewhere in the south, as well as Christian communities throughout the Muslim majority north, and violence has always been rare despite this demographic diversity. A variety of Muslim mosques and madrasas have been founded in the south, as have Christian churches and schools in the north. Religion is felt by many Nigerians to be a matter of personal choice, and it is possible for individuals to change faiths without being castigated, let alone executed.[151] Trust is stronger among members of a particular faith (e.g., a Muslim will prefer to have trade agreements with another Muslim), but cross-religious economic and social relations are as common in Nigeria as in any other country.

However, population growth, economic changes including oil revenues and globalization, corruption, and other forces over the last half century have contributed to a divergent experience for Nigerians according to their ethnic and religious identity. The concentration of resources and power in the hands of a tiny elite, as described in Chapter 2 of this monograph, creates a situation in which, as Philip Ostien describes, "The fighting is about access to resources controlled by the federal, state and local governments."[152] Further, as noted earlier, the wealthy elite throughout the country tend to be Christian, while the most impoverished communities in the country are found among the Hausa, Fulani, Kanuri, and other northern tribes—all of them primarily Muslim. As a result, the ethnic identity politics described in Chapter 3 exacerbate many kinds of inequalities and conspiracy theories that have laid the groundwork for the security challenges Nigeria faces in the north of the country today. It is certainly not a coincidence that the regions of the country where militant Islam has been most prominent are also the poorest of Nigeria.

From this perspective, the emergence of violent extremists like the Nigerian Taliban and Boko Haram can be viewed as a response in northern communities to insecurities about their spiritual and socioeconomic future. These same insecurities have also led to the creation of other kinds of religious militants like the Hisba-Muhtasif.[153] The Hisba, a name that used to refer collectively to various gangs of Islamic fundamentalist vigilantes, see themselves as a kind of religious police, and take it upon themselves to suppress a variety of behaviors they see as inconsistent with Sharia or socially undesirable.[154] Depending on the various state or region, they can reprimand, arrest, or even beat Nigerians caught violating Sharia law. Punishable offenses include drinking or selling alcohol, having premarital sex (most often revealed when the woman gets pregnant), or soliciting a prostitute. In some places, Hisba members also ensure that buses are segregated by gender. These gangs draw their membership from the huge population of unemployed youth, and are sometimes sponsored by local governments.[155] For example, the governor of Zamfara state has been the driving force behind the organization and funding of the Zamfara State Vigilante Service, a group that has been described as a "ragtag volunteer army" in which members known to wear red uniforms patrol Zamfara state arresting anyone suspected of violating Islamic law.[156]

Such forms of community-based policing and enforcement have a deep tradition in Nigeria[157] and West Africa more broadly, with roots in the tribal history of the region and colonial practices which often relied on tribal policing mechanisms for control.[158] Hisba gangs are not sanctioned by the national government, but by serving a role that the government has been unable to fulfill. According to Zachary Devlin-Foltz, they "gained popular support and made it easier for Islamist politicians to justify backing them and harder for non-Islamists to avoid, at minimum, condoning their work."[159] As described by Nigerian scholars Kayode Fayemi and Fummi Olonisaki, these non-state armed groups are in part tolerated by the state "because they respond to the security needs of communities that are far from the view of the state. As such, informal arrangements for security provision have been accorded different degrees of legitimacy by citizens and groups that exercise their demand for security through these informal sources. As a result, the state has lost a significant portion of its monopoly on the use of force as well as some degree of legitimacy as a security provider."[160]

This environment of socioeconomic and religiously-oriented insecurities, combined with the grievances described in Chapter 3 and a variety of other factors, have led to the emergence of militant Islamist groups including the Maitatsine sect and the Nigerian Taliban, a precursor to Boko Haram.[161] The first of these emerged during the late 1970s, when a young preacher from northern Cameroon known as Marwa started gathering a significant following in Kano, much to the consternation of the city's established religious elite.[162] He preached aggressively against Western influence and refused to accept the legitimacy of secular authorities over Muslim communities. In December 1980, a confrontation at a rally between his followers—who called themselves "the Maitatsine"—and police sparked massive rioting, causing destructive chaos in Kano for several weeks, leaving many hundred dead and spreading to other states.[163] Despite Marwa's death in the initial riots, pockets of violence continued for several years.[164]

A more violent religious militant group that was formed sometime around 2003 is the Al-Sunna Wal Jamma ("Followers of the Prophet," also sometimes called "the Nigerian Taliban" because of their claim to being inspired by the Islamist militants in Afghanistan).[165] Its stated objective was to transform Nigeria into an Islamic state and to introduce a more strict version of Sharia law. Its adherents were predominantly religious university students from northern regions of Nigeria. Some 200 members of this group took up arms for the first time on 24 December 2003,[166] when they attacked the village of Kanama in Yobe state, not far from Nigeria's northeast border with Niger. They destroyed government buildings and killed a policeman, then abducted about 30 villagers and took them to an encampment nearby, where they were held for about four days until the Nigerian military responded and destroyed the camp. According to several accounts from the freed villagers, the militants tried to recruit them, forced them to pray, and at least one of them was required to help build a defensive perimeter trench.

Nigerian Taliban militants also attacked police stations in a number of other towns nearby in Yobe and then in neighboring Borno state, burning buildings and stealing large quantities of weapons. At one state building they occupied, the militants pulled down the Nigerian flag and raised that of Afghanistan.[167] In September 2004, several dozen members of the group attacked a police patrol near Gwoza, close to the border with Cameroon; 28 were killed, while others fled across the border and were captured by authorities in that country and then returned to Nigeria for prosecution.[168] As described in the next chapter of this monograph, remnants of this militant group are considered by several observers as having been involved in founding the group known today as Boko Haram.

Another group—the so-called Islamic Movement of Nigeria (IMN), led by the radical cleric Ibrahim El-Zakzaki—was also prominent during the 1980s and 1990s, although their confrontations with the state were less frequent and less bloody than the other two groups mentioned above. Within the past decade, as Muhammad Isa notes, leaders of the IMN have become engaged more in politics than political activism, and its prominence among Islamists has been replaced by the more mainstream Sunni Wahhabi movement of Jama'atul Izalatul Bid'ah Wa Ikamatus Sunnah in northern Nigeria.[169]

These and other expressions of militant Islamism in Nigeria must be understood within the context of a confluence of socioeconomic and political grievances that have remained unaddressed over an extended period of time. Further, unlike the political violence witnessed in the south of the country, the violence in the north has also been fueled by a pervasive insecurity among Muslim communities about their religious and moral well-being, based in part on the fading influence of religious authority in a region that was once the center of a powerful Sokoto Caliphate. As examined further in the next chapter of this monograph, the combination of these environmental enablers has provided opportunities for Islamist extremists like Boko Haram to find ideological resonance and support.

Summary

To sum up, a combination of politically violent groups and organized crime networks in Nigeria creates a daunting mix of complex security challenges for the government.[170] In both the north and the south, terrorist attacks have involved members of Nigeria's growing youthful generation who have increasing access to information and higher expectations which are going unmet, resulting in levels of frustration that fuel the aggression and violence. The motivations for militancy include a variety of ethnic, socioeconomic, and other factors for which there may be no easy political solution. This should be of considerable alarm to the government as it suggests the conflicts could be sustained for many years to come.

In addition, as in many other West African countries, there has often been a blurred line in Nigeria between the state and the official political system on the one hand, and rebel groups and the illegal economy on the other. Prominent politicians and even military officers have often been directly linked to rebel groups—sponsoring, funding, and supervising them and then exploiting new lines of access to the various economies to improve or redefine their political status, power base, and expanded network of clients.[171] For example, MEND has had powerful patrons among the country's military officers and politicians who have encouraged and profited from its oil bunkering activities. As noted in the previous chapter, corruption is perhaps the most entrenched and endemic challenge Nigeria faces today. Together, a combination of security challenges and grievances exacerbate the fragile relationship between Nigerian citizens and their government. Vigilante groups are mushrooming in communities worst affected; the rich are investing in sophisticated security gadgets, tracking devices, and private security.[172] By extension, the unhealthy relationship between citizen and state greatly complicates the challenges of gathering the kinds of intelligence needed for combating crime and terrorism.

The contextual dimensions of grievances and security challenges inform our understanding of Boko Haram and the nature of the Nigerian government's response to it. As a national security problem, most Nigerians have until very recently viewed the radical Islamist threat in the north as less critical than the militant groups in the Niger Delta who have been damaging key economic targets, particularly oil infrastructure. However, a new appreciation for the threat posed by Boko Haram and other religious extremists has emerged following the August 2011 bombing of the UN building in Abuja, the spate of attacks in November 2011, and other related events. Further, when Western scholars analyze the modern security environment of Nigeria, they find a broad array of opportunities for groups like Boko Haram to find weapons, finances, safe havens, and new recruits. With this in mind, the discussion turns now to look at the history, recent evolution, and potential outlook for Boko Haram in Nigeria.

5. The Unique Case of Boko Haram

John Campbell, former U.S. ambassador to Nigeria, recently wrote that "Boko Haram, once an obscure, radical Islamic cult in the North, is evolving into an insurrection with support among the impoverished and alienated Northern population."[173] This one sentence reflects several of the key themes addressed in the previous chapters of this monograph. It is no coincidence that Boko Haram developed from a base in the north of the country, where a combination of socioeconomic isolation, politicized religious and ethnic identity, and conspiracy theories driven by fear and reinforced by a heavy-handed security response to protests all work together to create an enabling environment for radical Islamist ideologies to resonate. Having explored various kinds of enabling factors within the Nigerian context, we now turn to focus on the organization itself, and how it has taken advantage of this context to spread an ideology that resonates and leads to recruitment and financial support. Questions that guide the analysis include: How has Boko Haram come to be? What is its motivating ideology? What has it done thus far, and to what effect? Who funds and supports it? What are its linkages with other Islamist groups, or with al-Qaeda and the global Salafi-jihadist movement? After addressing these and other questions, the discussion turns to offer some thoughts about the potential future trajectory of Boko Haram.

A Brief History

As described in the previous chapter, there are some indications that key members of the Nigerian Taliban, including Aminu Tashen Ilimi, were integrally involved in the founding and early evolution of Boko Haram.[174] However, there are differences in opinion over the precise date and conditions under which the group that became known as Boko Haram was first established. A senior Nigerian military officer has suggested that the group has existed in some form or another since 1995,[175] while others have written that it was founded in 2003 or 2004. Nigerian reporter Isioma Madike contends that the group began in 1995 as Sahaba under the leadership of the conservative Islamist cleric Lawan Abubakar, who later left for the University of Medina in Saudi Arabia for further studies.[176] Isa Umar Gusau suggests that the origins of the group can be traced to a group of Muslim students who dropped out of the University of Maiduguri around 2002.[177]

Despite the existence of various conflicting accounts, it is agreed by most observers that in 2002, a 32-year old charismatic Muslim cleric, Ustaz Mohammed Yusuf, established a religious complex with a mosque and an Islamic boarding school in Maiduguri in Borno state, along with a prayer group which he called "Jama'atul Alhul Sunnah Lidda'wati wal Jihad" loosely translated from Arabic as "people committed to the propagation of the Prophet's teachings and jihad."[178] Adam Nossiter of the *New York Times* describes Maiduguri as "a hot, low-rise city of about one million people near the border with Cameroon. Exhortations to Allah are posted at traffic circles, women are veiled and bands of ragged boys carry plastic begging bowls."[179] The "ragged boys" he refers to are the *almajiri*, children sent by their parents to Islamic boarding schools in northern Nigeria, where they receive little education beyond rote memorization of the Koran. They receive no money, and are forced to beg in the streets in order to survive. Some teachers at these schools have been known to abuse these children, in some cases taking a portion of whatever people give them, and in other cases using them as foot soldiers in religious clashes.[180] This is the kind of school that was established by Yusuf.

Islamic Sharia law was adopted in Maiduguri during the late 1990s, as it was across Nigeria's northern states, but it was not enforced strictly enough for the conservative Yusuf.[181] A devout salafist, Yusuf embraced the view, first promulgated by the 13th century religious scholar Taqi al-Din Ibn Taymiyya, that the reason Muslim communities are made to suffer is because their leaders have not been true to the faith. He preached that it was necessary to engage in active jihad in order to defend the *ummah* (global community of Muslims) and spread the faith, and that a leader who does not enforce Sharia law completely, and wage active jihad against infidels, is unfit to rule. This was a much different conception of jihad than what the Sufi sects of Nigeria promoted, where the concept of "greater jihad" was viewed as being an internal struggle necessary for spiritual insight.

According to Toni Johnson of the Council on Foreign Relations, Yusuf originally intended his Salafist prayer and self-isolation movement to promote the religion of Islam and encourage the enforcement of Sharia law in the country's northern states.[182] He attracted mostly disaffected young people and unemployed university students and graduates, many of them animated by deep-seated socioeconomic and political grievances like poor governance and corruption. These are a similar breed of recruits—motivated by similar kinds of grievances—who participated in the Maitatsine riots of northeast Nigeria beginning in December 1980 described in the previous chapter.[183] In his preaching, Yusuf criticized northern Muslims for participating in what he believed to be an illegitimate state and encouraged his followers to protest and withdraw from society and politics.[184] Both the Maitatsine and Yusuf's followers rejected Western civilization and called for the strict enforcement of Sharia law.

In essence, Boko Haram—as the group came to be called by locals and eventually by the government, because of its anti-Western focus—sought to create a 'better' Nigeria through strict adherence to Islam. Over time, the group's members saw themselves increasingly at odds with the secular authorities, whom they came to view as representatives of a corrupt, illegitimate, Christian-dominated federal government. Their disappointment in local government leaders was worsened in the summer of 2009, when authorities in Bauchi refused to allow them to preach and recruit publicly.[185] Then on 11 June 2009 an encounter with the police turned violent. Nigeria had recently passed a law mandating the use of motorcycle helmets, but during a funeral procession to bury some of their members who died in a car accident, Boko Haram members refused to adhere to this law. This was perceived by the police as an open defiance of authority, reflecting a continuing pattern of behavior by Boko Haram that had to be dealt with. During the confrontation, 17 members of Boko Haram were shot; they

Figure 8. Photo obtained on 5 August 2009 shows the leader of the Boko Haram Islamic sect Mohammed Yusuf, 39, surrounded by soldiers at Giwa Barracks in Maiduguri, northeastern Nigeria, on 30 July 2009 shortly after his capture by Nigerian troops. Used by permission of Newscom.

were hospitalized at the University of Maiduguri Teaching Hospital, but none died.[186]

Anger at what were perceived to be heavy-handed police tactics then triggered an armed uprising in the northern state of Bauchi and spread into the states of Borno, Yobe, and Kano.[187] The violence began on 26 July when Boko Haram members attacked and destroyed the Dutsen Tanshi police station in Bauchi.[188] Over the next four days, in the towns of Maiduguri, Lamisulu, and Gamboru, members attacked the state police headquarters, a primary school, a maximum security prison, the national Directorate of Employment, the Makera police station, the Police Mobile College barracks, and several churches. The violence left at least 50 civilians, 22 suspected militants, two police officers, and one prison officer dead. On the same day, the group attacked several targets in nearby Yobe, including the Calvary Baptist Church, the National Population Commission, and the Federal Road Safety Commission office. And in Kano, members attacked the Wudil police station.[189]

The Nigerian army was deployed to reinforce and assist the overwhelmed local police forces, and when it was over more than 800 people were dead.[190] Many Boko Haram members were arrested, and some were paraded in humiliating fashion outside the police stations. Yusuf—along with his father in-law Baa Fugu and other sect members—were publicly executed on 30 July 2009 outside the police station in Maiduguri. The police initially claimed that they died after an intense gun battle with officers on duty, but video clips that later emerged showed that they were executed in cold blood.[191] Many observers and human rights advocates described these as extra-judicial killings, and eventually the Nigerian government agreed: in late 2011, five police officers were brought to trial for allegedly murdering Yusuf.[192]

This brief period marked a turning point for Boko Haram, whose new leaders—Imam Shekau, considered a spiritual leader and operational commander; Kabiru Sokoto, the alleged mastermind of the Christmas 2011 attacks described below; and Shaikh Abu Muhammed[193]—have been described by some observers as more radical and extremist than Yusuf was. For many members of the sect, the unjust circumstances surrounding the death of Yusuf served to amplify pre-existing animosities toward the government. Their communities, as Nigerian scholar Muhammad Isa notes, had been wrecked by "poverty, deteriorating social services and infrastructure, educational backwardness, rising numbers of unemployed graduates, massive numbers of unemployed youths, dwindling fortunes in agriculture... and the weak and dwindling productive base of the northern economy."[194] The accumulation of a broad range of socioeconomic and political grievances now justified, in their minds, a terrorist campaign. There are few other terms that could be used to describe the steady drumbeat of terrorist attacks that have taken place since 2009.

Attacks Attributed to Boko Haram

While it is beyond the scope of this monograph to provide an exhaustive catalog of all known attacks attributed to Boko Haram to date, the incidents listed in Appendix A exemplify the kinds of targets and lethality for which the group has established a reputation. In its early stages, the group mainly attacked Christians using clubs, machetes, and small arms as part of a strategy to provoke sectarian violence. By late 2010, Boko Haram had begun making and using crude but effective improvised explosive devices, often soft drink cans filled with explosives and a fuse that was lit and then thrown from a passing motorcycle.[195]

Analysis of attacks by Boko Haram over the last few years yields some important insights. To begin, it should be noted that while other groups described in the previous chapter have accumulated an extensive record of attacks over time—including the Niger Delta People Volunteer Force, the Iduwini Volunteer Force, and MEND—since 2009 Boko Haram has been responsible for more attacks and more casualties than any other armed group in Nigeria, as reflected in Figure 9. Further, since 2010, this group has been responsible for more terrorist attacks in Nigeria than all other groups combined.

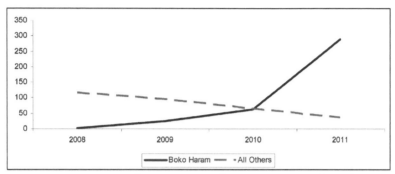

Figure 9: Proportion of Terrorist Attacks in Nigeria Attributed to Boko Haram. Source: Institute for the Study of Violent Groups, 2011

It is important to note that not only have Boko Haram's attacks increased in recent years, it accounts for a *rapidly increasing proportion* of all terrorist attacks that have occurred in the past few years. This should be taken into consideration when reviewing the Nigerian government's response to this group, as described in the next chapter of this monograph. Boko Haram has clearly become the most serious terrorist threat to Nigeria.

A majority of Boko Haram's attacks have come in just two forms: armed assaults and bombings. Over the past three years, as indicated in Figure 10, they have been responsible for more armed assaults than bombings, but there has been a very significant increase in bombings since mid-2011. Further, the number of casualties from Boko Haram bombings is now more than twice that of their armed assaults.

	All incidents (incl. robberies)	Bombings	Bombing Casualties	Armed Assaults	Armed Assault Casualties
2009	23	1	7	14	219
2010	57	11	127	35	107
2011	191	74	587	89	258

Figure 10: Terrorist Incidents Attributed to Boko Haram, 2009-2011. Source: Institute for the Study of Violent Groups, 2011

In addition to increasing frequency, Boko Haram's attacks have also spread geographically. Until recently, their attacks took place mainly in a handful of states in the northeast—Bauchi, Borno, Yobe, Plateau, and Kaduna—and mostly in and around the towns of Maiduguri, Damaturu,

Bama, and Potiskum. By the end of 2011, as indicated in Figure 11, the group's attacks had spread to the west and south of their original areas of operation, to include the towns of Kano, Katsina, Bauchi, Jos, Gombe, and the nation's capitol, Abuja.

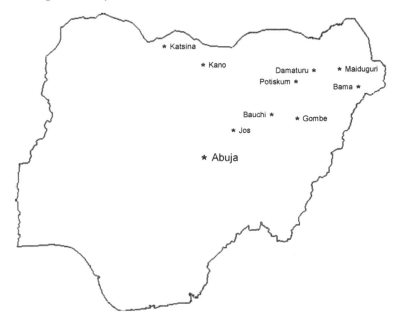

Figure 11: Map of Boko Haram Attack Locations in Nigeria, 2009-11 (author's figure)

All these developments indicate an expansion in Boko Haram's tactics, lethality, and geographic reach. Some observers have suggested al-Qaeda or one of its affiliates have played a role in this, as described later in this chapter. However, it is also equally likely that Boko Haram's increasing operational capabilities may have been derived from interactions with weapons traffickers and other criminal networks already indigenous to the northern regions of Nigeria.

They have also compiled a rather broad list of targets and victims. Members of Boko Haram have been responsible for attacks against government officials, military patrols, churches, politicians, academic institutions, police stations—from which they have stolen weapons used in subsequent attacks—and Christian and Muslim figures of traditional and religious authority who have been critical of its ideology.

As noted in Figure 12, Boko Haram's most frequent targets have been police stations, patrols, and individual policemen at home or in public who were off-duty or even retired. They have used petrol bombs, improvised explosive devices, and armed assaults in these attacks. A common tactic used by the group has been drive-by shootings and bombings. Almost all of the armed assaults were direct-fire, drive-by shootings, usually involving motorbikes, against unarmed individuals. They have also targeted a variety of politicians, including village chiefs and a member of parliament. On a few occasions, they have attacked prisons: in their 7 September 2010 attack against a large prison in Bauchi, guards were overpowered and an estimated 800 prisoners were released, including at least 120 Boko Haram members or supporters who were awaiting trial.[196] The group has also attacked individuals whom they deem to be engaged in un-Islamic activities, like drinking beer. But the category with the largest number of identified casualties have been churchgoers, clerics, and others affiliated in some way with organized religion.

	Target Categories				
	Political	Police or Military*	Religious	Educational	Other**
Number of Attacks	22	44	27	5	42
Est. Casualties	108	81	109	7	417

Figure 12: Victims of Attacks Attributed to Boko Haram, 2009-2011. Source: See list of attacks in Appendix A of this report.

* Includes other security personnel, like "prisons" and "guards"

** Includes "beer parlor," "shopping market," "public square," "bank" etc.

While most of the religiously-affiliated targets and casualties of these attacks have been Christian, there have also been several attacks by the group's members against prominent Muslims. For example, they are believed to be responsible for murdering Sheikh Ibrahim Birkuti, a prominent cleric who had publicly criticized Boko Haram for the increasing violence. He was shot dead as he left a mosque in Biu, approximately 125 miles south of Maiduguri.[197] Other Muslim leaders killed by Boko Haram include: Bashir Kashara, a well-known Wahhabi cleric, killed in October 2010; and Ibrahim Ahmad Abdullahi, a non-violent preacher, killed in June 2011.[198] Members of the group are believed to be responsible for killing the Shehu of Borno's brother; the Shehu is considered the most important traditional Islamic ruler in northeast Nigeria, generally regarded as second only to the Sultan of Sokoto among the Islamic emirate hierarchy.[199] Through these attacks, Boko Haram has demonstrated the kind of defensiveness about their ideology that we have seen among many other terrorist groups throughout history, including al-Qaeda.

Finally, the number of attacks against public targets (with no affiliation to any of the categories described above) has risen significantly in the past two years. In July 2009, shortly before his death, Yusuf claimed that Boko Haram did not "have any quarrel with the public, only the authorities, unless the general public supports the authorities."[200] However, the data clearly shows that a majority of their attacks from 2009 to 2011 have killed ordinary citizens, not authorities. In several recent instances, they have carried out mass casualty attacks, the intent of which can only be to kill indiscriminately. For example, on 29 May 2011, as newly elected Nigerian president Goodluck Jonathan took the oath of office, Boko Haram detonated three bombs at an army barracks in Bauchi state, killing at least 14 people.

Two weeks later, on 16 June, the first suicide bombing in Nigeria's history took place just outside the Nigeria Police Headquarters in Abuja.[201] The attack occurred as Inspector General of Police Hafiz Ringim was arriving at the building, called Louis Edet House. According to authorities, the driver of a car followed Ringim's convoy through the main gate and was heading toward the area where escort vehicles are parked when he was stopped and questioned by a guard, who then diverted the driver to a different part of the parking lot where the detonation took place.[202] Six people were killed, dozens more injured by debris and fire, and at least 40 cars were destroyed. This also highlighted the evolution of Boko Haram's tactical capabilities to include the kind of vehicle-born improvised explosive devices that security forces in Iraq and Afghanistan have become all too familiar with.

Then on 26 August 2011, Boko Haram carried out its most notorious attack to date using a suicide car bomber to blow up the United Nations building in Abuja. At least 18 people were killed, and many more were injured when the blast destroyed the lower floors of the building. According to one report, the driver rammed the car into an exit gate and then drove into a parking garage before detonating his explosives.[203] This is significant, according to Scott Stewart, because:

The U.N. compound was located in the diplomatic district of Abuja, where numerous high-profile facilities are located, demonstrating that Boko Haram possessed the ability to spot a soft target amid harder targets like foreign embassies and government buildings. The group also managed to successfully find and exploit the security gap at the exit gate. This indicates that some type of surveillance may have been conducted before the attack was launched.[204]

To date, Boko Haram has used car bombs in fewer than a dozen attacks, but each of these have attracted tremendous attention and with the exception of the attack on Nigeria's Police Headquarters, have been extraordinarily deadly.

In sum, Boko Haram was once viewed by authorities as a nuisance confined to the far northeast, attacking Christians with machetes and small arms. It has now become the most notorious armed group in Nigeria. It has expanded its attacks in terms of frequency and lethality, and its targets now include international ones like the UN building. While armed assaults were the predominant mode of attack in 2009, the group has recently added suicide bombings to its arsenal, beginning with the attack against the Abuja police barracks on 16 June 2011. These developments indicate an increasing level of capability and sophistication. In order to diminish the group's capabilities for causing more bloodshed and carnage, Nigeria's authorities must identify and interdict the financial sources of Boko Haram—a critical aspect of any terrorist group's operational capabilities.

Finances

Little is known publicly about Boko Haram's finances, though the U.S. and its allies have become increasingly engaged in a collaborative effort with Nigerian authorities to gather specific intelligence on the group's crossnational relationships, potential sources of funding and weapons, and other key operational aspects. Some investigations have led to members of the Nigerian diaspora living in places like Pakistan, Europe, and the U.S., but to date no major arrests have taken place in those countries.

Some reports suggest that the group finances its activities through robbing local banks.[205] For example, on 12 January 2010, four Boko Haram members attempted to rob a bank in Bakori Local Government Area of

Katsina state, according to the local Police Commissioner Umaru Abubakar Manko.[206] On 4 December 2011, Bauchi police commissioner Ikechukwu Aduba claimed that members of Boko Haram had robbed local branches of Guaranty Trust Bank PLC and Intercontinental Bank PLC.[207] And on 10 December 2011, Mohammed Abdullahi, spokesman of the Central Bank of Nigeria, claimed that "At least 30 bank attacks attributed to Boko Haram have been reported this year."[208]

The group's financing has also been allegedly linked to specific individuals with power and access to resources. Given the extensive system of patronage in Nigeria, this should come as no surprise. Several of these individuals have been arrested, but some were killed before any judicial process could determine their guilt or innocence. For example, on 31 July 2009 Alhaji Buji Foi—former Borno State Commissioner for Religious Affairs—was arrested and taken to Police Headquarters in Maiduguri, where he was publicly executed on 31 July 2009, a day after Yusuf was killed at the same location.[209] In January 2011, another suspected financier, local contractor Alhaji Bunu Wakil, was arrested in Maiduguri alongside 91 others suspected of being members or supporters of Boko Haram.[210] A month later, another alleged sponsor of the group, Alhaji Salisu Damaturu was killed during a shoot-out with police. According to Mohammed Jinjiri Abubakar, police commissioner for Borno state, Damaturu and another man, Mohammed Goni, had been named as financing the Boko Haram sect by an arms dealer, Mohammed Zakaria, who had been arrested in Maiduguri a week earlier.[211] And in November 2011, authorities arrested a member of the Nigerian Senate—Ali Ndume, a Peoples Democratic Party senator from Borno—and charged him with financing Boko Haram. Ndume's arrest came after he was fingered by Ali Sanda Umar Konduga, a Boko Haram spokesman who had been arrested a week earlier, and authorities claimed that Konduga's phone records indicated several communications between him and the legislator.[212] Figure 13 lists a handful of prominent individuals who have been accused by Nigerian authorities of being a sponsor of Boko Haram.

Alhaji Salisu Damaturu[213]	Sa'idu Pindar[217]
Alhaji Buji Foi[214]	Alhaji Ali Modu Sheriff[218]
Mohammed Goni[215]	Alhaji Bunu Wakil[219]
Ali Ndume[216]	

(Details on each are provided in the Notes section at the end of this chapter)

Figure 13: Individuals Accused of Being Financial Sponsors of Boko Haram

Finally, beyond bank robberies and individual financiers, there have also been rumors of Boko Haram's involvement in trafficking of illegal weapons and drugs, although there has to date been no firm evidence to support such claims. But whatever the sources of Boko Haram's financing, individuals involved in supporting the group do so largely because they find some resonance in the group's radical jihadist ideology. When this ideology resonates among individuals with access to resources, it clearly benefits the group's operational capabilities. Therefore, a thorough analysis of Boko Haram's ideology is necessary.

Socioeconomic and Religious Dimensions of Boko Haram's Ideology

In order to understand the emergence of Boko Haram, one must look for reasons why its ideology has found resonance among a small but increasingly capable group of young men in Nigeria. Drawing on the framework identified in Chapter 1 and the topics addressed in Chapters 2-4, we can see that an array of grievances and opportunities have laid the groundwork for Boko Haram to find some traction for its cause. These include rampant corruption among a political and wealthy elite that is heavily invested in the status quo; communities that see themselves politically and economically disadvantaged and marginalized; a lack of critical infrastructure and basic support services; a history with long periods of military dictatorship and political oppression; and a system in which entrenched ethnic identities are politicized and constrain opportunities for movement and meritocratic advancement.

In addition to these grievances, which are prevalent throughout the country, there are also specific political and socioeconomic frustrations found predominantly in northern Nigeria. Poverty, unemployment, and lack of education are much higher here than in the rest of the country. A recent report by the National Population Commission found that literacy rates are much lower among states in the North, and that 72 percent of children around the ages of 6-16 never attended schools in Borno state, where Boko Haram was founded.[220] As noted in earlier chapters, the lack of quality education is a core structural obstacle for individuals seeking a better future for themselves and their families.

The issue of schooling is particularly salient to understanding the ideology of Boko Haram. The Hausa word *boko* is derived from the English word 'book' and has come to mean the ability to read and write, especially in the Western-styled educational system, as distinct from the Islamic educational system that existed in northern Nigeria before being dislodged by colonialism.[221] As Muhammad Isa observes, the term implies a sense of rejection and "resistance to imposition of Western education and its system of colonial social organization, which replaced and degraded the earlier Islamic order of the *jihadist* state."[222] Further, according to Isa:

> Islamic scholars and clerics who once held sway in the caliphate state and courts assigned the name *boko* to northern elites who spoke, acted, ruled and operated the state like their Western colonial masters. It is not uncommon to hear in discussions among Islamist scholars and average northerners that poverty and collapsed governance—the bane of the region—can be blamed on the failures and corrupt attitudes of *yan boko* (modern elites trained at secular schools) who have acquired a Western education and are currently in positions of power. As such, the system represented by the *yan boko* is unjust, secular and has no divine origin. It is therefore un-Islamic, which in turn accounts for its ineptitude and corruptness.[223]

Of course, the Almajira system described earlier in this chapter—with schools attached to a Koranic teacher and emphasizing mainly rote learning of the Koran—remained available, with informal and fairly open criteria for admission, as opposed to the Western-oriented education system where access is restricted based on formal entry requirements. However, as a recent

UN report noted, these Islamic boarding schools offer "a kind of education which leaves students virtually unemployable in an increasingly globalizing economy in which Western education (communication, math, sociology, political science, history, etc.) is far more important."[224]

In essence, acquisition of a Western education was actively promoted in Nigeria during the colonial and post-colonial era as a means for achieving a better standard of living, an opportunity for uplifting one's position and access to power.[225] But during the late 1980s and early 1990s, the structural adjustment programs under the Babangida administration affected Nigeria's northern communities the most because the lack of education and infrastructure was the worst here. As Isa notes, "a new form of neo-liberal market economy was ushered in that privatized the state and resulted in university educated graduates struggling to find employment. Employment became a matter of a patron-client relationship, coupled with access to state power."[226] The deregulation of the nation's economy also set the stage for the sharp decline in farming in the north, as the government disposed of all land and programs they had maintained to support agricultural activities in the area.[227] Climate change and the country's increasing dependence on oil revenues also shaped the fortunes of the agricultural sector in the North.

All these socioeconomic changes combined to produce a sense of insecurity and vulnerability among northern Nigerians, and particularly among Muslim communities. This, in turn, offers insights into why Boko Haram's ideology has resonated among many, including frustrated university graduates who find legitimacy in their argument that Western society has failed them; their aspirations cannot be met by the system currently in place. As noted in Chapter 1, research by Andrew Kydd and Barbara Walter indicates that terrorist organizations are usually driven by political objectives, and in particular "five have had enduring importance: regime change, territorial change, policy change, social control and status quo maintenance."[228] These objectives have led to the formation of terrorist groups throughout the world. Research by Roy and Judy Eidelson identified what they call "belief domains" that also propel groups and individuals toward conflict, including superiority, injustice, vulnerability, distrust, and helplessness.[229] In the case of Boko Haram, several of these ideological components can be identified: the desire for policy change and social control; a religiously-based sense of superiority; distrust of authorities; perceptions of injustice; and shared feelings of vulnerability, particularly with regard to socioeconomic conditions and the status of Islam vis-à-vis other influences in the region. As Alex Thurston has observed, "Boko Haram has an entrenched sense of victimhood and now sees the state as both the main persecutor of "true" Muslims and the major obstacle to "true" Islamic reform.[230]

Religious Dimensions of Boko Haram's Ideology and Resonance

In the eyes of Boko Haram's members and supporters, the political and socioeconomic changes described above have corrupted Islamic society. As Boko Haram's founding leader Yusuf preached, "Our land was an Islamic state before the colonial masters turned it to a kafir land. The current system is contrary to true Islamic beliefs."[231] Throughout the Muslim communities of northern Nigeria today, there is a sense of unease and insecurity about the spiritual and moral future of their children, and concern about the fading influence of religious leaders like the Sultan of Sokoto.[232] The Sokoto Caliphate of the 19th century is remembered by locals as a fairly well-structured political system which melded politics, society, and Islamic education. In 1903, it was rapidly replaced by a Western European, Christian power with very different ideas about the relationship between governance and religion. Thus, a core element behind Boko Haram's ideological resonance is the simple fact that since the beginning of the 20th century, the historic *Dar-al-Islam* (house of Islam) built by dan Fodio has been ruled by non-Muslims.

As noted in the previous chapter, radicalization among Nigeria's Muslim communities is not exclusive to Boko Haram. To the contrary, there have been many groups throughout the country's history that have professed a belief system that rejects that status quo and actively aspires to an ideal past or envisioned future, and have incorporated violence as a means to achieve those aspirations. Many—but certainly not all—of these groups have been Islamist, meaning they have demanded that all Muslims be ruled by Muslim rulers and Sharia laws. In addition to the Maitatsine described in the previous chapter, another prominent entity in opposition to Islamic modernity in Nigeria is known as the Islamic Movement of Nigeria, a Sunni organization led by Shaykh Ibrahim el-Zakzaki.[233] According to RAND analyst Peter Chalk, "outside observers consider this group as the vanguard of a militant fundamentalist resurgence in Nigeria's northern states whose devotees remain committed to religious purity and counterdemocratic/capitalist objectives."[234] While Boko Haram has clearly overshadowed the IMN in recent years, it is important to note for a U.S. readership that in his sermons and statements, el-Zakzaki has portrayed U.S. military actions in Afghanistan and Iraq as a thinly veiled crusade aimed at Islam itself.[235]

In sum, Boko Haram's ideology is embedded in a deep tradition of Islamism, and is but one of several variants of radical Islamism to have emerged in northern Nigeria. Its followers are reportedly influenced by the Koranic phrase which says: "Anyone who is not governed by what Allah has revealed is among the transgressors."[236] However, the group's ideology resonates for many reasons beyond religion. Socioeconomic grievances include the huge gap between aspirations of Nigeria's youth and the opportunities provided by the system for achieving a better life. A swelling population amid economic despair creates an environment in which radical extremist ideologies can thrive.

In addition, the waning of Muslim leaders' power and influence in the region is a source of resentment; for a century, the elites of Northern Nigeria were Muslim community leaders, but this changed after the fall of the Sokoto Caliphate, and the new elites are seen by many as protecting and benefiting from a system of corruption and injustice. As Chris Ngwodo notes, Boko Haram "is a symptom of decades of failed government and elite delinquency finally ripening into social chaos."[237] Muhammad Isa provides an apt summary:

> The idea of *boko* is not just about rejecting Western education per se; it is a judgment of its failure to provide opportunities for better lives and thus became a symbol for the *Boko Haram* movement to capitalise on the shortcomings of *yan boko*. Subsequently it was coupled with *haram* (forbidden). The movement used the term to mobilise unemployed, unskilled and poverty-stricken youths to join its cause, dislodge the secular, boko-controlled state in Nigeria, and introduce the strict application of *Shariah* law and the creation of an Islamic state. This partly explains why *Boko Haram's* primary targets of attack were symbols of the state such as security agencies, which had become widely despised.[238]

The religious and socioeconomic dimensions of Boko Haram's ideology are amplified by the forces of western globalization, seen by many Islamists as a form of neo-colonialism. This, in turn, allows linkages to be made with the ideology of al-Qaeda and the global jihadist movement, where globalization is characterized as part of a perpetual war against the traditional beliefs and values of the *ummah* (global community of Muslims).

Linkages with al-Qaeda and the Global Jihadist Movement

Boko Haram is a small radical Sunni Islamist sect that finds only limited support among the mainly moderate Sufi Islamic communities of Nigeria, particularly the dominant Qadiriyya and Tijaniyaa brotherhoods. Because of this and its very anti-Western ideology, there have been growing concerns about the potential relationship between the group and Sunni extremist or terrorist groups elsewhere, including al-Qaeda or local affiliate groups like al-Shabaab in Somalia or al-Qaeda in the Islamic Maghreb (AQIM), located mainly in Algeria and Mali. If there is indeed growing collaboration between Boko Haram and al-Qaeda, it would benefit both in several ways. Boko Haram would gain access to expertise, weapons, and financing capabilities of individuals and affiliates of the global jihadist network, while al-Qaeda would gain an important foothold in West Africa with political impact, as Nigeria is a key strategic ally of the U.S. and Europe, and economic ramifications, particularly because of Nigeria's importance to global oil markets. In 2003, Osama bin Laden indicated that Nigeria was one of several countries "ready for liberation,"[239] suggesting that al-Qaeda would certainly welcome the establishment of an affiliate group in Nigeria. Thus, Western scholars and policymakers have recently begun looking for evidence to indicate whether Boko Haram is transforming from a local religious militant sect into an affiliate of the transnational al-Qaeda terrorist network.

On an ideological level, there is certainly some general alignment with al-Qaeda. The grievances that animate their violent attacks are similar in terms of portraying Western globalization and the status quo as inherently disadvantaging Muslims. Both groups promulgate the view that politicians and wealthy elites have destroyed the purity of Islamic societies by allowing vices like prostitution, pornography, and alcohol to corrupt mankind. Boko Haram and al-Qaeda members also share a belief in the superiority of governance by Sharia law instead of secular laws, and claim to be defending Islam against Western influences that constrain or prevent a Muslim from fulfilling his or her religious duties. Al-Qaeda's core ideology of "think globally and act locally"[240] is intended to inspire the kinds of attacks against authorities that Boko Haram has become known for. And, as noted in the previous chapter, Islamist extremists in Nigeria have also been inspired by the example of the Taliban in Afghanistan. The combination of these things suggests an ideological framework for collaboration between Boko Haram and al-Qaeda.

Views about the likelihood of operational ties between Boko Haram and al-Qaeda have changed over the last three years. Consider the following timeline of statements and reports:

- **August 2009:** The British Broadcasting Company (BBC) reported that "so far there has been no evidence of Osama Bin Laden's group in Nigeria, despite several arrests by the government and two warnings from the US about potential attacks on its interests in the country in as many years." According to Adam Higazi, a researcher on Nigeria at Oxford University, "Nigerian Islamic sects are relatively parochial and inward-looking, concentrating on fighting the Nigerian government rather than a worldwide jihad."[241]
- **February 2010:** AQIM announced its intent to train and arm Nigerian Muslims to fight against Nigerian Christians. According to an account published in Reuters, the statement was signed by AQIM "emir" Abu Mus'ab Abdelwadoud, and declared "We are ready to train your people in weapons and give you whatever support we can in men, arms and munitions to enable you to defend our people in Nigeria."[242]
- **June 2010:** A report broadcast on the Arab satellite news channel Al-Jazeera suggested that AQIM leader Abdalwadoud had agreed to provide Boko Haram "with ammunition and military gear to defend Muslims in Nigeria and face the march of the Crusader minority," and in return the Nigerian Islamist group would be expected to expand its operations and begin attacking foreign interests, including U.S. targets.[243]
- **October 2010:** A senior leader of Boko Haram, Shaykh Muhammed Abu Bakr Bin Muhammed al-Shakwa, reportedly responded to Abdalwadoud's invitation by pledging the group's allegiance to AQIM.[244]

- **February 2011:** In his testimony to Congress and his report "World-wide Threat Assessment of the U.S. Intelligence Community," U.S. Director of National Intelligence James Clapper stated that Boko Haram was "focused on local issues… [and] may be pursuing interests it shares with AQIM."[245]
- **June 2011:** The newly published National Strategy for Counterterrorism states that AQIM "has trained fighters from other allied organizations – such as Nigerian-based Boko Haram."
- **June 2011:** A spokesman for Boko Haram announced that members of the group had just returned from receiving militant training in Somalia, ostensibly provided by the al-Qaeda affiliated militant group al-Shabaab.[246] According to the IPT News service report, the statement read as follows: "We want to make it known that our jihadists have arrived in Nigeria from Somalia where they received real training on warfare from our brethren who made that country ungovernable."[247]
- **July 2011:** A report in a Nigerian newspaper suggested that British spies had uncovered a plot by al-Qaeda to make Nigeria their headquarters from where they could carry out attacks on Europe.[248] However, no corroborating reports or evidence of this has since emerged.
- **August 2011:** General Carter Ham—commander of the U.S. Africa Command—stated that several sources of information indicate the group has had contacts with AQIM as well as al-Shabaab in Somalia.[249] "What is most worrying at present," he said, is "a clearly stated intent by Boko Haram and by al-Qaeda in the Islamic Maghreb to coordinate and synchronize their efforts."[250]

Then came the attack against the United Nations Building in Abuja on 26 August killing at least 23 people and injuring 80 others. According to Nigeria's State Security Service, Boko Haram member Mamman Nur is accused of masterminding the attack, and is believed to have links with the al-Qaeda affiliate group al-Shabaab in Somalia.[251] Following this attack, General Ham stated that Boko Haram, al-Shabaab, and AQIM have each "very explicitly and publicly voiced an intent to target Westerners and the U.S. specifically."[252] To some observers, the attack indicated an expansion from ideological alignment to strategic and operational coordination. In September 2011, Gilles de Kerchove, the European Union's Counterterrorism

Coordinator, noted that "there is still nothing structural. There are efforts at contacts, and small transfers of money. It seems that some members of Boko Haram and al Shabaab were trained by AQIM."[253]

In November 2011, the Algerian deputy foreign minister, Abdelkader Messahel, stated that he had "no doubts that coordination exists between Boko Haram and al-Qaeda. The way both groups operated and intelligence reports show there is cooperation."[254] Also in November 2011, the U.S. Embassy in Nigeria issued an emergency warning to its citizens living in or visiting the country about potential Boko Haram attacks on major hotels in Abuja, including the Transcorp Hilton Hotel, Sheraton Hotels and Towers, and Nicon Luxury Hotels.[255] Al-Qaeda affiliates have attacked Western hotels elsewhere in the world, including Kenya, Indonesia, the Philippines, Turkey, and Pakistan.

On 24 November a purported spokesman for Boko Haram, Abul Qaqa, stated: "It is true that we have links with al-Qaeda. They assist us and we assist them."[256] And on 30 November 2011 the U.S. House of Representatives Committee on Homeland Security released a headline-grabbing report, *Boko Haram: Emerging Threat to the U.S. Homeland*, which claimed:

> Perhaps the most troubling aspect of the rise of Boko Haram in Nigeria is the reports of increasing collaboration between the group and al Qaeda in the Lands of the Islamic Maghreb (AQIM) and al Shabaab. The rapid evolution of Boko Haram may point to the sharing of weapons and expertise among various terrorist organizations across the African continent.[257]

Thus, a synthesis of available research indicates that ideological agreement between Boko Haram and al-Qaeda is fairly straightforward. What is less clear is the extent to which strategic or operational collaboration exists. The fact that Boko Haram attacked an international target, the UN building in Abuja, is evidence to some that the group is now fully engaged in the global jihadist movement. Further, the increasing sophistication of attacks and its adoption of suicide car bombings may be a sign that Boko Haram is indeed receiving tactical and operational assistance from a foreign militant group. Since AQIM has attacked UN targets in Algeria, and al-Shabaab has attacked UN targets in Somalia, Boko Haram's decision to attack the UN building in Abuja is unlikely a coincidence. At the very least, the argument goes, this attack on a distinctly non-Nigerian target was a first for Boko Haram, and may indicate a major shift in its ideology and strategic goals. In his February 2012 testimony to Congress, the U.S. Director of National Intelligence expressed concern "that Boko Haram—elements of which have engaged with al-Qa'ida in the Islamic Maghreb (AQIM)—is interested in hitting Western targets, such as the US Embassy and hotels frequented by Westerners."[258]

However, it must also be noted that the dozens of attacks by Boko Haram since August 2011 have exclusively targeted local Nigerians (see Appendix A). Even the attacks in the first two months of 2012 have all targeted locals, like the 20 February 2012 attack which killed 30 people at the Baga Market in Maiduguri, and the 26 February suicide bomb attack against a Nigerian church in Jos. Unless the group launches a campaign against U.S. or Western targets, it remains to be seen whether the attack against the UN Building was a one-off—perhaps a form of payment in kind to al-Qaeda in return for materials or services provided—or whether Boko Haram has indeed embraced the global jihadist targeting strategy and ideological objectives.

Of course, any alleged links between Boko Haram and a broader Islamist extremist movement worldwide lead naturally to increasing concerns, both to the Nigerian government specifically and to the U.S. and Western governments in general. However, a few things must be noted about the nature of these links, if they exist. First, while Boko Haram's media capabilities have clearly advanced as evidenced by their online propaganda efforts, it is noteworthy that they do not post their communiqués, videos, and so forth on al-Qaeda-affiliated web forums, blogs, or websites. Instead, their videos are being posted to YouTube, bypassing the as-Sahab media network that has been so central to al-Qaeda's propaganda efforts for many years. As well, these videos have not shown Boko Haram leaders praising the leaders of al-Qaeda, or characterizing their fight within the context of a global jihad, a basic tenet of al-Qaeda's ideology. Further, a review of the most prominent al-Qaeda websites does not reveal Boko Haram linkages among members or aspiring young supporters of the global jihad. And, while we have seen a few statements from Ayman al-Zawahiri offering moral support to the group, we have not seen al-Qaeda videos heralding a presence in Nigeria, or using battlefield footage (ala Iraq or Afghanistan) as a tool to mobilize Muslims in other countries to come join Boko Haram in their struggle.

Given the statements noted above, certain members of AQIM may be involved in some kind of ad-hoc coordination or knowledge sharing with Boko Haram. However, the primary interest of AQIM these days appears to be smuggling, kidnapping, and other forms of raising finances. A relationship with members of AQIM could facilitate weapons trading or other kinds of transactions, but at the same time these same kinds of transactions could be facilitated by trusted agents within the Kanuri tribal networks north of the border in Niger. Meanwhile, some observers have suggested Boko Haram may have established linkages with—and perhaps learned some of their recent explosives designs from—al-Shabaab, the radical Islamist group in Somalia that was declared an affiliate of al-Qaeda. However, there is no clear evidence yet that Nigerians have gone to Somalia to fight or receive training, nor have there been cases of Somali militants captured or killed in confrontations with security forces in Nigeria. As the dominant insurgent group in Nigeria, Boko Haram is currently attracting the lion's share of the country's media and security attention, which would seem to make it a prime candidate for al-Qaeda to offer it an affiliation type of relationship. It is at least curious that to date they have not.

Conclusion and Potential Future Trajectory of Boko Haram

In sum, Boko Haram can be seen as the most recent and violent form of militant Islam that has been active in the north of Nigeria for decades. It is rooted in a much deeper history of Islamism in the region, stemming from the dan Fodio militant campaign to establish the Sokoto caliphate in the 19th century. Its ideological resonance is fueled in part by a perceived decline of religious authority in a place where for centuries Islam was a much more powerful force in political, legal, and social relations. They offer a vision of the future that rejects modernization and Western globalization, and they use violence as a weapon in their struggle for influence among the Muslim communities of Nigeria. The ideology of Boko Haram has spread in part because of many socioeconomic grievances that have produced a perceived marginalization and insecurity (physical and spiritual) among northern Muslim communities. Further, its animosity toward the Nigerian government is shared broadly among Nigerians, regardless of faith but particularly in the north and especially among Muslim communities.

Beyond ideological resonance, there are also several kinds of environmental factors that provide opportunities for Boko Haram to engage in violent activity. As noted in Chapter 4, these include a security environment that provides access to weapons, funds, and safe havens among sympathizers and supporters; widespread organized criminal activity which undermines the authority of the state; and historical traditions of organized religious piety and opposition to the values of Western liberal democratization. Population growth without infrastructure or employment opportunities has created an environment in which scores of young Nigerians have nothing productive or meaningful into which their energies can be directed, a problem that is particularly acute in large urban areas. And permeating all of this is a widespread sentiment that the government at the federal, state, and local levels is either weak or ineffectual, at best, or worse is hostile toward the Muslim communities of the north and intentionally tries to keep them marginalized and disadvantaged.

The combination of ideological resonance and operational capability has culminated to produce the modern threat of Islamist terrorism in Nigeria, a threat which many observers in the U.S. and other western countries have grown increasingly concerned about. Like an array of contemporary terrorist groups throughout history, Boko Haram started small, but over time their operational capabilities and impact have grown, spreading like a cancer from Borno to neighboring states, eventually reaching all the way to Abuja. Its presence is not yet felt south of Abuja, where the all-important oil extraction and other economic activities take place. Surely, attacks against targets in the south could help them advance their strategy of provoking sectarian conflict, but thus far Boko Haram has not shown a capability for operations further south than Abuja. And as noted earlier in this monograph, a central goal of Boko Haram has been to provoke conflict in Middle Belt, where the seams of north-south differences are most pronounced, and where the seat of political power is located.

...a central goal of Boko Haram has been to provoke conflict in Middle Belt, where the seams of north-south differences are most pronounced, and where the seat of political power is located.

However, the challenges for Boko Haram to plan and carry out an operation in the south would be akin to the challenges of doing this in another country. Without the assistance of sympathizers within the southern Muslim communities, the operators would have limited knowledge of the area, and limited situational awareness about local law enforcement and intelligence agencies. They would attract suspicion as foreigners. All these things would leave them highly vulnerable to the kinds of intelligence gathering that would in all likelihood prevent them from succeeding. From a strategic viewpoint, it makes better sense to stay closer to home, where there are greater chances that planned attacks can be carried out successfully.

There are other potential constraints on Boko Haram's trajectory as well, including condemnation by respected leaders in the Muslim world. For example, the leader of the Islamic community in Nigeria, Sultan Abubakar Saad, has denounced Boko Haram's actions as un-Islamic. Beyond the religious realm, it is important to remember that Boko Haram has found virtually no support among northern elites, including traditional and tribal leaders. Perhaps the perceived dominance of the Kanuri tribesmen within Boko Haram is an important reason for this. Or perhaps it is simply the case that while the northern elites may have their suspicions about the Nigerian government, they feel they have far more to lose than to gain from the kind of sectarian violence Boko Haram has been attempting to provoke.

And of course, Boko Haram's ideology has found very limited resonance among a youthful non-Kanuri population in the north, most of whom are far more concerned about jobs, education, and economic issues than the religious insecurities that are central to Boko Haram's motivations for using violence. In truth, most Nigerians throughout the country see Boko Haram as an obstacle to a better future, rather than a group fighting to bring about a better future. Thus, Boko Haram's vision of the future and its strategy to bring about that future is seen as beneficial by almost no one in Nigeria, north or south, Muslim or Christian. Perhaps this limited ideological appeal is its most vulnerable shortcoming, which will be addressed further in the next chapter.

> *In truth, most Nigerians throughout the country see Boko Haram as an obstacle to a better future, rather than a group fighting to bring about a better future.*

Boko Haram's core ideology and its attacks to date suggest it is poised to remain a primarily Nigerian threat; they claim to seek a better world for Nigerians, specifically Nigerian Muslims, and there are many things they feel they can do within their local surroundings that would have a much greater effect on that goal than launching an attack against a target in a foreign country, ala al-Qaeda. However, according to General Ham, Boko Haram may be splitting, with one subgroup focused on domestic issues and another on violent international extremism.[259] An *Associated Press* report published 4 November 2011 indicates that the group may have even split into three factions: one that remains moderate and welcomes an end to the violence; another that wants a peace agreement; and a third that refuses to negotiate and wants to implement strict Shariah law across Nigeria.[260] There is at the very least evidence of disagreements among some Boko Haram members. On 19 July 2011, a group calling itself the Yusufiyya Islamic Movement distributed leaflets widely in Maiduguri denouncing other Boko Haram factions as "evil." The authors of the leaflet, asserting the legacy of founder Mohammed Yusuf, distanced themselves from attacks on civilians and on houses of worship.[261]

According to Jon Gambrell, "The split in Boko Haram appears to be so serious that one representative of its moderate faction was killed after negotiating with former Nigeria President Olusegun Obasanjo."[262] The event he referred to occurred on 18 September 2011, when after meeting with Obasanjo in Maiduguri—ostensibly as part of a government-sponsored attempt to negotiate with Boko Haram—Alhaji Babakura Fugu, a former brother-in-law of Mohammed Yusuf, was shot and killed. Boko Haram claimed responsibility for the killing in a text message sent to journalists in Maiduguri a day later. Before his death, Fugu had released a statement outlining three conditions that Boko Haram had identified as necessary for establishing peace: the rebuilding of their mosque, which had been demolished during the 2009 riots; the payment of compensation to his family as ordered by the court over the extra-judicial killing of their father, Yusuf's father-in-law; and the directive that the security agencies should desist from further harassment of the sect members.[263]

If there is indeed a split among the main ranks of Boko Haram, it could be a good thing for hastening its defeat, as one faction turns on another in a struggle to dominate the militant Islamist agenda. However, it could also mean something worse is in store. We have seen this kind of splintering before in the terrorist world: the Irish Republican Army (IRA) spawned several splinter groups like the Provisional IRA, Continuity IRA, and Real IRA, while the Salafist Group for Preaching and Combat, the pre-cursor to AQIM, was a splinter group of the Armed Islamic Group in Algeria. Analysis of those cases suggests that splinter groups often seem to feel the need to be more violent than the original group. From this perspective, it is feasible to envision a variant of Boko Haram morphing into something new, like "Al Qaeda in West Africa," and if such a splinter group were to follow the trajectory of other al-Qaeda affiliates like AQIM, al-Shabaab, the Indonesian group Jemaah Islamiyah, or the Yemen-based al-Qaeda in the Arabian Peninsula, it could feasibly be primed to expand its target set to include U.S. targets, as suggested in the November report by the House of Representatives.[264] The U.S. and the West should monitor events closely, but should also be careful not to overreact to the perceived threat, elevating it to an international stature that in some ways could actually benefit Boko Haram or an al-Qaeda-affiliated splinter of it in terms of attracting new sources of financing and recruitment from abroad.

Certainly, the group's long-term prospects depend greatly on how the Nigerian government responds to it. Unfortunately, the ways in which authorities have responded to Boko Haram, and to Islamist extremism in general—as described in the next chapter of this monograph—may in some cases have made the counterterrorism effort more difficult. The one thing that Nigerian forces should not do is act in such a manner that would give validation to Boko Haram's ideology.

6. Responding to Boko Haram

The first chapter of this monograph described how terrorism is largely contextual: there are political and socioeconomic grievances that provide ideological resonance and a security environment in which a group can attract recruits, funds, materiel, and safe havens. Defeating a terrorist group thus requires attention to those grievances and elements of the security environment that allow the group to operate. Unfortunately, the grievances in Nigeria that have fueled unrest and political violence over the past decades, in both the south and the north, are so many and so great that the government may be overwhelmed. In conducting field research for this monograph, one interviewee described the Nigerian government's response to the current security challenges as "buying time and loyalty with oil money in the south and north… what they need to do instead is reduce corruption, emphasize infrastructure development, especially electric power, support education, and assure affordable housing options."[265] Various sources have described the country's political system as one in which government leaders "buy off" potential threats to their power and use public resources to influence the population. According to another interviewee, "the system depends entirely upon oil revenues; take that away, chaos will result."[266]

Significant reforms are needed in many areas, including the legal sector. The appeal among many Muslims of Sharia law is that the secular laws are seen as serving only the elites of Nigeria. Corruption is so rampant that the wealthy and connected are perceived as able to get away with virtually any kind of injustice. As John Campbell notes, Boko Haram's ideology "draws on a long-standing local tradition of Islamic radical reform that emphasizes the pursuit of justice for the poor through the imposition of Sharia. Adherents generally despise Nigeria's secular leadership and the country's traditional Muslim elites, whom they see as having been co-opted by the government."[267] In his analysis of extremist groups in Nigeria, Chris Ngwodo noted, "It is their advocacy of the poor and their opposition to social injustice that lends these groups their appeal."[268]

Inequitable application of the rule of law exacerbates an already deeply problematic system of ethnic identity politics, which detracts from any significant sense of national unity or shared journey. As noted in Chapter 3, the emphasis on differences in heritage precludes the development of a shared cultural heritage among Nigerians. And of course, the government must also address the myriad socioeconomic demands like poverty, health and educational services, unemployment, infrastructure, and so forth. The link between these many kinds of grievances and the rise of violent extremism is particularly prominent in the north, where the people have higher poverty, illiteracy, unemployment, health problems, and overall insecurity than elsewhere in Nigeria. This was highlighted in the September 2011 report by the Presidential Committee on Security Challenges in the North-East Zone, which noted the need to address issues of governance and the delivery of services to people.

Beyond the preconditions described earlier, there are also potential triggers for violence outbreaks: a belief that elections are not free and fair, or a government's inability to respond effectively when faced with economic shocks or environmental disasters. And in the global environment, Nigeria must collaborate with others to combat regional and global trafficking networks that could be used to help finance terrorist groups in their country. In truth, there is an extensive list of complex issues that need to be addressed in fighting Boko Haram and the underlying conditions that enable its ideological resonance and operational capabilities.

Jennifer Cooke, Director of the Africa Program at the Center for Strategic and International Studies, described in her recent Congressional testimony how "the Nigerian government's response to Boko Haram will need to be integrated into a comprehensive political, economic, and security strategy that offers some promise of real improvement to northern populations and communities and limits the appeal of Boko Haram and its potential successors."[269] Her perspective, endorsed in this monograph, reflects a common theme in the contemporary security studies literature that a whole-of-government approach is necessary for successfully defeating a terrorist group. In the case of Boko Haram, however, a broader perspective is needed: defeating this group will require a "whole of Nigeria approach" in which government forces and nongovernmental entities are engaged in a complementary effort, in some cases with the support and assistance of the U.S. and the international community. Success will come from working together to understand all we can about Boko Haram and the environment that has sustained them, and then craft a strategy that employs this knowledge to maximum benefit. This chapter identifies what Nigeria's government and civil society entities are doing (but could do to better) to confront Boko

Haram, and then explores some ways in which the U.S. and the international community can assist them in these efforts.

Nigeria's Government

Policies enacted by President Goodluck Jonathan's administration may have alienated some northern military leaders and other elites, and this could exacerbate north-south elite rivalries. But for now this seems to be a separate issue from the threat of Boko Haram. To ensure it remains unconnected to the sectarian conflict being provoked in the north, Jonathan could incorporate more northerners into government leadership positions. This, in turn could lead to more northern efforts to confront the Boko Haram threat through local powerbrokers, because more powerful people would have a vested interest in preserving the status quo rather than pursue change through violence. Further, as described below, the government could identify and leverage culturally specific factors in a comprehensive counterterrorism strategy. In particular, Muslim leaders in northern Nigeria are seen by many in their communities as powerbrokers and trusted mediators of disputes. They draw tacit authority by nature of a deep historical Muslim influence in social and political life throughout the region. Not only do these religious leaders have an important role to play in confronting the threat of Boko Haram, they also can have a positive impact on the future of the country, if involved in discussions about economics, security, and development projects. To promote stability, address religious insecurities, and to provide a conduit for locals to voice their grievances about the government in a non-threatening environment, channels of communication between government and religious leaders are vital at both the public level and the private, behind the scenes level, in some cases to ensure the safety of religious leaders who might become exposed to targeting by Boko Haram.

At the same time, the anti-corruption efforts that began under the Obasanjo regime are fundamental to the long-term building of trust and legitimacy among Nigerian citizens. It is a positive sign that Jonathan's administration is not only committed to continuing these efforts, but it has also identified the fuel subsidy issue as a contributor to the corruption problem. As noted in Chapter 3, however, this must be handled after reliable electricity is provided throughout the country, thereby reducing people's reliance on generators and the fuel for them. On a positive note,

Nigeria's future looks relatively bright, certainly when compared to the past. Its annual GDP growth has exceeded 7 percent for the last several years.[270] The banking, finance, and information technology sectors are contributing more to this growth than the oil sector, which is good because the oil sector employs very few Nigerians. And there is relative political stability in Nigeria. As described in Chapter 2, the governing political party has been in power since 1999, and maintains a north-south political balance of sorts via an alliance within the party, which includes an agreement that the presidency will alternate between a northern candidate and a southern candidate. Despite events surrounding the election of Jonathan, a southerner, Nigerians have demonstrated that the country can withstand a modification to this arrangement.

In short, the political and economic conditions in Nigeria have been improving considerably, and in most cases are far better than adherents of Boko Haram's ideology would have you believe. This, in turn, aids the government in undermining that ideology and reducing its resonance. Clearly, as described in previous chapters, Boko Haram is an enemy of moderation and stability; they have chosen to promote a violent ideology shrouded in religious language, and portray themselves as a vanguard of an epic struggle between good and evil. As such, they cannot be bombed into submission, nor can all Boko Haram members and sympathizers be identified and captured or killed. Just like many other religious terrorist groups around the world, the eventual demise of Boko Haram will come through a combination of kinetic force, law enforcement, local intelligence, and diminishing the local resonance of the group's ideology.

> ...the eventual demise of Boko Haram will come through a combination of kinetic force, law enforcement, local intelligence, and diminishing the local resonance of the group's ideology.

To date, however, the Nigerian government has responded to Boko Haram—and to previous manifestations of violent religious extremism, like the Maitatsine riots—primarily with a show of force. In addition to routine police searches, Nigeria's military forces have been deployed on multiple occasions to find and apprehend members of the group, search for weapons, enforce curfews, and other counterterrorism missions. But perhaps it can be said that Nigeria's leaders are learning that successfully confronting the threat of Boko Haram will require more than a traditional kill/capture counterterrorism strategy. They have already attempted a basic organizational decapitation approach—in which it is assumed that capturing and/or killing the leaders will cause the group to disintegrate—but following the public execution of Boko Haram's leaders and financiers, the problem has only gotten worse.

Further, as former Inspector General of Police Alhaji Ibrahim Coomassie observed in a July 2011 report, quality intelligence gathering in support of the government's counterterrorism efforts is deficient.[271] The biggest obstacle here, according to Jonah Fisher, is "the lack of cooperation from the local population. Boko Haram members live among the community but people are either too scared or unwilling to inform on them."[272] Intelligence gathering in support of the government's counterterrorism efforts is made difficult by the immense distrust toward the government that is found among many Muslim communities in the north. This distrust is in part a response to actions taken by the police and military that damaged an already fragile perception of government legitimacy.

A recent UN report described Nigeria's Joint Task Force as "a federal unit comprising army, police and customs officials, who make up for their lack of operational intelligence with a wholly counterproductive willingness to use lethal force."[273] An Amnesty International report describes how the Nigerian police force is responsible for hundreds of extra-judicial killings and disappearances each year across the country that largely "go uninvestigated and unpunished."[274] As described earlier in this monograph, a good deal of public attention has been focused on the brutal way in which the local police responded to the August 2009 Boko Haram uprising, in particular the extra-judicial killing of the group's original leader Mohammed Yusuf and other members.[275] One video, widely circulated online, appears to show the police parading individuals in public with their hands bound behind them, and then summarily executing them in front of the gathered crowds. But this was but one of several notable instances. During a November 2008 disturbance in the city of Jos, the local governor ordered the police and army to simply shoot suspected rioters on sight.[276] In another instance, after Boko Haram militants attacked an army patrol in Maiduguri with explosives and gunfire on 9 July 2011, injuring two soldiers, locals reported that the army began burning homes and shooting unarmed civilians. In one account published by the United Nations Integrated Regional Information

Networks news service, "Soldiers began shooting in the air...breaking into homes, singling out male occupants and shooting them, and driving women out of the houses which they set ablaze."[277]

According to a BBC News report, the governor of the Nigerian state of Borno "admitted that the army has been guilty of excesses during operations to counter Boko Haram."[278] On 12 July 2011, a group of 18 local members of the respected Borno Elders Forum called for the withdrawal of troops from the city, saying the soldiers had worsened the security situation.[279] At the very least, these actions have not fostered a healthy relationship between Nigeria's security forces and the community members they are ostensibly there to protect. The perceived lack of legitimacy, in turn, weakens the government's counterterrorism efforts.

Nigeria's corruption problem, discussed earlier, also plays a particularly troubling role in undermining the state's ability to permanently solve the security challenges in the north, including the threat of Boko Haram. A recent eyewitness account published by the BBC describes how "harassment from checkpoints, or as some residents call them 'toll booths,' has helped alienate the police from the Maiduguri population."[280] In conducting field research for this monograph, corruption was particularly noted by interviewees in their depictions of the police. As one put it, "Any mistake you make, from speeding to making a spelling mistake on a permit application, is an opportunity for a policeman or someone else in the government to make money."[281] Others described the selective application of rules and laws based on an individual's status, with bribery playing a significant role in law enforcement, or lack thereof. One interviewee told of a story in which a local child was abducted, and instead of going to the police for help, the father went to see a local tribal leader, who was successful in finding and retrieving the stolen child and did not charge any kind of fee or reward—whereas he felt the policemen surely would have.

Most observers of Nigeria would agree that the police are well-armed, but many are corrupt and not properly trained. Because of this, the military has been called upon to provide various domestic security duties, and this has not been welcomed by anyone in or out of the military. One interviewee offered a personal story about a conference that was being planned in the Niger Delta. The convening organization was advised to ask for a security presence, but the head of the local police demanded a bribe, a lump sum for each police officer he would assign to provide security. Further, the conference organizer was informed that if the bribe was not paid, the police would make it very difficult for people to come to this conference. In the end, the Nigerian military forces were contacted, and agreed to provide security for the conference—of course, leading to a great deal of anger among members of the local police department. For their part, members of the Nigerian Army have come to despise the local police, for whom they have no respect. While there are surely examples where a cordial or collaborative relationship exists, this study found that in general the relations between military and police are often marked by competition for resources, and sometimes even violent clashes between police and military officers. In one case, a policeman slapped a military officer, and shortly thereafter an entire barracks came to beat the policeman, whose injuries required hospitalization.

The cumulative result of these problems within Nigeria's security sector is that the current strategy for dealing with Boko Haram—stationing large numbers of military and police in the north, especially in Maiduguri—is an approach that, as John Campbell, U.S. ambassador to Nigeria from 2004 to 2007, noted, "could do more harm than good."[282] Without perceived legitimacy of those forces among the people they are meant to protect and gather intelligence from, it remains an enabling environment for Boko Haram to draw support. In essence, as described earlier in this monograph, this is a struggle for influence over the minds and hearts of countless Muslim communities in northeast Nigeria. The legitimacy of the Nigerian government and its actions has direct implications for its ability to counter the narrative of radical Islamists like Boko Haram.

Legitimacy and trust are key aspects of any audience's willingness to accept a message; if the government of Nigeria loses or has lost it, Boko Haram and others with a competing message have an opportunity to gain influence among their target audience. To overcome the state security forces' fractured coercive capacity, the Nigerian government must establish a level of moral and political legitimacy that will help them gain the support of local Muslim communities in the north. The research literature on conflict and security supports the notion that as legitimacy of a political regime declines, their citizens are more likely to rebel.[283] In addition to putting an end to corruption, the government must also address the many grievances mentioned earlier by becoming more transparent, efficient, and effective with regard to delivery of services, rule of law, accountability, and justice for all. It must foster nationwide respect toward all religious faiths, equitable distribution

Nigerians must come to trust their government more than they have previously had reason to.

of resources, improvements in education and economic opportunity, and much more. Nigerians must come to trust their government more than they have previously had reason to. In this regard, it is noteworthy that in July 2011 the Nigerian authorities put on trial five police officers connected to Yusuf's killing and in August 2011 began the court martial of a military commander responsible for troops that killed 42 sect members during the July 2009 uprising.[284]

Beyond addressing the grievances that underscore Boko Haram's ideology, there are also additional ways in which the tools of influence warfare can be used to impact the group's "street perception" in ways that will diminish ideological resonance and increase the number of locals willing to provide information and intelligence about the radical sect.[285] To begin with, Boko Haram is not only Islamist, it is also Salafist, which means its interpretations of the Koran, the Hadith, and the guidelines for a proper Muslim life are highly conservative, not just by local Sufi standards, but by even the standards of other Islamists. They feel threatened by religious moderation; they view the cooperative relationship between religious leaders and the secular government in Nigeria as selling out, accepting a less powerful or dominant role for religion than these Islamist extremists feel should exist. However, their views on this matter are distinctly unpopular among most Nigerians. Recent polls have found very limited support among Nigerians—13 percent nationwide—for the notion that Sharia should be the only source of legislation.[286] In essence, there are aspects of the group's ideology that undermine its long-term resonance and viability. And, of course, the violent means by which Boko Haram seeks to achieve its objectives also further alienates many. Most Nigerians—north, south, Muslim, Christian— live peacefully side by side and do not want sectarian violence. In essence, Boko Haram is articulating and pursuing a vision of the future that few Muslims in Nigeria want, particularly considering the deep traditions of moderate Sufi Islam throughout West Africa. Further, through its actions Boko Haram has shown itself to be an enemy to all Nigerians, regardless of religion or ethnicity.

A counterideology narrative that the Nigerian government should emphasize here is that positive changes for Muslim communities in the north can and will come without the need for violence. Further, engaging in violence undermines the kind of positive future that can be obtained. In truth, most Nigerians see Boko Haram as an obstacle to a better future, not a group fighting to bring about positive change. Those who find some resonance in the group's ideology must be convinced that the leaders of Boko Haram are not the vanguard of a movement toward positive change; they are murderers of Muslims, seeking power to shape and control the future in a way that adheres to their fundamentalist version of Islam, a version which is foreign to Nigeria and anathema to the teachings of Nigeria's leading Islamic scholars. Usman dan Fodio, founder of the Sokoto Caliphate, is revered in Nigeria, and the murdering marauders of Boko Haram are motivated by ideals that run counter to what he stood for. They have killed indiscriminately, including many Muslim men, women, and children, and in doing so, they have alienated themselves from mainstream Nigerian society. Further, they do not provide social or welfare services—a key to the success of Hezbollah.[287] Hamas, and other terrorist groups who have sought to win over local hearts and minds—even though these things are in dire need within their areas of operation. And Boko Haram members have also killed well-respected Muslim leaders like Ibrahim Birkuti[288] simply because they dared criticize the group's ideology and use of violence, suggesting that the group's leaders must be afraid of these criticisms; perhaps because they recognize their own ideological vulnerabilities.

These and many other topics can be addressed in Nigeria's effort to diminish Boko Haram's influence among the northern Muslim communities. In addition to addressing the core issues of legitimacy and the many socioeconomic grievances described above, the government can weaken its terrorist adversary by identifying and exploiting their ideological weaknesses and vulnerabilities. Individual doubts and fears within any organization undermine confidence and diminish the organization's operational capabilities. Within Boko Haram, there are already a wide variety of faults and ideological contradictions that make it difficult to attract new recruits or financial support. As discussed in the previous chapter, differences over ideology and strategy may have led to a splintering of the group in several types of Boko Haram, with the original Kanuri-dominated group remaining the most violent and inflexible. When their indiscriminate bombings serve to further undermine the credibility and resonance of the group's ideology, Boko Haram's difficulties are exacerbated. The Nigerian government's overall objective should be to not only locate and apprehend members of Boko

Haram and disrupt its financing streams, but to also degrade its capacity for influencing Muslim communities. This is an area in which nongovernmental entities can play a major role in countering the threat of Boko Haram.

The Role of Civil Society and Nongovernmental Entities

While a government is surely expected by its citizens to lead the fight against terrorism, there are many kinds of nongovernmental entities that can also help address the kinds of conditions that give legitimacy to the grievances articulated in a terrorist group's ideology. Further, in several cases, nongovernmental actors may be perceived on a local community level as having more legitimacy than the government, and as such they are in a unique position to have influence in those communities. In the struggle against Boko Haram, these entities play an important role in providing services and development assistance to compensate for the deficiencies of the state. As a result, the proposition offered here is that where human security is better, regardless of who is responsible for improving it, Boko Haram's ideological resonance is weakened, and their influence challenges are made more difficult.

Given Nigeria's environment of widespread grievances and insecurity, it is unsurprising to find a system of locally-oriented cultural, religious, and ethnic allegiances. This is a common phenomenon in a variety of struggling states, where local nongovernmental entities like civil society organizations (CSOs) are providing services to many whom the government has been unable or unwilling to take care of. These services could include dispute resolution, health and welfare, or even security. Some CSOs work to expose and battle corruption, while others encourage dialogue and unity across ethnic and religious lines. As a recent report on governance and security by the International Peace Institute noted, "civil society groups have been at the forefront of the relentless struggles against dictatorship and bad governance in West Africa over the years and continue to lead the process to strengthen human security."[289] Recognizing the important role that these entities play throughout West Africa, several governments in the region have recently established the West Africa Civil Society Forum with the objective of facilitating capacity building and networking among CSOs.[290]

To be sure, government forces in Nigeria clearly have significant capabilities for the use of force in responding to security challenges. But as noted above, when the legitimacy of that capacity and those who deploy it is undermined by brutal excesses or by endemic corruption among government agencies at all levels, including local police forces, it can be expected that many Nigerians prefer to involve nongovernmental entities in resolving disputes or addressing security problems. This aspect of the citizen-state relationship in Nigeria also has implications for countering the threat of violent extremism. In addition to reporting suspicious activities to the authorities, CSOs can also offer alternatives to the messages of violent extremism. They can take the lead in confronting and debating those individuals in their community who would use their words to inspire and encourage violence against others. According to a recent report by the Center on Global Counterterrorism Cooperation, "CSOs can help to give voice to marginalized and vulnerable peoples, including victims of terrorism, and provide a constructive outlet for the redress of grievances. They have important roles to play in activism, education, research, oversight, and even as potential assistance and service providers."[291]

As noted earlier, Nigeria's population of over 155 million is Africa's largest, which naturally means this country has a very complex civil society with thousands of organizations and tremendous diversity among them in terms of size, capabilities, and community influence. Thus, a comprehensive analysis of who they all are and how they impact the lives of Nigerians is far beyond the scope of this study. Instead, three categories of civil society entities (and specific examples of each) will be described here to illustrate the phenomenon of how they influence individuals' behavior and help reduce the likelihood of violent extremism: 1) religious leaders; 2) traditional and tribal rulers; and 3) other community organizations that are committed to objectives of security, peace-building, and social services. Following a brief description of each category, the discussion will focus on some clear trends and relationships—particularly involving the state and the governed—that can be discerned within the broader context of mitigating grievances and countering the threat of violent extremism.

1) Religious Leaders

As noted earlier in this monograph, the religious dimension of Boko Haram's ideology is central. The group is but the most recent manifestation of a longer history of conflict between the state—viewed by many in the north as corrupt and illegitimate—and religious extremism. In modern Nigeria, spiritual insecurities combine with the other kinds of grievances addressed in Chapter 3 to create a sustainable environment for radical Islamist groups like Boko Haram. Thus, leaders within the Muslim community must be involved in any successful approach to defeating the group. In fact, because Boko Haram's ideology draws on religious beliefs derived from their strict interpretation of Islam and the Koran, the most important nongovernmental entity that must be involved in the fight against them is the collection of authority figures in Nigeria's Muslim communities. These are largely organized around two "Brotherhoods"—the Qadiriyya and Tijaniyya. Although there are no accurate figures as to how many members each brotherhood may have, they are counted in the millions and can be found the length and breadth of Islamic West Africa. For this reason, their leaders can be significantly influential through their proclamations and religious edicts. They appear regularly on television, and as such have a powerful platform from which to counter Islamist radicalization. They also finance and run a range of religious and social programs that, according to Jonathan Hill, "have the effect of preventing men, women and children from turning to radical factions" of Islam.[292]

The older of these Brotherhoods, the Qadiriyya, named for the Islamic scholar and jurisprudent Abdul-Qadir al-Jilani, was founded during the 12th century in Baghdad, and had spread to Nigeria according to some estimates by at least the 14th century. The Tijaniyya was founded in Morocco by Ahmad at-Tijani in 1781 and was introduced to what became northern Nigeria in the 19th century.[293] It is important to note that the presence of these brotherhoods in Nigeria represents local chapters of international religious movements.[294] Further, their histories are closely connected: al-Tijani was at one time a member of the Qadiriyya, but he left after growing frustrated with what he saw as its rigid hierarchy and failure to provide greater support to the poor.[295]

The early 19th century was also when the Sokoto Caliphate was established by Usman dan Fodio, as described in Chapter 4. Today, however, only a shadow of the Sokoto Empire remains. The current Sultan of Sokoto, Alhaji Muhammad Sa'ad Abubakar, still functions primarily as the paramount leader of the traditional institutions in Sokoto state, but he has no direct rule over any emirate or chiefdom.[296] However, his supreme authority in Islamic matters transcends territorial boundaries as he is considered the overall leader of Nigerian Muslims, and carries the title of President General of the Nigerian Supreme Council for Islamic Affairs. Further, although the Sultan has no formal political powers, his influence is still considerable. Presidents continue to seek both his opinions and his support, for his command of the faithful means that he can make the government of the north extremely difficult if he so chooses.[297]

In essence, the Sultan is only one of several major players in Nigeria's contemporary Islamic landscape. Others include the Izala movement, which runs a charity and first aid organization and has links with Wahhabi religious leaders in Saudi Arabia; the Salafiyya movement, which runs schools, internet cafes, and business outlets; and the Islamic Movement in Nigeria, originally established under the banner of the Muslim Brotherhood, which runs schools and clinics and publishes newspapers.[298] In 1978, a cleric in Jos named Sheikh Ismaila Idris established a conservative Islamist movement called the *Jama't Izalat al Bid'a Wa Iqamat as Sunna*,

translated roughly as the "Society for the Removal of Innovation and the Reinstatement of Tradition," or commonly referred to as Izala. Some scholars have described the Izala as a reform movement because of its opposition to innovation and its emphasis on strict adherence to the *sunna* of the Prophet Muhammad.[299] Jonathan Hill has characterized it as a salafist organization because it "embraces a legalist and scripture-centered understanding of Islam."[300] The writings of Sheikh Gumi are also said to have influenced the Izala movement. However, according to Peter Chalk, leaders and followers do not believe that traditional Islam and modernity are incompatible.[301] Also, in contrast to the traditional Sufi brotherhoods and their spiritually pre-selected leaders, the Izala are characterized by elected

Figure 14. The Nigerian Sultan of Sokoto watches traditional water sports during the Argungu fishing festival in northern Nigeria 14 March 2008. Photo used by permission of Newscom.

officials, a written constitution, and a deliberative bureaucratic decision-making process. And perhaps most importantly, when compared with Boko Haram's ideology, the Izala advocate a thoroughly modern, inclusive education system, in which Arabic culture and Islamic studies are integrated with Western-oriented courses in mathematics, English, history, and general world knowledge.[302]

A series of internal debates within the movement during the 1980s, often over finances, leadership, and defining "true Islam," at one point resulting in two opposing Izala factions in Jos and Kaduna, weakened its perceived authority in the Muslim community. However, it is still an influential movement today, and bears mention in discussing the diverse religious landscape of northern Nigeria. Certain Izala leaders, including Sheikh Alhassan Saidu of the Sultan Bello Mosque, have a significant following in Jos and the surrounding region. According to published reports, Umaru Abdul Mutallab—father of Farouk Abdulmutallab, who attempted to bomb a U.S.-bound airliner in December 2009—contacted Sheikh Ahmad Gumi, the son of Abubakar Gumi, with an urgent request to try to steer his son away from extremist influences.[303] These and other examples illustrate the complex diffusion of influence in the Muslim communities of northern Nigeria.

Leaders in Muslim communities exercise power through a number of means, including a system of Islamic courts in which disputes are mediated and punishments meted out to members of the community deemed guilty of a major offense.[304] As described earlier in this monograph, this environment of self-policing can support efforts to counter extreme radicalization of the type promoted by Boko Haram and other Salafist elements. The Qadiriyya and Tijaniyya brotherhoods, the Izala, and the Sokoto Caliphate are all opposed to extreme radical interpretations of Islam like the salafi-jihadist ideology of al-Qaeda. Further, as Charlie Szrom and Chris Harnisch point out, Islamic authority for northern Nigerians is the Sultan of Sokoto, not a collection of salafist preachers in the Middle East and their fatwas. Nigerians in general have resisted the revisionist worldview promoted by al-Qaeda that downplays traditional authority structures such as the Sokoto Caliphate.[305] Thus, the extreme radicalism of the salafi-jihadist variant is considered rare and an unwelcome foreign influence by most Nigerians. In fact, several Muslim clerics and Islamic associations have denounced al-Qaeda's and Boko Haram's perversions of Islam.[306]

As Jonathan Hill observes, the head of the Qadiriyya, Sheikh Qaribullahi Nasiru Kabara, and the head of Tijaniyya, Sheikh Ismail Ibrahim Khalifa, acknowledge that the challenge confronting them and everyone else seeking to stem the tide of Islamist radicalism is at once both ideological and practical.[307] As crucial to the religious arguments they marshal are the various community outreach programs they finance and run. Not only do they help mitigate the shortcomings of public services, they form alternatives to those offered by the Islamists. Yet arguably, the Brotherhoods' task is made all the more difficult by their desire to work with the authorities whenever possible. Unlike the Islamists who simply condemn the federal, state, and local governments, the Brotherhoods try to engage with them.[308]

Christian leaders can also play a role in addressing the underlying conditions that have helped Boko Haram's ideology resonate among some Muslim communities. One way is in addressing the "spiritual insecurities" (described in the previous chapter) that have animated radical Islamists in the north for many years. According to a report by the U.S. Institute of Peace, there are a variety of efforts on both the national and grassroots levels to promote interfaith dialogue and communication between Muslims and Christians to prevent future outbreaks of violence and promote ethno-religious tolerance and federal cohesion.[309] On the national level, the leaders of the Christian Association of Nigeria have stated their commitment to interfaith dialogue and some form of peacebuilding between the two communities. At the local level, one of the most promising efforts has been the Interfaith Mediation Council. Started by James Wuye, a Christian pastor, and Mohammed Ashafa, an Imam, this organization has been effective in working with communities to mitigate religious conflict, and promote tolerance and coexistence.[310]

A recent report by the United Nations describes how some CSOs are helping to build networks of moderate Muslim leaders by working with religious, education, government, and media leaders on projects aimed at promoting a pluralistic, tolerant Islam. For example, one CSO is working with a major Indonesian popular music star to create an album promoting Islam as a religion of peace. This work is an important contribution to efforts to counter distortions of Islam being propagated by terrorists and discredit the notion that Islam or any other religion justifies terrorism.[311]

Another report, by the Center on Global Counterterrorism Cooperation, describes how religious leaders can contribute to addressing conditions conducive to the spread of terrorism through their work within and among different communities of faith. The report's authors note that religious leaders at all levels representing different faiths have an essential role to play in promoting inter- or intra-religious dialogue, tolerance, and understanding among religions—all of which are important. For example, compared with other segments of civil society, the clergy is often in the unique position of both having access to those in high-level government positions and engaging with the masses on the ground.[312]

In sum, religious leaders and their organizations—both Muslim and Christian—provide a broad range of services within their communities, from free schools for children and literacy education programs for adults to food, shelter, and dispute resolution. Religious leaders in Nigeria are widely seen as essential parts of the social fabric, and they have a vital role to play in responding to the threat of Boko Haram; some have been outspoken critics of the group, and unfortunately have been attacked in an effort to coerce the behavior of others through fear and intimidation. Efforts like the Interfaith Mediation Council are critical for ensuring that Boko Haram's attempts to provoke sectarian violence do not succeed. Credible religious leaders can pose a threat to the abilities of Boko Haram to spread its ideology, and as such are an asset in any counterterrorism effort. This has not been overlooked by the Nigerian government, but has not yet played a central role in the struggle against Boko Haram. Given the nature of Boko Haram's ideology and strategy, there must be a more concerted effort to involve religious leaders in de-legitimizing their ideology and diminishing their potential ability to attract local support. Just as the U.S. has learned from recent experiences in Iraq and Afghanistan, a sustained and consistent religious leader engagement program can be integral to achieving the objectives of a counterterrorism strategy.

2) Traditional Rulers

Another influential nongovernmental entity in Nigeria is the local traditional ruler. Centuries before Nigeria was colonized by the British, social and political life was organized around dozens of kingdoms—including the kingdom of Borno; the Hausa kingdoms of Katsina, Kano, Zaria, and Gobir in northern and central Nigeria; Yoruba kingdoms of Ife, Oyo, and Ijebu in the southwest—and thousands of small communities.[313] Many of these were kingdoms administered by traditional rulers based on family ancestry with titles like Oba, Emir, Sarki, Shehu, Mai, Lamido, and so forth.[314] British colonialism, roughly 1861-1960, brought a system of indirect rule in which traditional and religious rulers—particularly in the northern parts of Nigeria—were allowed to retain their power and influence in return for cooperating with British political and economic interests.[315]

Indirect rule was common throughout Britain's African colonies, an approach based on a recognition that direct governance of vast territories would have to overcome tremendous cost and logistical challenges. According to one historian's account, "From the point of view of the colonial authorities, supporting traditional governance was a convenient and cheap method of both maintaining order and collecting tax with limited resources. Nonetheless, it remained very clear where the ultimate power lay; leaders who demonstrated any significant independence of mind were rapidly hustled into exile and replaced with more pliant substitutes."[316] But when Britain granted independence to its various African colonies, in several cases the new governments abolished all remnants of traditional rule. Tanzania, for example, passed a law eliminating the authority of traditional leaders in 1963; by 1965, residual authority of chiefs in Ghana had also been eliminated. However, according to Sklar, post-independence Nigeria saw the emergence of a "mixed government" system, a symbiotic relationship between traditional and state-derived institutions.[317]

Today, the Nigerian government has a complex relationship with traditional rulers. According to William Miles, "Traditional rulers play useful roles in brokering between the people and the state, enhancing national identity, resolving minor conflicts and providing an institutional safety-valve for often inadequate state bureaucracies."[318] Scholars have identified over 350 ethnic groups in Nigeria, and each has its own system of authority structures, culture, and ancestry. Three of them—Hausa-Fulani, Yoruba, and Igbo—dominate the Nigerian landscape, and are largely concentrated in specific regions of the country. But security researchers and policymakers must recognize the importance of traditional leaders within these ethnic groups, large or small, particularly in terms of sociopolitical decision-making and perceptions of justness and legitimacy. According to Blench et al.,

The daily business of most traditional leaders is the settling of disputes involving family, communal and religious life, and in many ways this is both useful to the community and valuable to the state, as many disputes that might otherwise clog up the court system are settled informally and usually in ways that accord with the local community's sense of appropriateness.[319]

Titles like the Ooni of Ife, Aareonokankafo of Yorubaland, Deji of Akure, Bobagunwa ilu Egba, and Alaafin of Oyo bring a great deal of respect, influence, and power among particular communities of Nigerians.[320] According to Nigerian scholar Ali Yahaya, traditional authorities "exercise considerable influence and are consulted by the federal, state and local governments."[321] However, the role of traditional and religious rulers in addressing Nigeria's security challenges is mixed. According to the interviews conducted for this research, as well as other published accounts, a majority of these rulers merely reinforce longstanding patronage relationships and will only do what they believe is in their own self-interests. If they perceive that confronting violent extremism would lead to significant risks, especially to their survival, they will do nothing. Further, when government forces respond to political violence, or even political activism such as peaceful street protests, in a heavy-handed manner, traditional and religious rulers must distance themselves from any perception that they support the government, or risk losing their own legitimacy in the eyes of those whom they seek to influence. Overall, as a recent Department for International Development Nigeria report noted, "When a traditional ruler maintains his integrity, he will receive the cooperation of his subjects."[322] The same can be said about CSOs and religious leaders as well. For their part, civil society organizations not associated with traditional or religious rule have considerably less power and influence within their communities, but are far less likely to be perceived as tainted or co-opted by a corrupt government.

Certainly, the role that traditional rulers play in conflict prevention and mediation throughout Nigeria can be seen as an important component of a comprehensive counterterrorism effort. In areas where the government's capacity to provide services or rule of law may be limited, traditional rulers offer a means for local individuals to pursue justice and can also help provide services to those in need. In doing so, they can have an impact on grievances that could otherwise lead local youth to be receptive to the radical messages of Boko Haram.

3) Non-Affiliated Community Organizations

In addition to traditional and religious rulers, there are hundreds of community-based nongovernmental organizations that also play a prominent role in the lives of ordinary Nigerians. Some, like the Center for Environment, Human Rights and Development, investigate conflicts in rural areas and work to bring public and government attention to cases of human rights

Name	City/Region	Name	City/Region
Africa Centre for Rural Development & Environment	Enugu	Global HIV/AIDS Initiative, Nigeria (GHAIN)	Sokoto
African Foundation for Prevention and Protection Against Child Abuse & Neglect	Rivers	Greenwatch Initiative	Benue
Baobab for Women's Rights Borno	Maiduguri	Human Rights & Community Development Initiative	Kano
Borno Coalition for Democracy and Progress	Maiduguri	Justice, Development & Peace Commission	Abuja
Community Action for Popular Participation	Abuja	Living in the Environment	Benue
Centre for Campaign Against Drug Abuse & Trafficking	Sokoto	Mobgal Hore Women Development Association	Adamawa
Centre for Peace Projects & Development	Kaduna	National Youth Council of Nigeria Ogun State	Ogun
Community Youth Organization Nigeria	Ogun	New Nigeria Youth Association	Owerri, Imo
Community Emergency Response Project	Abuja	Nigeria Red Cross Society	Lagos
Commonwealth Youth Organization Nigeria	Abeokuta, Ogun	Osa Foundation	Benue
Community Life Project	Lagos	Peace Corps Nigeria	Ibadan, Oyo
Economic Empowerment & Development Initiative	Enugu	Security, Justice & Growth Programme	Kano
Fantsuam Foundation	Kaduna	Women Advancement Network (WOFAN)	Kano

Figure 15. Examples of Community Organizations in Nigeria[323]

abuses. Others, like the Kebetkache Women Development and Resource Center, run workshops to build leadership and conflict resolution skills, or offer democracy education and participation programs for Nigerian youth, as does the Youngstars Development Initiative. Figure 15 lists a small sampling of these organizations to illustrate the topical and geographic diversity among them.

Almost all of these CSOs receive funds from private donors, Western governments, and philanthropic organizations. None of them would attest to having enough resources to do what their communities need from them, but they serve a critical role in helping to mitigate the shortcomings of the Nigerian government. Some of these organizations were established specifically because Western donors have increasingly preferred to support indigenous civil society partners in the developing world. Similarly, faith-based community service organizations receive some support from Muslim or Christian communities in wealthy donor countries.

Many Nigerian CSOs are run out of private homes, led by members of families with a longstanding reputation in their surrounding community, educators at a local university, or by prominent political or social activists. Some successful business and political leaders also contribute to these organizations, but as described earlier, the systemic nature of corruption and patronage in Nigeria could threaten to undermine the perceived legitimacy of a particular organization if seen to be merely a tool for propaganda or influence.

Of course, there are also hundreds of foreign and intergovernmental aid organizations working to help Nigerians address an array of environmental, health, and other challenges. For example, the United Nations Development Program is heavily involved throughout Nigeria. However, they are comparatively much less influential in the daily lives and decision-making of ordinary Nigerians. From the analysis conducted for this JSOU monograph, little evidence was found that these non-Nigerian organizations play a significant role in countering the efforts of violent extremists. In some cases, they have even become targets of those extremists; the August 2011 attack on the UN building in Abuja is a poignant example of this. Further, an attack like this not only diminishes the institutional knowledge and capabilities of an organization, but it also has a dampening effect on the enthusiasm of other international players to remain engaged in helping Nigeria tackle its many challenges. The long-term impact of the deteriorating security environment in Nigeria remains to be seen, but it is highly likely that in the short-term, at least some foreign aid organizations will determine that a safer and more productive use of their resources is found elsewhere.

In sum, many kinds of nongovernmental organizations can have a direct impact on the daily lives of Nigerians, particularly in areas of providing assistance, dispute resolution, and information throughout their communities. They can play a significant role in addressing underlying grievances and conditions that sustain Boko Haram's ideological resonance. But like the religious leaders and traditional rulers, they must be supported in their efforts. Perhaps this is an area in which the U.S. and our allies can assist.

Regional and International Contributions

Boko Haram is a Nigerian entity that will eventually be defeated by Nigerians. However, there are ways in which regional and international actors can contribute meaningfully to those efforts. To begin with, several countries— including Egypt, Algeria, Morocco, Spain, the U.K., and the U.S.—have extensive experience confronting the threat of domestic terrorism. Nigerian authorities should welcome expertise from these countries. Also, while Nigeria's military is the largest and most well-equipped in West Africa, specialized skills are needed to combat terrorism. The U.S. Department of Defense has recently provided more than $8 million to Nigeria for the development of a counterterrorism infantry unit.[324] According to Lieutenant General Azubuike Ihejirika, the Nigerian Army Chief of Staff, the United States, France, Pakistan, and Britain have also offered to assist with counterterrorism training.[325] General Ham has proposed that the development of Nigeria's counterterrorism capabilities could include providing non-lethal equipment and training, and helping security forces to be more precise in their use of force.[326]

Of course, these international contributions should strengthen Nigeria's military and police capabilities but should not reflect an endorsement of an exclusively kinetic response to the threat of terrorism. In fact, Nigeria receives a tremendous amount of foreign aid from the international community, including $614 million from the U.S. in 2010, which supports programs in democratic governance, economic reform, security service reform and professionalization, and education and healthcare services.[327] Given the underlying grievances and conditions that have contributed to the rise of Boko Haram and other extremist groups, regional and international actors can also help Nigeria with policing and judicial system reforms, agricultural and infrastructure development—particularly the delivery of electricity—and most importantly, combating corruption. Further, these are areas in which aid to nongovernmental organizations may have the greatest impact. By empowering and improving community-level efforts at mitigating the grievances described throughout this monograph, regional and international assistance can help diminish Boko Haram's ideological resonance and degrade their capacity for influence, and by extension their operational capabilities.

An additional area of assistance focuses on addressing broader security challenges, like combating regional and global trafficking networks, and thwarting AQIM's attempts to gain influence in northern Nigeria. Regional and international actors can help ensure weapons from the recent Libyan conflict do not find their way into northern Nigeria. The monitoring and surveillance capabilities of other countries may be particularly useful here. The international community must also ensure that Boko Haram is unable to draw financial support from sympathizers in the global Nigerian diaspora. Overall, however, while regional and international actors can play an important support role in the fight against Boko Haram, it is at the local community level within Nigeria that this group will eventually be defeated.

Summary

This analysis highlights the importance of perceptions and beliefs in the study of terrorism and counterterrorism. An individual's choice to engage in—or disengage from—terrorism occurs at the intersection of ideas, perceptions, and opportunities.[328] Successful terrorist organizations capitalize on an environment in which their ideology resonates and their grievances are considered legitimate by smart, competent individuals. From this perspective, it becomes clear that Nigeria's counterterrorism strategy—which has mostly focused on killing or capturing individuals, interdicting finances, and so forth—will not lead to victory unless combined with a concerted effort to discredit the organization, its leaders, and ideology, and influence the perceptions of potential supporters within the community targeted by the organization. Combating terrorism effectively is not only a matter of appropriately directing kinetic force to identified targets; rather, the primary challenges involve acquiring contextually-relevant intelligence and affecting perspectives and belief systems in ways that create significant difficulties for a terrorist organization's ideology to find local resonance.

Counterterrorism strategy should focus on at least three areas: organizations, environmental conditions, and perceptions. It involves attacking terrorist organizations and their members, degrading their functional capabilities, encouraging "leaving" alternatives, and supporting sociopolitical entities that draw support away from them. It also involves mitigating sociopolitical conditions and other grievances which have historically been used by terrorist organizations to justify their use of violence. Here, the instruments of soft power are just as important in helping combat terrorism as a nation's security forces. Legitimacy in effort is also critical, in that it affects the quality of intelligence needed to identify and take away from the terrorist group the things that facilitate their operations, like safe havens, weapons proliferation, weak border controls, and illicit financial networks.

Boko Haram has evolved over the past three years into a type of threat the Nigerian government has not dealt with before. In the recent past, militant groups employing terrorist tactics were mainly confined to the Niger Delta, were focused on economic grievances and targets, and could be bought off. Some observers have been quick to point out the promising potential of the government's "amnesty" program, launched in 2009 under the Yar 'Adua regime as an attempt to quell the violence in the Niger Delta, based on recommendations made by the Niger Delta Technical Committee in 2008.[329] One report estimated that 20,192 militants surrendered their weapons, though others have suggested that there are still tens of thousands of weapons available throughout the Niger Delta, many in the hands of small gangs who are either engaging in low-level criminal activity or adopting a "wait and see" attitude toward the new administration of Goodluck Jonathan. Of note, though, the amnesty program has focused only on former militants—it did not address future generations of militants. To do that, the government must address the grievances that motivate those militants to organize and launch violent attacks, as well as the enabling environmental factors that sustain the resonance of these groups' political ideologies.

The same grievances and factors must also be addressed in a comprehensive effort to defeat Boko Haram. Interestingly, in May 2011 the new governor of Borno state—Kashim Shettima—offered an amnesty deal to Boko Haram, but a spokesman for the sect rejected the deal during an interview on a BBC Hausa radio program, stressing that the group's reasons of not accepting the amnesty are: "First we do not believe in the Nigerian constitution and secondly we do not believe in democracy but only in the laws of Allah."[330] It is highly unlikely that Boko Haram can be appeased by any amnesty program, or a policy to bring better employment and education prospects to their home region. Theirs is an intractable ideology, with a broad array of potential targets, and most importantly of all, a belief that their religious devotion will result in victory.

Further, unlike the Niger Delta militant groups, Boko Haram has opportunities to garner assistance from established jihadist groups in other parts of Africa, and perhaps even the global jihadist network, through which they could acquire weapons, knowledge, finance, and additional ideological support. In short, Nigeria is now facing a kind of terrorist threat that has become tragically familiar to the U.S. and other western allies who have been targets of radical Salafi-jihadist violence in recent years. There is much that external actors could offer in the form of lessons learned, including the need to protect influential moderates within the Muslim communities of the north against retributional attacks by Boko Haram. The situation in northern Nigeria requires a sense of urgency and cooperation—interagency, regional, and international—among both governmental and nongovernmental entities. For the sake of all Nigerians, one hopes that all those who can contribute to the solution will rise to the occasion before the situation deteriorates further.

7. Conclusion and Implications for SOF

This study of Boko Haram is intended first and foremost as a useful backgrounder for members of U.S. Special Operations Forces, particularly those with interests or mission assignments in sub-Saharan Africa. Much of the analysis illustrates the complex and intersecting kinds of information needed to understand the phenomenon of modern religiously-inspired domestic terrorism, so it should hopefully be useful to the general counterterrorism practitioner as well. Clearly, no terrorist group has ever emerged in a vacuum; there are dynamic contexts—political, social, economic, temporal, spatial, even spiritual—that must be taken into account. Thus, a considerable amount of emphasis has been placed throughout the monograph on identifying the array of environmental conditions and grievances among members of the local population that facilitate opportunities for Boko Haram to muster support and orchestrate acts of political violence. The government of Nigeria has struggled to deal effectively with these grievances and sources of tension throughout the country, and there is a pervasive belief particularly among northern Nigerians that the government continually fails to address critical needs of those who aspire for a better future. While resources are surely constrained, it is the inequitable distribution of those resources, and the widely acknowledged levels of corruption among elites, that detract from the government's effectiveness. In turn, patronage and corruption fuel a general perception that government officials—to include law enforcement—cannot be trusted, and this further undermines the government's ability to influence the behavior of local community members in positive directions, away from the lure of radical extremist ideologies like that of Boko Haram.

An overwhelming majority of problems identified in this study can be tackled, but only by a capable government that is seen by its citizens as legitimate and trustworthy. There is much that Nigeria's government can and must do to reduce alienation and build trust and legitimacy among its citizens—particularly in the northern region—and address other enablers of terrorism described in this study. At the core of the problem is perceived government legitimacy, or lack thereof, and how this provides opportunities for non-state actors like Boko Haram to capture loyalties, hearts, and minds in pursuit of their radical vision of the future. In essence, it is what the Irregular Warfare Joint Operating Concept calls "a violent struggle among state and nonstate actors for legitimacy and influence over the relevant populations."[331] As U.S. Army officers Cindy Jebb and Madelfia Abb note, "The most challenging society for a polity to rule is one that has reinforcing cleavages such that loyalties to a group or tribe supercede loyalties to the state or the political system. How a political system interacts with a society will determine if it can overcome these divisions."[332]

Legitimacy is central to ensuring security; if corruption is not tackled effectively, and the use of force among military and police is viewed as illegitimate by locals, the counterterrorism effort against Boko Haram will be much more difficult and much less successful than it should be. For these reasons, according to a recent Congressional report, the U.S. has begun to publicly pressure Nigeria's government to tackle corruption, encourage greater investment in the north, address poverty and joblessness, and promote government accountability and transparency.[333] Of course, the government of Nigeria does not need the U.S. or anyone else to tell them they have a corruption problem; the country's leaders have acknowledged it for many years. Furthermore, there are people within the Nigerian government who want to do something about it, and in some cases are actively trying. They need and deserve support and protection for their courage. But based on this analysis of the underlying problems that have given fuel to the rise of Boko Haram, it seems evident that strengthening trust and legitimacy between state and citizen should be a top priority for the Nigerian government.

Beneath the corruption, however, lies a much deeper and complex structural challenge: the politicization of ethnic identities. Issues of ethnic representation in positions of power and authority have dominated Nigerian political discourse for decades. Every ethnic group wants more representation for themselves; politics is seen as a zero-sum game in which one group's gains are seen as another group's loss. It is a political system that pits ethnic groups against each other in a constant struggle over limited resources. This constant focus on who has what, who does not have what, who should have what, and so forth undermines the potential effectiveness of the nation-state to ensure an equitable distribution of resources. Compared to the U.S., where the "melting pot" approach of cultural integration has been encouraged for centuries and has fostered a sense of national pride in being "American" across many diverse ethnicities, the situation in Nigeria seems hopelessly counterproductive to nation-building. Addressing this system of structural ethnic cleavages should also be a priority of Nigeria's government.

Obviously, meeting the needs of all Nigerians is a central goal of the government, but as noted throughout this monograph, there is much that nongovernmental entities do to make up for the deficiencies of the state. Further, in many parts of the country the government is viewed as having less legitimacy than nongovernmental entities. Thus, while the international community should certainly find ways to help Nigeria's government better serve its people, it should also embrace the many opportunities to address environmental conditions and grievances through a community-level engagement strategy. As noted earlier, a state-centric approach to combating Boko Haram and its ideological resonance will be only partially effective. Some of Nigeria's security challenges have deep socioeconomic and structural roots. For example, large numbers of unemployed young men provide a fertile breeding ground for armed groups and extremists. With governmental and nongovernmental resources properly deployed, the energies of a youthful population could be directed toward more productive pursuits, like critical infrastructure and development efforts. A collaborative and networked approach—combining the strengths of the public and private sector, and particularly of civil society organizations—should be a cornerstone of the effort to combat Boko Haram, as each actor has unique resources to contribute.

Beyond the need to mitigate environmental conditions and grievances, however, the characteristics of Boko Haram must also be studied, particularly its ideology and operational capabilities, and how these are viewed by members of the local environment. In essence, Boko Haram's success or failure can be seen as a product of individual relationships and interactions within its operating environment over a period of time. Examining these patterns of interaction can yield insights about the choices individuals make toward or against engaging in any kind of terrorist activity. From this knowledge, efforts can be made to exploit the vulnerabilities of Boko Haram's ideology and actions. It must be remembered that both governments and militant groups struggle to establish "street credibility" and legitimacy in the influence warfare battlespace. This struggle impacts the kind and quality of intelligence provided by community members to local authorities attempting to combat terrorism and organized crime. This monograph highlights how and why a central goal of the strategy to defeat Boko Haram should be to degrade its capacity for influencing Muslim communities. Eventually, it will cease to be relevant, just like all terrorist groups who have come before it. And it is here that we may find ways in which U.S. Special Operations Forces can assist our Nigerian allies in bringing about this end state sooner than later.

Implications for SOF

As noted in the introduction to this monograph, helping Nigeria confront the terrorist threat of Boko Haram is in the interests of the U.S. and the international community. Of course, there is much that needs to be done that is well outside the purview of SOF, the U.S. government in general, or any other outside entity. For example, reducing alienation and strengthening trust and legitimacy between the state and citizen, and several of the other recommendations highlighted above, can only be achieved by the Nigerian government. But to be sure, the U.S. military has amassed significant experience in helping a fledgling young democracy establish legitimacy, combat corruption, and improve economic and political stability, infrastructure, and the provision of services. Our troops have experience developing and implementing confidence-building measures in small villages as part of an overall strategy to improve civil-military relations, and by extension improving perceptions of a government's legitimacy.[334] One particular area in which SOF could be useful is in providing training and helping security forces to be more precise in their use of force, as General Ham proposed.[335]

SOF teams could also serve as trusted brokers between Nigerian forces and local communities, helping to forge healthier relationships between the government and traditional leaders, religious leaders, and civil service organizations. SOF could also work with local community organizations in ways that would help strengthen their capacity to provide social services. In doing so, they would contribute to building a sense among the community members that things are getting better, a sense that undermines the resonance of Boko Haram's ideology which claims that change will only come through the use of violence and terrorism. In this role, SOF would forge their own beneficial partnerships with local, community-based organizations, providing a source of intelligence and a means by which targeted financial support can be most effective in helping mitigate the grievances and conditions that animate supporters of Boko Haram's ideology. From a SOF intelligence-gathering perspective, local nongovernmental entities offer a uniquely valuable source of information on the world of militants, information that could be useful for preventing or responding to an attack against a U.S.-related target. This view has already been incorporated into U.S. strategy, which is why the U.S. government has been working to develop ties with Yemen's most influential tribes in an effort to develop new networks of sources on al-Qaeda in the Arabian Peninsula.[336] Because of their "on the ground" presence and expertise, Russ Howard noted that nongovernmental entities can make excellent sources of intelligence.[337] They "understand the sensitivities of the local culture and the immediate needs and vulnerabilities of the populace," and "often have access to individuals who for any number of reasons would not speak with military or intelligence personnel." [338]

Engaging with the West Africa Civil Society Forum is one of many pathways through which SOF can identify CSOs that are influential in their communities, and can thus play a role in any local counterterrorism or counter-trafficking mission. On the national level, most nations in West Africa have ministries of cultural affairs, interior affairs, or some other entity that presumably has ample visibility on the CSOs within their country, and thus offer another conduit for information on potential community-based SOF partners. However, a word of caution is necessary about working with government agencies or local entities in Nigeria. When forging a working relationship, the SOF operator must take into consideration several factors, including: Does this individual have historical legitimacy? What might be this person's hidden agenda? Upon what factors is their influence based (e.g., is this person widely respected for the kind of person they are and what they do, or is their power derived simply due to their title or access to resources)? Do locals show respect toward this person regardless of ethnic or tribal affiliation? Do they have a track record of reconciliation/conflict mediation? It can be expected that some people will be quite influential in a local context yet not have the best interests of all Nigerians in mind. Obtaining "ground truth" is essential in all areas of SOF deployment, and it is the same here with regard to identifying the kinds of traditional rulers, religious leaders, and nongovernmental organizations that deserve U.S. support and assistance in countering local terrorist threats.

As described throughout this monograph, legitimacy and influence are central dimensions in the fight against Boko Haram. Jessica Turnley describes how "in all cases of influence… key interactions happen at the local level" with "authority vested in local leaders such as tribal elders, or in the leaders of unincorporated, informal groups such as insurgent groups or religious communities."[339] Engaging the local population in the fight against Boko Haram will be vital to the success of Nigeria's counterterrorism strategy. To assist local leaders, U.S. Special Operations Forces (SOF) can draw lessons from a tribal engagement strategy that has been a prominent component of success in Afghanistan and Iraq. Boko Haram, like any other terrorist group, faces considerable challenges and difficulties, and often these are well understood by local leaders. Thus, a central part of an effective counterterrorism strategy should be to work with these local leaders to amplify and exacerbate these challenges, and make them even more difficult for the enemy to overcome.

Further, as noted in the previous chapter, understanding and exploiting the vulnerabilities of Boko Haram's ideology and actions should be a prominent component of a comprehensive counterterrorism strategy. However, resonance is made possible when the "message" is delivered by a credible "messenger," and from this perspective the government may have less effectiveness in the influence warfare battlespace than nongovernmental entities. Here, SOF can help train local community and religious leaders on how the tools of strategic communication can be used to counter Boko Haram's ideology, crafting and disseminating a range of competing narratives that draw support away from the terrorist group and toward a different vision of the future.

...understanding and exploiting the vulnerabilities of Boko Haram's ideology and actions should be a prominent component of a comprehensive counterterrorism strategy.

In the context of northern Nigeria, radio is a particularly important source of information and influence. Several Hausa language broadcasts are available, including the Voice of America, the BBC, and similar news services sponsored by Germany, China, Iran, and other countries. Freedom Radio, the largest radio station in northern Nigeria, is a privately-owned station in Kano with approximately 75 percent of the population as listeners. Radio offers an important means for communicating the counter-narratives that weaken Boko Haram, and for highlighting the contradictions in the group's ideology and actions that weaken it even more. Unfortunately, some Islamic clerics who have dared to criticize Boko Haram—in their sermons, in newspapers, or on radio programs—have been killed.[340] If Nigeria's government is unable or unwilling to provide security for these influential voices—essential in the fight against Boko Haram—then perhaps this is another area in which SOF can assist.

There may also be a need for SOF expertise in manhunting terrorist suspects in targeted operations. Drawing on years of experience advising Iraqi and Afghan forces and leading small unit raids to capture or eliminate key leaders, SOF could certainly be of assistance to Nigerian forces in their efforts to track down Boko Haram's most lethal threats. But there must be great caution before considering such actions: a U.S. troop presence on Nigerian soil, particularly if there for the sole purpose of helping to confront a radical Islamist group, could give Boko Haram a source of legitimacy that they could capitalize on. It could also lead to a shift in targeting away from locals and toward Western or international targets. The U.S. should avoid sending SOF on any mission that could inadvertently benefit the terrorists' ability to generate resonance for its ideology.

In general, over the last decade SOF has learned many lessons from Iraq, Afghanistan, and other kinds of tribal environments with low government legitimacy, armed militants—some of whom are religiously inspired—available weapons, financial support, safe havens, and other elements seen in northern Nigeria. SOF operators have confronted violent non-state actors in urban and rural environments where poverty, illiteracy, and anti-government sentiment is high, and have come to appreciate the critical importance of information operations, public diplomacy, infrastructure development, and civil affairs as part of a comprehensive counterterrorism strategy. In the event that SOF are called upon for strategic intervention in northern Nigeria, in cooperation with Nigerian forces, these lessons will surely inform an effective approach.

This kind of security challenge is one for which SOF are uniquely prepared. Compared with conventional military forces, SOF is better equipped for working with traditional and religious leaders in a comprehensive effort to combat Boko Haram and the local conditions that sustain it. Thus, the research and analysis in this monograph is intended to provide useful insights about Boko Haram and its operating environment for a SOF readership, because the most powerful weapon in the SOF arsenal is knowledge. SOF operators are already well-versed in the research on "cross-cultural competency," "human terrain analysis" and "layered social networks."[341] Research in this area emphasizes that within any human terrain, interdependent actors and complex networks must be accounted for in order to understand the behavior of citizens, particularly in response to the demands of its government. Human interactions and meaningful transactions—economic, social, political, et cetera—in a complex society like Nigeria's are made possible through constantly negotiated and renegotiated relationships. As former USSOCOM Commander Admiral Eric Olson noted in his 2009 testimony before Congress, "The complexity of today's and tomorrow's strategic environments requires that our SOF operators maintain not only the highest level of warfighting expertise but also cultural knowledge and diplomacy skills."[342]

Essentially, SOF operators must develop a comprehensive understanding of the environments in which terrorist organizations' ideologies have found resonance. This kind of context-specific research on a group's ideological resonance differs from the more traditional approach of gathering information on a group's operational capabilities. In the case of Boko Haram, this includes studying the fragile nature of the relationship between the state and the citizen, the diffusion of power and competing loyalties within Nigerian society, the societal and informal governance networks, the politicized ethnic identities, and the overarching competition for influence among Muslim communities. It also includes gathering information on insecurities that local community members have about their physical and spiritual future, and how these insecurities can be manipulated by charismatic leaders with a radical ideology.

Research is needed on situation-specific factors that contribute to political violence in a particular location, in order to develop context-appropriate counterterrorism strategies. We need to identify the most prominent influencers in a community, and determine how/where youth congregate and learn from peers; how social networks develop and evolve in different cultural contexts; which groups enjoy strategic influence, and why; what interactions matter most in motivating individuals to conduct violence; and other central questions. With this knowledge, counterterrorism strategists should craft appropriate ways to assess the resonance of a terrorist organization's messages, themes, and communication mechanisms, and determine ways to reduce the resonance of these messages and themes within a given context.[343] As support for terrorism wanes, intelligence tends to increase on terrorist activities, penetrations occur, and operations become more difficult.[344] Reducing an organization's ideological resonance requires addressing an array of environmental conditions that may span a broad socioeconomic and political landscape.[345]

Knowledge must also be developed on the history of other violent non-state actors in northern Nigeria with similar ideology, motivating grievances, membership, finances, and so forth that have challenged the government for supremacy and control over a particular territory. How a local environment sustains a terrorist organization depends largely on how individuals within that environment perceive the opportunities for the organization's success. The past matters: Is there a history of political violence either locally or within the surrounding region? Are there regional examples of success or failure of terrorism? By the same token, we must also study the history of how the government has responded to those groups, and whether these responses have been effective at the tactical and long-term strategic levels. Where a government has historically used force to deal with problems in communities as seen in Nigeria, research should focus on how these actions may exacerbate the grievances of the governed and motivate other violent non-state actors. At the same time, the impact of non-kinetic responses to terrorism must also be examined to determine their applicability. For example, the amnesty program implemented as a way of reducing the violence in the Niger Delta is unlikely to be effective in confronting the threat posed by Boko Haram.

SOF operators also need to develop a context-specific "map of influences" to identify the groups, individuals, and institutions that have the most power and influence within a local community. In several parts of Africa, nongovernmental entities play a larger role than governments in providing human security and basic services. Gaining a complete picture of the diverse influence landscape requires that we determine whether certain actors are perceived as legitimate within their areas of operation. In turn, these perceptions of legitimacy comprise one of several criteria for determining which local entities would be most beneficial to establish relationships and partnership with in pursuit of SOF counterterrorism objectives.

Final Thoughts

As a relatively young democracy with a very large and diverse population, Nigeria should anticipate the emergence of politically violent groups from time to time. All countries, even advanced Western democracies, have had to deal with such challenges. Some have dealt with the challenges of terrorism more effectively than others, but in all cases there have been lessons to be learned. Collectively studying these lessons, and drawing from them what seems to be most useful in confronting today's terrorist threats, is one of the most important security missions of our time. Furthermore, sharing the lessons and experiences with other countries fighting a lethal terrorist group like Boko Haram is in our best interests.

But the real heroes in defeating Boko Haram will be the Nigerian people themselves. There should be no doubt that an overwhelming majority of Nigerians want the problem of Boko Haram to go away, and that they will have the courage and determination to contribute meaningfully toward that shared goal. The end of Boko Haram, like all terrorist groups, will be a matter of time. Sooner or later, the resonance of its ideology will fade, it will cease to attract young men to its cause, or support among local community members who have already grown weary of the group's attempts to provoke sectarian violence. This, in turn, will have a direct impact on the kinds of intelligence that will play a central role in defeating Boko Haram. Currently there are pockets of sympathizers for Boko Haram's ideology and grievances, if not its actions. As these diminish, so too will the organization.

The major contributors to the demise of Boko Haram will be Muslim community leaders and nongovernmental leaders with local legitimacy, more so than the heavy-handed tactics of the police and military. Surely, as this monograph illustrates, the problem of Boko Haram will not go away solely through the use of force. To some observers, Nigeria's heavy-handed response to the group has been counterproductive, "hastening its transformation into a menacing transnational force" as a recent *New York Times* article noted.[346] The U.S. can provide assistance to our Nigerian allies in reversing the trajectory of Boko Haram, but they must be willing to incorporate a more comprehensive approach to the fight. Various assets of the U.S. government, including SOF, can assist with the influence warfare aspects of countering Boko Haram. For example, the U.S. Agency for International Development funds several programs in the northern states of Bauchi and Sokoto,[347] including a program called Leadership, Empowerment, Advocacy, and Development, through which northern governments build partnerships between state and local governments and the private sector to improve accountability, governance, and the delivery of essential services.[348] By working together to address fundamental issues of human security, we can mitigate the grievances of the governed that animate recruits and local supporters of Boko Haram. The same kind of comprehensive approach to combating terrorism can also guide SOF assistance in responding to security challenges elsewhere in sub-Saharan Africa. ↑

Bibliography

Adesoji, Abimbola O. 2011. "Between Maitatsine and Boko Haram: Islamic Fundamentalism and the Response of the Nigerian State," *Africa Today* 57(4), pp. 99-119.

Alexander, John B. 2009. *Africa: Irregular Warfare on the Dark Continent*, JSOU Report 09-5. Tampa, FL: JSOU Press.

Amnesty International. 2009. *Killing At Will: Extrajudicial Executions and other Unlawful Killings by the Police in Nigeria* (London: Amnesty International). Online at: http://www.amnesty.org/en/library/asset/AFR44/038/2009/en/f09b1c15-77b4-40aa-a608-b3b01bde0fc5/afr440382009en.pdf

Baker, Bruce. 2004. "Protection from Crime: What is on Offer for Africans?" *Journal of Contemporary African Studies*, 22(2), pp. 165-188.

Baker, Bruce. 2002. *Taking the Law into Their Own Hands*. Aldershot: Ashgate.

Bandura, Albert. 2005. "Mechanisms of Moral Disengagement," in *The Making of a Terrorist, Vol. 2: Training*, edited by James J.F. Forest. Westport, CT: Praeger Security International.

Barber, Benjamin R. 2005. "Terrorism, Interdependence and Democracy," in The Making of a Terrorist, Volume 3: Root Causes, edited by James J.F. Forest. Westport, CT: Praeger.

Barber, Benjamin R. 1995. *Jihad vs. McWorld*. New York: Times Books.

Barrett, Roby C. 2011. *Yemen: A Different Political Paradigm in Context*, JSOU Report 11-3 (May). Tampa, FL: JSOU Press.

Benjamin, Daniel and Steve Simon. 2002. *The Age of Sacred Terror*. New York: Random House.

Blench, Roger, Selbut Longtau, Umar Hassan and Martin Walsh. 2006. *The Role of Traditional Rulers in Conflict Prevention and Mediation in Nigeria*. DFID Nigeria, September.

Bloom, Mia. 2005. *Dying to Kill: The Allure of Suicide Terrorism*. New York: Columbia University Press, 2005.

Bonat, Zuwaqhu A. "Economic Deregulation, the Peasantry and Agricultural Development in Nigeria: A Kaduna State Case Study," in *The Political Economy of Nigeria Under Military Rule*: 1984-1993, edited by Said A. Adejumobi and Abubakar Momoh. Harare: Sapes, 1995.

Campbell, John. 2011. *Nigeria: Dancing on the Brink*. Plymouth, UK: Rowman & Littlefield.

Campbell, John. 2011. "To Battle Nigeria's Boko Haram, Put Down Your Guns," *Foreign Affairs* (September 9).

Campbell, John and Asch Harwood. 2011. "Nigeria's Challenge," *The Atlantic* (June 24).

Carr, Christopher. 2007. "Combating the International Proliferation of Small Arms and Light Weapons," in *Countering Terrorism and Insurgency in the 21st Century (Vol. 2: Combating the Sources and Facilitators)*, edited by James J.F. Forest. Westport, CT: Praeger.

Chalk, Peter. 2004. "Islam in West Africa: The Case of Nigeria," in *The Muslim World After 9/11*, edited by Angel M. Rabasa, Cheryl Benard, Peter Chalk et al. Santa Monica, CA: RAND Corporation.

Chenoweth, Erica. 2005. "Instability and Opportunity: The Origins of Terrorism in Weak and Failed States," in *The Making of a Terrorist, Vol. 3: Root Causes*, edited by James J.F. Forest. Westport, CT: Praeger Security International.

Clapper, James R. "Statement for the Record on the Worldwide Threat Assessment for the U.S. Intelligence Community," Statement of the Director of National Intelligence, February 10, 2011, pg. 18. Available at: http://www.dni.gov/testimonies/20110210_testimony_clapper.pdf

Cockayne, James and Phil Williams. 2009. *The Invisible Tide: Towards an International Strategy to Deal with Drug Trafficking Through West Africa*. New York: The International Peace Institute.

Cooke, Jennifer. 2011. Statement before the U.S. House of Representatives, Subcommittee on Counterterrorism and Intelligence, "Hearing on Boko Haram – Emerging Threat to the U.S. Homeland" (November 30). Online at: http://homeland.house.gov/hearing/subcommittee-hearing-boko-haram-emerging-threat-us-homeland

Cordesman, Anthony H. 2002. "Saudi Security and the War on Terrorism: International Security Operations, Law Enforcement, Internal Threats, and the Need for Change." Center for Strategic and International Studies. Online at: http://www.csis.org/media/csis/pubs/saudiwarterr030302.pdf

Cragin, Kim and Peter Chalk. 2003. *Terrorism and Development: Using Social and Economic Development to Inhibit a Resurgence of Terrorism*. Santa Monica, CA: RAND Corporation.

Cragin, Kim and Scott Gerwehr. 2005. *Dissuading Terror: Strategic Influence and the Struggle Against Terrorism*. Santa Monica, CA: RAND Corporation.

Crenshaw, Martha. 1998. "The Logic of Terrorism: Terrorist Behavior as a Product of Strategic Choice," in *Origins of Terrorism: Psychologies, Ideologies, Theologies, States of Mind*, edited by Walter Reich. Baltimore: Woodrow Wilson Center Press, pp. 7-24.

Crenshaw, Martha. 1995. *Terrorism in Context*. College Station, PA: Pennsylvania State University Press.

Crenshaw, Martha. 1981. "The Causes of Terrorism," *Comparative Politics* (July), pp. 379-399.

Danjibo, D. N. 2010. *Islamic Fundamentalism and Sectarian Violence: The "Maitatsine" and "Boko Haram" Crises in Northern Nigeria*. Peace and Conflict Studies Programme, Institute of African Studies, University of Ibadan. Online at: http://www.ifra-nigeria.org/spip.php?article156

Davidson, Basil. 1967. *A History of West Africa, 1000-1800: The Growth of African Civilization*. London: Longman.

Devlin-Foltz, Zachary. 2010. "Africa's Fragile States: Empowering Extremists, Exporting Terrorism," *Africa Security Brief* 6.

Eidelson, Roy J. and Judy I. Eidelson. 2003. "Dangerous Ideas: Five Beliefs that Propel Groups Toward Conflict," *American Psychologist* 58, no. 3 (March), pp. 182-192.

Ellis, Stephen. 2009. "West Africa's International Drug Trade," *African Affairs*, 108(431), pp. 171-196.

Esposito, John. 1995. *The Oxford Encyclopedia of the Modern Islamic World*, 4th Ed. Oxford University Press, 1995.

Falola, Toyin and Matthew Heaton. 2008. *A History of Nigeria*. Cambridge University Press.

Fayemi, J. Kayode and Fummi Olonisakin. 2008. "Nigeria," in *Challenges of Security Sector Governance in West Africa*, Alan Bryden, Boubacar N'Diaye and 'Funmi Olonisakin (eds.). Geneva Centre for the Democratic Control of Armed Forces.

Felbab-Brown, Vanda and James J.F. Forest. 2012. "Political Violence and Illicit Economies of West Africa," *Terrorism and Political Violence* 24(1).

Flanigan, Shawn Teresa. 2006. "Charity as Resistance: Connections between Charity, Contentious Politics, and Terror," *Studies in Conflict and Terrorism*, 29(7).

Florquin, Nicolas and Eric G. Berman (eds.). 2005. *Armed and Aimless; Armed Groups, Guns, and Human Security in the ECOWAS Region*, Geneva.

Forest, James J.F. 2012. "Al Qaeda's Inconvenience Truths: A Study of Influence Warfare," *Perspectives on Terrorism*, 8(1).

Forest, James J.F. 2007. "Combating the Sources and Facilitators of Terrorism," in *Countering Terrorism and Insurgency in the 21st Century* (Vol. 2), edited by James J.F. Forest. Westport, CT: Praeger, pp. 1-22.

Forest, James J.F. 2009. "Influence Warfare and Modern Terrorism," *Georgetown Journal of International Affairs*, 10(1).

Forest, James J.F. 2010. "Terrorism as a Product of Choices and Perceptions," in *Terrorizing Ourselves*, edited by Benjamin H. Friedman, Jim Harper, and Christopher A. Preble. Washington, DC: Cato Institute, pp. 23-44.

Forest, James J.F. 2006. "The Final Act: Ideologies of Catastrophic Terror," published by the Fund for Peace Expert Series, online at: http://www.fundforpeace.org/web/images/pdf/forest.pdf

Forest, James J.F. (ed.). 2009. *Influence Warfare: How States and Terrorist Struggle to Shape Perceptions*. Westport, CT: Praeger.

Forest, James J.F. and Matthew V. Sousa. 2006. *Oil and Terrorism in the New Gulf: Framing U.S. Energy and Security Policies for the Gulf of Guinea*. New York: Lexington Press.

Guichaoua, Yvan 2006. "The Making of an Ethnic Militia: The Oodua People's Congress in Nigeria," CRISE Working Paper No. 26. Center for Research on Inequality, Human Security and Ethnicity, Queen Elizabeth House, Oxford University. Online at: http://www.crise.ox.ac.uk/pubs/workingpaper26.pdf

Gurr, Ted Robert. 1970. *Why Men Rebel*. Princeton University Press.

Habermas, Jurgen. 1975. *Legitimation Crisis*. Boston: Beacon Press.

Hafez, Mohammed. 2005. "Political Repression and Violent Rebellion in the Muslim World," in *The Making of a Terrorist: Recruitment, Training and Root Causes*, edited by James J.F. Forest. Westport, CT: Praeger.

Hamden, Raymond H. 2005. "Unresolved Trauma and the Thirst for Revenge: The Retributional Terrorist," in *The Making of a Terrorist (Vol. 1: Recruitment)*, edited by James J.F. Forest. Westport, CT: Praeger.

Hamill, Todd J. Richard F. Drecko, James W. Chrissis, and Robert F. Mills. 2008. "Analysis of Layered Social Networks," *IO Sphere* (Winter).

Hill, Jonathan. 2010. *Sufism in Northern Nigeria: Force for Counter-Radicalization?* Carlisle, PA: Strategic Studies Institute.

Hoffman, Bruce. 2006. "The Use of the Internet By Islamic Extremists." Testimony presented to the House Permanent Select Committee on Intelligence (May 4). Online at: http://rand.org/pubs/testimonies/CT262-1

Hoffman, Bruce. 2006. *Inside Terrorism*, 2nd edition. New York: Columbia University Press.

Horgan, John. 2003. "The Search for the Terrorist Personality," in *Terrorists, Victims and Society: Psychological Perspectives on Terrorism and its Consequences*, edited by Andrew Silke. Chichester, England: John Wiley and Sons.

Horgan, John. 2005. "The Social and Psychological Characteristics of Terrorism and Terrorists," in *Root Causes of Terrorism: Myths, Realities and Ways Forward*, edited by Tore Bjorgo. London: Routledge.

Howard, Russell D. 2007. *Intelligence in Denied Areas*, JSOU Report 07-10. Tampa, FL: JSOU Press.

Hudson, Rex A. 2001. *Who Becomes a Terrorist and Why: The 1999 Government Report on Profiling Terrorists*. Guilford, CT: The Lyons Press, 2001.

Human Rights Watch 2011. "Corruption on Trial: The Record of Nigeria's Economic and Financial Crimes Commission. Available online at: http://www.hrw.org/reports/2011/08/25/corruption-trial

Human Rights Watch. 2008. "Nigeria: Arbitrary Killings by Security Forces in Jos." Online at: http://www.hrw.org/news/2008/12/19/nigeria-arbitrary-killings-security-forces-jos

Ibaba, Ibaba Samuel. 2011. "Terrorism in Liberation Struggles: Interrogating the Engagement Tactics of Movement for the Emancipation of the Niger Delta" *Perspectives on Terrorism*.

International Crisis Group. 2010. "Northern Nigeria: Background to the Conflict," *Africa Report no. 168*.

Isa, Muhammad Kabir. 2010. "Militant Islamist Groups in Northern Nigeria," in *Militias, Rebels and Islamist Militants: Human Insecurity and State Crises in Africa*, edited by Wafulu Okumu and Augustine Ikelegbe. Pretoria: Institute for Security Studies.

Issaka K. Souare. 2010. "A Critical Assessment of Security Challenges in West Africa," *ISS Situation Report*.

Jane's Intelligence Review. 1999. "African Struggle over Smuggled Weapons" (November 23). London: Jane's Intelligence Service.

Jasparro, Christopher. 2007. "Sociocultural, Economic and Demographic Aspects of Counterterrorism," in *Countering Terrorism and Insurgency in the 21st Century (Vol. 2: Combating the Sources and Facilitators)*, edited by James J.F. Forest. Westport, CT: Praeger.

Jebb, Cindy R. and Madelfia A. Abb. 2005. "Human Security and Good Governance: A Living Systems Approach to Understanding and Combating Terrorism," in *The Making of a Terrorist, Volume 3: Root Causes*, edited by James J.F. Forest. Westport, CT: Praeger.

Johnston, Hugh. 1967. *Fulani Empire of Sokoto*. Oxford University Press, 1967.

Keen, David. 2005. *Conflict and Collusion in Sierra Leone*. Palgrave Macmillan.

Kandeh, Jimmy D. 2005. "The Criminalization of the RUF Insurgency in Sierra Leone," in *Rethinking the Economics of War: The Intersection of Need, Creed, and Greed*, Cynthia A. Arnson and I. William Zartman, eds. Washington, DC: Woodrow Wilson Center, pp. 84-107.

Khalil, Lydia. 2007. "Authoritarian and Corrupt Governments," in *Countering Terrorism and Insurgency in the 21st Century (Vol. 2: Combating the Sources and Facilitators)*, edited by James J.F. Forest. Westport, CT: Praeger, 2007.

Killingray, David. 1986. "The Maintenance of Law and Order in British Colonial Africa," *African Affairs*, 85(340), pp. 411-437.

Kirschke, Joseph. 2008. "The Coke Coast: Cocaine and Failed States in Africa," *World Politics Review* (September 9).

Krueger, Alan B. and Jitka Maleckova. 2003. "Education, Poverty and Terrorism: Is There a Causal Connection?" *Journal of Economic Perspectives* 17(4), pp. 119-144.

Kydd, Andrew H. and Barbara F. Walter. 2006. "The Strategies of Terrorism," *International Security* 31(1), pp. 49-80.

Lacquer, Walter. 2001. "Left, Right and Beyond: The Changing Face of Terror," in *How Did This Happen? Terrorism and the New War*, edited by James Hoge and Gideon Rose (Oxford: Public Affairs, 2001), pp. 71-82.

Last, Murray. 2007. "Muslims and Christians in Nigeria: An Economy of Panic," *The Round Table: The Commonwealth Journal of International Affairs*, 96(392), pp. 605-616.

Leigh, Karen. 2011. "Nigeria's Boko Haram: Al-Qaeda's New Friend in Africa?" *TIME Magazine* (August 17).

Leiter, Michael E. 2008. Testimony (Statement for the Record) before the Senate Committee on Homeland Security and Governmental Affairs (July 10).

Liotta, Peter H. and James F. Miskel. 2005. "Digging Deep: Environment and Geography as Root Influences for Terrorism," in *The Making of a Terrorist, Vol. 3: Root Causes*, edited by James J.F. Forest. Westport, CT: Praeger Security International.

Loimeier, Roman. 1996. *Islamic Reform and Political Change in Northern Nigeria*. Evanston, IL: Northwestern University Press.

Love, James B. 2010. *Hezbollah: Social Services as a Source of Power*, JSOU Report 10-5. Tampa, FL: JSOU Press.

Maier, Karl. 2000. *This House Has Fallen: Crisis in Nigeria*. London: Penguin.

Marr, Jack John Cushing, Brandon Garner and Richard Thompson. 2008. "Human Terrain Mapping: A Critical First Step to Winning the COIN Fight, *Military Review* 88 (March/April), pp. 37-51.

McCauley, Clark. 2008. "Pathways Towards Radicalization," START Research Brief. National Consortium for the Study of Terrorism and Responses to Terrorism.

McCauley, Clark. 2004. "Psychological Issues in Understanding Terrorism and Response to Terrorism," in *Psychology of Terrorism: Coping with the Continuing Threat* (Condensed Edition), edited by Chris Stout. Westport, CT: Praeger.

McCue, Colleen and Kathryn Haahr. 2008. "The Impact of Global Youth Bulges on Islamist Radicalization and Violence," *CTC Sentinel* 1(1) (October) pp. 12-14.

McFate, Montgomery. 2005. "The Military Utility of Understanding Adversary Culture." *Joint Forces Quarterly* 38, pp. 42-48.

Meehan, Patrick and Jackie Speier. 2011. *Boko Haram: Emerging Threat to the U.S. Homeland*, U.S. House of Representatives Committee on Homeland Security, Subcommittee on Counterterrorism and Intelligence (November 30).

Merrari, Ariel. 1990. "The Readiness to Kill and Die: Suicidal Terrorism in the Middle East," in *Origins of Terrorism: Psychologies, Ideologies, Theologies, State of Mind*, edited by Walter Reich. Baltimore: Woodrow Wilson International Center Press.

Miles, William F.S. 1993. "Traditional rulers and development administration: Chieftaincy in Niger, Nigeria, and Vanuatu," *Studies in Comparative International Development*, 28(3), pp. 31-50.

Moghadam, Assaf. 2008. "The Salafi-Jihad as a Religious Ideology." *CTC Sentinel* 1(3), pp. 14-16.

Moghadam, Assaf. 2006. *The Roots of Terrorism*. New York: Chelsea House.

Moghaddam, Fathali M. 2005. "The Staircase to Terrorism: A Psychological Exploration," *American Psychologist* 60, pp. 161-169.

Mousseau, Michael. 2005. "Terrorism and Export Economies: The Dark Side of Free Trade," in *The Making of a Terrorist, Vol. 3: Root Causes*, edited by James J.F. Forest. Westport, CT: Praeger Security International.

Musah, Abdel-Fatau. 2009. *West Africa: Governance and Security in a Changing Region*. New York: International Peace Institute.

Mustapha, Abdul Raufu. 2005. "Ethnic Structure, Inequality and Governance of the Public Sector in Nigeria," CRISE Working Paper No. 18. Center for Research on Inequality, Human Security and Ethnicity (Queen Elizabeth House, Oxford University). Online at: http://www.crise.ox.ac.uk/pubs/workingpaper18.pdf

Naghshpour, Shahdad Joseph J. St. Marie, and Samuel S. Stanton, Jr. 2007. "The Shadow Economy and Terrorist Infrastructure," in *Countering Terrorism and Insurgency in the 21st Century*, edited by James J.F. Forest. Westport, CT: Praeger.

Northrup, David. 1978. *Trade Without Rulers: Pre-Colonial Economic Development in South-Eastern Nigeria*. Oxford University Press.

O'Neil, Bard and Donald J. Alberts. 2007. "Responding to Psychological, Social, Economic and Political Roots of Terrorism," in *Countering Terrorism and Insurgency in the 21st Century (Vol. 2: Combating the Sources and Facilitators)*, edited by James J.F. Forest. Westport, CT: Praeger.

Olson, Eric T. 2009. *USSOCOM Posture Statement* (June 4).

Onuoha, Freedom C. 2010. "The Islamist Challenge: Nigeria's Boko Haram Crisis Explained," *African Security Review* 19(2).

Osaghae, Eghosa. 1989. "The Federal Cabinet, 1951-1984," in *Federal Character and Federalism in Nigeria*, edited by Peter P. Ekeh and Eghosa E. Osaghae. Ibadan: Heinemann.

Otite, Onigu. 1990. *Ethnic Pluralism and Ethnicity in Nigeria*. Shaneson, Ibadan, pp. 44-57.

Pape, Robert A. 2003. "The Strategic Logic of Suicide Terrorism," *American Political Science Review* 97(3), pp. 343-361.

Paul R. Ehrlich and Jianguo Liu. 2005. "Socioeconomic and Demographic Roots of Terrorism," in *The Making of a Terrorist, Vol. 3: Root Causes*, edited by James J.F. Forest. Westport, CT: Praeger.

Pauly, Robert J. Jr. and Robert W. Redding. 2007. "Denying Terrorists Sanctuary Through Civil Military Operations," in *Countering Terrorism and Insurgency in the 21st Century (Volume 1: Strategic and Tactical Considerations)*, edited by James J.F. Forest. Westport, CT: Praeger Security International, pp. 273-297.

Pegg, Scott. 2003. "Globalization and Natural Resource Conflicts," *Naval War College Review* 61(4).

Pillar, Paul. 2005. "Superpower Foreign Policies: A Source for Global Resentment," in *The Making of a Terrorist, Vol. 3: Root Causes*, edited by James JF Forest. Westport, CT: Praeger Security International.

Pillar, Paul. 2007. "The Democratic Deficit: The Need for Liberal Democratization," in *Countering Terrorism and Insurgency in the 21st Century (Vol. 2: Combating the Sources and Facilitators)*, edited by James J.F. Forest. Westport, CT: Praeger.

Ploch, Lauren. 2011. "Nigeria: Elections and Issues for Congress," Congressional Research Service (May 17). Online at: http://assets.opencrs.com/rpts/RL33964_20110401.pdf

Post, Jerrold M. 2005. "When Hatred is Bred in the Bone": The Socio-Cultural Underpinnings of Terrorist Psychology," in *The Making of a Terrorist (Vol. 2: Training)*, edited by James J.F. Forest. Westport, CT: Praeger, 2005.

Post, Jerrold M. 1998. "Terrorist Psycho-logic: Terrorist Behavior as a Product of Psychological Forces," in *Origins of Terrorism: Psychologies, Ideologies, Theologies, States of Mind*, edited by Walter Reich. Baltimore: Woodrow Wilson Center Press, pp. 25-40.

Pratten, David. 2008. "Introduction to the Politics of Protection: Perspectives on Vigilantism in Nigeria," *Africa* 78(1), pp. 1-15.

Rapoport, David C. 2004. "The Four Waves of Terrorism," in *Attacking Terrorism: Elements of a Grand Strategy*, edited by Audrey Kurth Cronin and James M. Ludes. Washington, DC: Georgetown University Press.

Reno, William. 2000. "Clandestine Economies, Violence, and States in Africa," *Journal of International Affairs*, 53(2), pp. 433-459.

Richardson, Louise. 2006. *What Terrorists Want*. New York: Random House, 2006.

Robins, Robert and Jerrold Post. 1997. *Political Paranoia: The Psychopolitics of Hatred*. New Haven, CT: Yale University Press.

Rosand, Eric, Alistair Millar and Jason Ipe. 2008. *Civil Society and the UN Global Counter-Terrorism Strategy: Opportunities and Challenges*. Washington, DC: Center on Global Counterterrorism Cooperation.

Ross, Jeffrey Ian. 1993. "Structural Causes of Oppositional Political Terrorism," *Journal of Peace Research* 30(3), pp. 317-329.

Rotimi T. Suberu. 1996. *Ethnic Minority Conflicts and Governance in Nigeria*. Ibadan: Spectrum Books Limited.

Sageman, Marc. 2004. *Understanding Terror Networks*. Philadelphia: University of Pennsylvania Press.

Schwartz, Stephanie. 2010. "Is Nigeria a Hotbed of Islamic Extremism?" USIP Peace Brief 27. Washington, DC: U.S. Institute of Peace.

Sharabi, Hisham. 1998. *Neopatriarchy: A Theory of Distorted Change in Arab Society*. London: Oxford University Press.

Silke, Andrew. 1998. "Cheshire-Cat Logic: The Recurring Theme of Terrorist Abnormality in Psychological Research," *Psychology, Crime and Law* 4, pp. 51-69.

Silke, Andrew. 2004. "An Introduction to Terrorism Research," in *Research on Terrorism: Trends, Achievements and Failures*, edited by Andrew Silke. London: Frank Cass.

Singer, Peter W. 2002. "Corporate Warriors: The Rise of the Privatized Military Industry and its Ramifications for International Security," *International Security* 26(3).

Sklar, Richard L. 2003. "The Premise of Mixed Government in African Political Studies," in O. Vaughan (ed.) *Indigenous Political Structures and Governance in Africa*. Ibadan: Sefer Books Ltd., pp. 3-25.

Sprinzak, Ehud. 1998. "The Psychopolitical Formation of Extreme Left Terrorism in a Democracy: The Case of the Weathermen," in *Origins of*

Terrorism: Psychologies, Ideologies, Theologies, States of Mind, edited by Walter Reich. Baltimore: Woodrow Wilson Center Press, pp. 65-85.

Stout, Chris. 2004. "Introduction," in *Psychology of Terrorism: Coping with the Continuing Threat* (Condensed Edition), edited by Chris Stout. Westport, CT: Praeger.

Szrom, Charlie and Chris Harnisch. 2011. *Al Qaeda's Operating Environments: A New Approach to the War on Terror*. Washington DC: The American Enterprise Institute.

Taylor, Max and John Horgan. 2006. "A Conceptual Framework for Addressing Psychological Process in the Development of the Terrorist." *Terrorism and Political Violence* 18(4).

Taylor, Maxwell. 1988. *The Terrorist*. London: Brassey's, 1988.

The Economist. 2011. "Groping Forward: Nigeria's New Government" (November 12).

The Economist. 2011. "A Man and a Morass" (May 28).

Thurston, Alex. 2011. "Nigeria's Terrorism Problem," *Foreign Policy* (August 26).

Turnley, Jessica Glicken. 2011. *Cross-Cultural Competence and Small Groups: Why SOF are the Way SOF are*. JSOU Report 11-1. Tampa, FL: JSOU Press.

U.S. Department of Defense. 2007. *Irregular Warfare (IW) Joint Operating Concept (JOC)* (September 11). Online at: http://www.fas.org/irp/doddir/dod/iw-joc.pdf

U.S. Department of Defense. 2009. United States Special Operations Command (USSOCOM) *Strategic Plan*. (December 18).

U.S. Directorate of National Intelligence, 2008. *Global Trends 2025: A Transformed World* (Report of the National Intelligence Council's 2025 Project. Online at: http://www.dni.gov/nic/NIC_2025_project.html.

UN Office for Coordination of Humanitarian Affairs. 2011. "Analysis: What Will Follow Boko Haram?" *IRIN News* (November 24).

United Nations Office on Drugs and Crime. 2009. *Transnational Trafficking and the Rule of Law in West Africa: A Threat Assessment*. Vienna: UNODC, July.

Watts, Michael, Ike Okonta, and Dimieari Von Kemedi. 2004. "Economies of Violence: Petroleum, Politics and Community Conflict in the Niger Delta, Nigeria." Washington, DC: U.S. Institute of Peace.

Weimann, Gabriel. 2005. "Terrorist Dot Com: Using the Internet for Terrorist Recruitment and Mobilization," in *The Making of a Terrorist, Vol. 1: Recruitment, edited by James J.F. Forest.* Westport, CT: Praeger.

Wellington, Bestman. 2008. "Nigeria and the Threat of Al-Qaeda Terrorism," *Terrorism Monitor* 6(12).

Wood, Geoffrey. 2004. "Business and Politics in a Criminal State: The Case of Equatorial Guinea," *African Affairs*, 103(413), pp. 547-567.

Yahaya, Ali D. 2005. "Traditional leadership and institutions" in *Northern Nigeria: A Century of Transformation, 1903-2003*, edited by Alhaji M. Yakuba, Ibrahim M. Jumane, Asmain G. Saeed. Kaduna, Nigeria: Arewa House, Ahmadu Bello University.

Zuhur, Sherifa. 2005. "Saudi Arabia: Islamic Threat, Political Reform, and the Global War on Terror." Carlisle, PA: Strategic Studies Institute. Online at http://www.strategicstudiesinstitute.army.mil/Pubs/display.cfm?pubID=598

Appendix A: Recent Attacks Attributed to Boko Haram

The following list exemplifies the kind of targets and lethality for which the group has established a reputation:[349]

- September 21, 2010: In the Gwaidomari neighborhood in Maiduguri, militants riding motorcycles fired upon and killed two people (a local chief and a trader) with Kalashnikov style rifles. A man claiming to be a chieftain of Boko Haram claimed responsibility on behalf of the group.
- September 5, 2010: In the town of Bama, Borno, unidentified armed assailants on a motorcycle fired on and killed a retired police officer. A man claiming to be a chieftain of Boko Haram claimed responsibility. The group also claimed responsibility for another attack on the same day in Mauduguri, when unidentified gunmen riding a motorcycle fired upon the district head of Kalari area in Limanti Ward of Maiduguri, Lawan Zanna Mohammed Kagu, wounding Kagu and another person and killing a trader. And near the Maiduguri New Prisons, unidentified militants riding a motorcycle fired upon locals, injuring two people.
- September 7, 2010: Boko Haram attacked a large prison in Bauchi; guards were overpowered and an estimated 800 prisoners were released, including at least 120 Boko Haram members or supporters who were awaiting trial.[350]
- October 6, 2010: In Maiduguri, unidentified militants riding motorcycles entered the house of Awana Ali Ngala, the national vice chairman of the All Nigeria Peoples Party, and killed him in his living room. On the same day, unidentified militants riding motorcycles fired upon the house of Ali Modu, the speaker of the Borno state House of Assembly, killing one policeman.*
- October 9, 2010: In Maiduguri, two unidentified militants riding a motorcycle fired upon and killed Sheikh Bashir Mustapha, an Islamic scholar who was teaching in his home, and one other person.*
- October 19, 2010: In Maiduguri, three unidentified militants fired upon and killed Police Inspector Kashim Bukar as he walked home.*

- October 22, 2010: In the village of Kandahar near Ganuwa, unidentified militants attacked and killed a local village head, Mohammed Tukur.*
- November 19, 2010: In Maiduguri, two unidentified militants riding motorcycles and armed with Kalashnikov style rifles fired upon and killed three people in front of the Gomari Jumat Wahabi mosque.*
- November 29, 2010: In Borno, a militant armed with a firearm, two swords, and a knife attempted to kill a village chief in the chief's compound.*
- December 24, 2010: In Jos, 38 people were killed and 74 others were injured when militants detonated four improvised explosive devices made with dynamite in the Kabong shopping market just minutes apart from one another. Boko Haram claimed responsibility for the attack. Meanwhile, a private security guard in Maiduguri was killed by militants in two vehicles when they fired on him with unknown firearms and threw an unknown number of petrol bombs at the Sinimari Church of Christ. The group also threw petrol bombs at the Dala Baptist Church, setting it on fire. Five people including a pastor were killed and 25 other people were injured when militants attacked the Victory Baptist Church with firearms and petrol bombs. Boko Haram claimed responsibility for these attacks as well.
- December 24, 2010: Triple bomb blasts in the city of Jos killed over 80 people and wounded several dozen others, while over 100 people were killed in the reprisal attacks in its aftermath. In a statement published on what is thought to be its website, http://mansoorah.ne, Boko Haram claimed responsibility.[351]
- December 28, 2010: In the Zinnari area of Maiduguri, unidentified militants fired on a teaching hospital and killed one policeman and two civilians.*
- December 31, 2010: In the neighborhood of Jikowyi in Abuja city, unidentified militants detonated an improvised explosive device at the Dunamis Church.*
- January 28, 2011: the Borno state candidate of the All Nigeria People's Party (ANPP) for the April 2011 gubernatorial elections was assassinated, along with his brother, four police officers and a 12-year old boy. Boko Haram was blamed for the killings, though there is some debate about this.[352]

- April 9, 2011: A polling center in Maiduguri was bombed by suspected members of Boko Haram.
- April 15, 2011: Members of the sect bombed the Independent National Electoral Commission headquarters in Niger state.
- April 20, 2011: Boko Haram killed a Muslim cleric and ambushed several police officers in Maiduguri.
- April 22, 2011: Boko Haram freed 14 prisoners during a jailbreak in Yola, Adamawa state.[353]
- May 29, 2011: On the day of President Goodluck Jonathan's inauguration, three bombs exploded within minutes of each other at an artillery brigades in Bauchi killing 13 people and injuring more than 40 others. Later that evening, another explosion occurred at a nearby drinking establishment in Shadawanka, killing six people.[354]
- May 30, 2011: Three men shot and killed Abba-Anas Umar Garbai, the younger brother of the Shehu of Borno, the most prominent traditional and Islamic spiritual leader in northeastern Nigeria.[355] A spokesman for Boko Haram later claimed responsibility.
- June 6, 2011: During a week of attacks on a church and police stations in Maiduguri, at least 14 people were killed in three explosions, including three people outside St Patrick's Catholic Church; David Usman, pastor of the Church of Christ in Nigeria, was shot dead by gunmen on motorcycles; and Ibrahim Birkuti, a Muslim cleric who had criticiszd Boko Haram, was shot dead outside his home in the town of Biu, roughly 120 miles south of Maiduguri.[356]
- June 7, 2011: In Maiduguri, gunmen attacked three police stations and the Ramat Square parade ground. Four explosions went off at Gwange police station, two at Dandal police station while the seventh bomb exploded near St. Patrick's (Catholic) church. A spokesman for Boko Haram also claimed responsibility, acknowledging that three of its members who attacked the Gwange police station were killed.[357]
- June 16, 2011: Four children were killed in a church playground in an explosion in the town of Damboa, south of the state capital Maiduguri, Borno state.[358] *
- June 16, 2011: Boko Haram used a suicide car bomber to attack Nigeria's police headquarters (Louis Edet House) in Abuja. The explosion killed eight people, shattered the glass windows of the seven-story police headquarters and destroyed dozens of vehicles in the parking lot.[359]

– June 20, 2011: Five people were killed in an attack on a community centre in Gomari, Maiduguri by Boko Haram members firing from the back of motorbikes.[360] In a separate attack on the same day, suspected Boko Haram gunmen killed a police officer in Maiduguri.[361] Boko Haam may have also been responsible for other attacks against a bank and police station in Kankara town in Katsina state, though there are conflicting reports and nobody took credit for those attacks.[362]

– June 26, 2011: Men riding motorcycles threw bombs into outdoor beer gardens on Sunday night in the Dala area of Maiduguri, killing at least 25 people.[363]

– June 27, 2011: Two girls were killed and three customs officers wounded at the Custom House in Maiduguri. *

– July 3, 2011: An explosion killed at least 10 people and injured many others yesterday at a bar close to a police barracks in Maiduguri, Borno state. On the same day, gunmen shot dead Mustafa Baale, the chairman of Jere Local Government Area, after trailing him to his mother's house in Maiduguri.[364]

– July 4, 2011: Suspected members of Boko Haram killed a policeman and three staff of Shani local government area of Borno state and stole a significant amount of cash that was meant for paying the salaries of local government employees.[365] Police subsequently raided an alleged hideout of suspected Boko Haram members, during which three people were killed.

– July 5, 2011: After attacking the Toro Divisional Police Station (in Bauchi state) and chasing off the handful of police on duty, suspected members of Boko Haram ransacked the station's armory, carting away guns and ammunition.[366]

– July 6, 2011: Boko Haram members on a motorcycle threw a bomb at a military patrol vehicle, injuring three soldiers. On the same day, two policemen were trailed to their homes and killed; an Assistant Superintendent of Customs was killed at his house in Ummarari area of the state capital, Abuja; and three others were killed, including a customs officer.[367]

– July 10, 2011: A bombing at the All Christian Fellowship Church in Suleja, Niger state killed three people and wounded seven.[368] Authorities also claimed that 11 members of Boko Haram were killed and two soldiers wounded on Saturday night when the group attacked a military patrol in Maiduguri with explosives. And half a dozen people were wounded by an explosion near a popular hotel in the Obalende district of Kaduna.

- July 22, 2011: An explosion at the Budun market in Maiduguri, Borno state, injured three soldiers. *
- July 23, 2011: A bomb exploded in Maidugri, close to the home of Abubakar Ibn Umar Garbai El-kanemi, the Shehu of Borno, leaving three soldiers wounded. *
- July 26, 2011: Boko Haram members shot and killed Mohammed Ali Lawal, the district head of Bulabulin in Maiduguri, as well as his 9 year-old daughter.
- August 2, 2011: A bomb exploded at Gomari Airport Ward in Maiduguri, killing at least one person. *
- August 4, 2011: An explosion in Maiduguri killed two people. *
- August 8, 2011: A 40-year-old school teacher, Nurudeen Algoni Umar was shot dead by suspected members of Boko Haram.[369]
- August 9, 2011: Members of Boko Haram attacked a police station on Baga Road in Maiduguri, injuring two people.[370]
- August 12, 2011: Prominent Muslim Cleric Liman Bana was shot dead by Boko Haram members while walking home from conducting prayers at the main mosque in Ngala.[371]
- August 15, 2011: A man was shot dead by Nigerian police on Monday in a failed attempt to bomb police headquarters in Maiduguri.[372]
- August 19, 2011: Members of Boko Haram shot dead three policemen and a civilian after breaking into the house of one of the officers in Maiduguri.[373]
- August 25, 2011: Boko Haram gunmen attacked two police stations and two banks in Gombi, in northern Nigeria, leaving 16 people dead.[374]
- August 26, 2011: At least 18 people were killed in a suicide car bombing at the U.N. building in Abuja. The driver entered the compound by ramming an exit gate, then maneuvered his vehicle into a parking garage before detonating it. This attack was Boko Haram's first attack against a transnational target rather than against a government or sectarian target .[375]
- September 4, 2011: Two Boko Haram gunmen shot dead an Islamic cleric Maiduguri.[376]

- September 12, 2011: Six policemen and a civilian were killed by Boko Haram militants in Misau, Bauchi state following simultaneous attacks on a commercial bank and a police station in the area.[377]
- September 13, 2011: Boko Haram gunmen shot dead four people in a bar in Maiduguri.[378]
- October 1, 2011: Attackers used explosives and gunfire to target an army patrol near a wedding in Maiduguri, killing three civilians.[379]
- October 3, 2011: Suspected Boko Haram gunmen shot dead three people at a market in Maiduguri.[380]
- October 9, 2011: A roadside bomb in the Gwange area of Maiduguri was detonated as a military patrol vehicle was passing by, followed by shots fired by suspected Boko Haram militants.[381]
- October 12, 2011: Authorities say members of Boko Haram attacked a bank in Damboa, in northeast Nigeria, killing one police officer and stealing an undisclosed sum of money.[382]
- October 13, 2011: Suspected members of Boko Haram shot and killed a prison guard at his home in Maiduguri.[383]
- October 15, 2011: Gunmen Saturday killed Ali Banga, the leader of the Borno State Vigilante Association, after trailing him to his home in Maiduguri.[384] *
- October 16, 2011: Police suspect Boko Haram was responsible for the assassination of Modu Bintube, an MP in Borno state legislature, outside of his home in Maiduguri.[385]
- October 16, 2011: A bomb explosion killed three people at a police station in Gombe, northern Nigeria. Gombe Police Commissioner G.E. Orubebe said it was not clear who was behind the attack but it bore the hallmarks of similar strikes carried out by Boko Haram.[386]
- October 19, 2011: A Muslim cleric and his student were killed in Layin Tanki, in Gwange area of Maiduguri.[387]
- October 21, 2011: Alhaji Zakariya Isa, a reporter for Nigerian Television Authority, died after being shot in the head and chest at his home in Maiduguri. A day later, Boko Haram spokesman Abu Qaqa indicated that his group had carried out the attack.[388]
- October 27, 2011: A bomb was used to attack a military patrol in Maiduguri. *
- October 29, 2011: Suspected Boko Haram gunmen killed a cleric in Maiduguri identified as Goni Ali Gana'a.[389]

- October 30, 2011: A roadside bomb was used in an attack against a military patrol in Maiduguri.[390]
- November 4, 2011: Several explosions took place throughout Maiduguri, including one at a military office. A soldier was also killed at the popular Monday Market in Maiduguri.[391]
- November 5, 2011: A series of coordinated attacks in Borno and Yobe states, primarily around Damaturu, killed at least 67 people, leaving a new police headquarters in ruins, and government offices burned. A Boko Haram spokesman told *The Daily Trust* newspaper that it was responsible for the attacks and promised more.[392]
- November 9, 2011: Four policemen were killed in Mainok (northern Nigeria), and a police station and the rescue unit of the Federal Road Safety Commission (FRSC) were destroyed by suspected members of Boko Haram.[393] The group also stormed the residence of the Mainok village head; he was not home, but they killed his brother.[394]
- November 13, 2011: A roadside bomb exploded in Bauchi, injuring four people.[395] On the same day, three gunmen killed a man near the home of the Shehu of Borno.[396] *
- November 14, 2011: Three suspected Boko Haram gunmen attacked the residents of an Islamic scholar in Borno state and killed an 18-year-old Islamic student.[397]
- November 21, 2011: Members of Boko Haram attacked a Joint Task Force base in the Bulumkutu Market area of Maiduguri and engaged officers in a shootout lasting several hours.[398] Meanwhile, in the Gwange area of Maiduguri, gunmen killed Kala Boro a protocol officer at the Borno state Government House.[399]
- December 4: Boko Haram gunmen attacked police area command headquarters in Bauchi state, killing six people and injuring five others.
- December 25, 2011: At least 42 people are killed at several churches around Nigeria, including St. Theresa Catholic Church in Madalla, a town near Abuja, as well as churches in Jos and Gadaka; the attacks are claimed by Boko Haram.[400]
- January 20, 2012: Bomb attacks and shootings in Kano, Nigeria's second largest city, killed 186 people in the group's most deadly attacks to date.[401]

- January 29, 2012: Boko Haram members attacked a police station in Kano, and issued a warning that if group members who had been captured in the north-western Sokoto state were not released, Kano-style attack would be launched there.[402]
- February 16, 2012: Armed gunmen stormed a federal prison, killing a guard and freeing 119 inmates; Boko Haram later claimed 7 of those freed were members.[403]
- February 20, 2012: Suspected Boko Haram militants killed at least 30 men, women and children at the Baga market in Maiduguri.[404]
- February 26, 2012: Dozens were killed and injured in attacks on churches in Jos and Gombe states, and seven suspects were arrested while attempting to bomb a church in Bauchi.[405]
- February 26, 2012: Motorcycle-mounted gunmen killed three police officers at a checkpoint in Borno state.
- February 27, 2012: Boko Haram members attacked a police station in Adamawa state.[406]
- February 28, 2012: Susspected Boko Haram militants set fire to the Gamboru Primary School in Maiduguri, and claimed responsibility for burning down another primary school in Maiduguri two days earlier.[407]

* Indicates attacks have taken place for which no group claimed responsibility, but authorities believe that Boko Haram may be linked to these as well.

Appendix B: Additional Resources for Information on Boko Haram and Violence in Northern Nigeria

Websites and Blogs

African Union Center for Studies on Research and Terrorism
   http://www.caert.org.dz/an/apropos.php

Beegeagle's Blog
   http://beegeagle.wordpress.com

Council on Foreign Relations Blog: Africa in Transition
   http://blogs.cfr.org/campbell

Institute for Security Studies, Pretoria
   http://www.iss.co.za

Nigeria Security Tracker
   https://nigeriasecuritytracker.crowdmap.com

Sahel Blog
   http://sahelblog.wordpress.com

U.S. Africa Command (AFRICOM)
   http://www.africom.mil

U.S. Department of State, Bureau of African Affairs
   http://www.state.gov/p/af

U.S. Department of State, Bureau of Conflict and Stabilization Operations
   http://www.state.gov/g/cso

News

BBC Africa
   http://www.bbc.co.uk/news/world/africa

Daily Trust
   http://dailytrust.com.ng

Guardian
   http://www.ngrguardiannews.com

Leadership
   http://www.leadership.ng/nga

The Nation
   http://issuu.com/thenation/

Panapress
   http://www.panapress.com

Reuters Africa
   http://af.reuters.com
Vanguard
   http://www.vanguardngr.com
Also, see http://allafrica.com for a daily collection of news stories from a
   variety of African newspapers.

Other Online Resources

Christian-Muslim Relations in Nigeria
John Campbell discusses the relations between Muslims and Christians in
Nigeria. Campbell emphasizes that where religious divisions correspond
to ethnic and economic differences, conflict often acquires a religious
coloration.
http://www.youtube.com/watch?v=9DMRvqwZ588&feature=player_
embedded

Extrajudicial killing of Boko Haram Financier
http://www.liveleak.com/view?i=aab_1286378932
 and http://www.clickafrique.com/Magazine/ST010/CP0000003972.aspx

Extrajudicial killing of Boko Haram leader Yusuf
http://www.aljazeera.com/news/africa/2010/02/2010298114949112.html
and http://www.youtube.com/watch?v=ePpUvfTXY7w
(see http://allafrica.com/stories/201110250374.html for news article)

John Campbell, "Nigeria's Battle with Boko Haram" – Audio (MP3) recorded
September 26, 2011. Online at: http://www.cfr.org/nigeria/nigerias-battle-
boko-haram-audio/p26027

Sounding the Alarm on Boko Haram: John Campbell says deteriorating economic and social conditions in Northern Nigeria are behind the recurring
upsurge in Boko Haram's activity. Campbell cautions that the circumstances
enabling Boko Haram to operate may be taken advantage of by international
terrorists, though that has not happened yet.
http://www.youtube.com/watch?v=RA0dQoAWBSU

U.S. House of Representatives, Subcommittee on Counterterrorism and Intelligence, "Hearing on Boko Haram – Emerging Threat to the U.S. Homeland" (November 30, 2011), online at: http://homeland.house.gov/hearing/subcommittee-hearing-boko-haram-emerging-threat-us-homeland

Books and Journal Articles

Abbink, Jon. 2004. "Violence and State (Re)Formation in the African Context: Global and Local Aspects of Crisis and Change," in Robert E. Westerfield, ed. Current Issues in Globalization. Hauppauge, NY: Nova Science Publishers, pp. 137-49.

Adamu, Fatima. 2003. Globalization and Economic Globalization in Northern Nigeria. Development Studies Association, UK.

Adebajo, Adekeye. 2008. Hegemony on a Shoestring: Nigeria's Post-Cold War Foreign Policy. In Adekeye Adebajo and Abdul Raufu Mustapha, eds. Gulliver's Trouble: Nigeria's Foreign Policy after the Cold War. Pietermaritzburg: University of KwaZulu-Natal Press, pp. 1-37.

Adesoji, Abimbola 2010. "The Boko Haram Uprising and Islamic Revivalism in Nigeria." Africa Spectrum 45(2), pp. 95-108.

Adesoji, Abimbola O. and Akin Alao. 2009. "Indigeneship and Citizenship in Nigeria: Myth and Reality," The Journal of Pan African Studies, 2/9, pp. 151-165, available at http://www.jpanafrican.com/docs/vol2no9/2.9_Indigeneship_and_Citizenship_in_Nigeria.pdf

Agbese, Pita. 2003. "Federalism and the Minority Question in Nigeria," in Aaron Gana and Samuel Egwu, eds., Federalism in Africa. Trenton: Africa World Press, pp. 237-61.

Akomolafe, Soji 2006. "Nigeria, the United States and the War on Terrorism: the Stakes and the Stance," in Olayiwola Abegunrin and Olusoji Akomolafe, eds. Nigeria in Global Politics. New York: Nova Science Publishers, pp. 225-244.

Albert, Isaac O. 1993. Inter-Ethnic Relations in a Nigerian City: A Historical Perspective of the Hausa-Igbo Conflicts in Kano 1953-1991. Ibadan: Institute of African Studies.

Aliyu, Sanusi. 1996. Religious-Based Violence and National Security in Nigeria: Case Studies of Kaduna State and the Taliban Activities in Borno. Masters Thesis, Ft. Leavenworth, KS: U.S. Army Command and Staff College.

Ambe-Uva, Terhemba Nom. 2010. "Identity Politics and the Jos Crisis: Evidence, Lessons, and Challenges of Good governance." African Journal of History and Culture. 2(3), pp. 42-52.

Bach, Daniel. 1997. "Indigeneity, Ethnicity and Federalism," in Larry Diamond et al., eds., Transition Without End: Civil Society Under Babangida. Boulder, CO: Lynne Rienner, pp. 333-350.

Bach, Daniel. 2006. "Inching Towards a Country Without a State: Prebendalism, Violence and State Betrayal in Nigeria," in Christopher Clapham, Jeffrey Herbst and Greg Mills, eds., Big African States. Johannesburg: Wits University Press, pp. 63-96.

Beckett, Paul A. and Crawford Young, eds. 1997. Dilemmas of democracy in Nigeria. Rochester: University of Rochester Press.

Beckford, J. 2003. Social Theory and Religion. Cambridge University Press.

Beckford, James A. and John Walliss, eds. 2006. Theorizing Religion: Classical and Contemporary Debate. Aldershot, UK: Ashgate Publishing.

Blench, Roger, Selbut Longtau, Umar Hassan and Martin Walsh. 2006. The Role of Traditional Rulers in Conflict Prevention and Mediation in Nigeria. A study prepared for the UK Department for International Development (DfID), available at http://www.rogerblench.info/Development/Nigeria/ Conflict percent20resolution/Final percent20Report percent20TRs percent20September percent2006.pdf

Campbell, John, "Nigeria on the Brink," Foreign Affairs, September 9, 2010.

Castells, Manuel. 1997. The Power of Identity. Oxford: Blackwell Publishers.

Cline, L. E. 2011. "Today We Drink Blood: Internal Unrest in Nigeria," Small Wars and Insurgencies, 22(2), pp. 273-289.

Danfulani, Umar H.D. and Sati Fwatshak (2002), "Briefing: the September 2001 Events in Jos, Nigeria," African Affairs 101, 243.

Danfulani, Umar H.D. (2006), —The Jos peace conference and the indigene/ settler question in Nigerian politics, given at a seminar on interreligious conflict in Nigeria, at the African Studies Centre, Leiden on March 2, 2006, available at http://www.ascleiden.nl/Pdf/paper-Danfulani.pdf

Danjibo, D. N. 2010. Islamic Fundamentalism and Sectarian Violence: The "Maitatsine" and "Boko Haram" Crises in Northern Nigeria. Peace and

Conflict Studies Programme, Institute of African Studies, University of Ibadan. Online at: http://www.ifra-nigeria.org/spip.php?article156

Diamond, Larry. 1988. Class, Ethnicity and Democracy in Nigeria: The Failure of the First Republic. Basingstoke, UK: Macmillan.

Dudley, Billy J. 1968. Parties and Politics in Northern Nigeria. London: Frank Cass.

Egwu, Samuel G. 2003. "Ethnicity and Citizenship Rights in the Nigerian Federal State," in Aaron Gana and Samuel Egwu, eds., Federalism in Africa. Trenton: Africa World Press, pp. 37-53.

Ekeh, Peter P. and Eghosa E. Osaghae, eds. 1989. Federal Character and Federalism in Nigeria. Ibadan: Heinemann.

Ellis, Stephen and Haar, Gerrie Ter. 2004. Worlds of Power: Religious Thoughts and Political Practice in Africa. London: Hurst and Company.

Falola, Toyin. 1998. Violence in Nigeria: The Crisis of Religious Politics and Secular Ideologies. Rochester, NY: University of Rochester Press.

Harnischfeger, Johannes (2004), "Sharia and control over territory: conflicts between 'settlers' and 'indigenes' in Nigeria," African Affairs 103, pp. 431-52.

Higazi, Adam. 2008. "Social Mobilization and Collective Violence: Vigilantes and Militias in the Lowlands of Plateau State, Central Nigeria," Africa: Journal of the International African Institute, 78(1), pp. 107-135.

Human Rights Watch. 2001. Jos: A City Torn Apart. New York: Human Rights Watch.

Human Rights Watch. 2005. Revenge in the Name of Religion: The Cycle of Violence in Plateau and Kano States. New York: Human Rights Watch.

Human Rights Watch. 2006. "They do not own this place": Government Discrimination Against "Non-Indigenes" in Nigeria. New York: Human Rights Watch.

Human Rights Watch. 2008. Nigeria: Arbitrary Killings by Security Forces in Jos. Online at: http://www.hrw.org/en/news/2008/12/19/nigeria-arbitrary-killings-security-forces-jos

Ibrahim, Jibrin. 1989. "The Politics of Religion in Nigeria: The Parameters of the 1987 Crisis in Kaduna State," Review of African Political Economy. 16(45), pp. 65-82.

Ifeka, Caroline. 2000. "Ethnic Nationalities, God and the State: Whither the Federal Republic of Nigeria?" Review of African Political Economy, 27(85), pp. 450-459.

Isichei, Elizabeth. 1987. "The Maitatsine Risings in Nigeria 1980-85: A Revolt of the Disinherited." Journal of Religion in Africa 17(3), pp. 194-208.

James, Ibrahim, ed. 2000. The Settler Phenomenon in the Middle Belt and the Problem of National Integration in Nigeria. Jos: Midland Press Ltd.

Joseph, Richard A. 1987. Democracy and Prebendal Politics in Nigeria: The Rise and Fall of the Second Republic. New York : Cambridge University Press.

Kazah-Toure, Toure. 2003. Ethno-Religious Conflicts in Kaduna State. Kaduna: Human Rights Monitor.

Kazah-Toure, Toure. 2004. "A Discourse on the Citizenship Question in Nigeria," Democracy and Development: Journal of West African Affairs, 4(1), pp. 41-63.

Khuri, Fuad I. 1990. Imam and Emirs: State, Religion and Sect in Islam. London: Saqi Books.

Kraxberger, Brennan. 2005. "Strangers, Indigenes and Settlers: Contested Geographies of Citizenship in Nigeria," Space and Polity, 9(1), pp. 9-27.

Kukah, Matthew Hassan. 1994. Religion, Power and Politics in Northern Nigeria. Ibadan: Spectrum Books.

Maier, Karl. 2000. This House has Fallen: Nigeria in Crisis. London: Penguin.

Mazrui, Ali. 2002. "Shariacracy and Federal Models in the Era of Globalization: Nigeria in Comparative Perspective." In: Edward R. McMahon, and Thomas A.P. Sinclair, eds. Democratic Institution Performance: Research and Policy Perspectives. Westport, CT: Praeger, pp. 63-76.

Mustapha, Abdul Raufu. 2009. "Nigeria since 1999: A Revolving Door Syndrome or the Consolidation of Democracy?" in Abdul Raufu Mustapha, and L. Whitfield, eds. Turning Points in African Democracy. Rochester, NY: James Currey, pp. 71-93.

Nwachukwu, Ijeoma. 2005. "The Challenge of Local Citizenship for Human Rights in Nigeria," African Journal of International and Comparative Law, 13(2), pp. 235-261.

Odinkalu, Chidi Anselm. 2004. "From Nativity to Nationality: Understanding and Responding to Africa's Citizenship Crises," Democracy and Development: Journal of West African Affairs, 4(1), pp. 31-40.

Ohadike, Don. 1992. "Muslim-Christian Conflict and Political Instability in Nigeria," in John O. Hunwick, ed. Religion and National Integration in Africa: Islam, Christianity and Politics in the Sudan and Nigeria. Illinois: Northwestern University Press.

Ojukwu, Chris C. and C.A. Onifade. 2010. "Social Capital, Indigeneity and Identity Politics: The Jos Crisis in Perspective," African Journal of Political Science and International Relations 4(5), pp. 173-180.

Okpanachi, Eyene. 2010. Ethno-religious Identity and Conflict in Northern Nigeria: Understanding the Dynamics of Sharia in Kaduna and Kebbi State. Ibadan: IFRA, Nigeria. Online at: http://www.ifra-nigeria.org/spip. php?article167

Olayode, Kehinde. 2010. Self-Determination, Ethno-Nationalism, and Conflicts in Nigeria. Ibadan: University of Ibadan Press. Online at: http:// www.ifra-nigeria.org/spip.php?article156

Onuoha, Freedom C. 2010. "The Islamist Challenge: Nigeria's Boko Haram Crisis Explained," African Security Review 19(2), pp. 54-67.

Osaghae, Eghosa E. and Rotimi R. Suberu. 2005. A History of Identities, Violence and Stability in Nigeria. Centre for Research on Inequality, Human Security and Ethnicity (CRISE). Online at: http://www.crise. ox.ac.uk/pubs/workingpaper6.pdf

Osaghae, Eghosa. 1991. "Ethnic Minorities and Federalism in Nigeria," African Affairs 90, pp. 237-258.

Osaghae, Eghosa (1998), "Managing Multiple Minority Problems in a Divided Society: The Nigerian Experience," Journal of Modern African Studies 36(1), pp. 1-24.

Oyeniyi, Adeyemi Bukola. 2010. "Terrorism in Nigeria: Groups, Activities, and Politics," International Journal of Politics and Good Governance, 1(11), pp. 1-16.

Paden, John. 2008. Faith and Politics in Nigeria: Nigeria as a Pivotal State in the Muslim World. Washington, D.C. United States Institute for Peace (USIP).

Pillay, Anton M. 2011. Suicide Terrorism in Nigeria: A Look At the Boko Haram. Consultancy Africa Intelligence, 2011. Online at: http://www. consultancyafrica.com/index.php?option=com_content&view=

article&id=785:suicide-terrorism-in-nigeria-a-look-at-the-boko-haram-&catid=57

Plotnicov, Leonard. 1967. Strangers to the City; Urban Man in Jos, Nigeria. Pittsburgh: University of Pittsburgh Press.

Plotnicov, Leonard. 1971. "An Early Nigerian Civil Disturbance: The 1945 Hausa-Ibo Riot in Jos," The Journal of Modern African Studies, 9(2), pp. 297-305.

Plotnicov, Leonard. 1972. "Who Owns Jos? Ethnic Ideology in Nigerian Urban Politics," Urban Anthropology, 1(1), pp. 1-13.

Post, Kenneth and Vickers, Michael. 1973. Structure and Conflict in Nigeria, 1960-1966. Madison: University of Wisconsin Press.

Sanusi, Lamido Sanusi. 2007. "Politics and Sharia in Northern Nigeria," in Benjamin Soares and Rene Otayek, eds. Islam and Muslim Politics in Africa. New York: Palgrave, Macmillan.

Sodiq, Yushua. 2009. "Can Muslims and Christians Live Together Peacefully in Nigeria?" The Muslim World 99, pp. 646-688.

Suberu, Rotimi T. 2001. Federalism and ethnic conflict in Nigeria. Washington, D.C.: United States Institute of Peace. Online at: http://bookstore.usip.org/resrcs/chapters/1929223285_otherchap.pdf

Suberu, Rotimi T. 2009. "Religion and Institutions: Federalism and the Management of Conflict over Sharia in Nigeria", Journal of International Development, 21(4), pp. 547-560.

Ukiwo, Ukoha. 2003. Politics, Ethno-Religious Conflicts and Democratic Consolidation in Nigeria. The Journal of Modern African Studies, 41(1), pp. 115-138.

Wunsch, James S. 2003. "Nigeria: Ethnic Conflict in Multinational West Africa," in Joseph R. Rudolph, Jr., Encyclopedia of Modern Ethnic Conflicts. Westport, Conn. Greenwood Publishing Group, pp. 169-182.

Endnotes

1.   Mike Oboh, "Boko Haram leader tape threatens Nigeria forces," *Reuters*, January 27, 2012. Online at: http://www.reuters.com/article/2012/01/27/us-nigeria-bokoharam-tape-idUSTRE80Q1YL20120127?feedType=RSS&feedName=worldNews.

2.   Scott Stewart, "Nigeria's Boko Haram Militants Remain a Regional Threat," STRATFOR (January 26, 2012). Online at: http://www.stratfor.com/weekly/nigerias-boko-haram-militants.

3.   U.S. House of Representatives Committee on Homeland Security, Subcommittee on Counterterrorism and Intelligence, "Boko Haram: Emerging Threat to the U.S. Homeland" (November 30, 2011), pp. 17-19.

4.   Patrick Meehan and Jackie Speier, *Boko Haram: Emerging Threat to the U.S. Homeland*, U.S. House of Representatives Committee on Homeland Security, Subcommittee on Counterterrorism and Intelligence (November 30, 2011), p. 13.

5.   Jon Gambrell, "Nigeria: Radical Muslim Sect Grows More Dangerous," Associated Press, November 4, 2011. Online at: http://www.breitbart.com/article.php?id=D9QQ3V200&show_article=1.

6.   See John Campbell, "Boko Haram Splits?" Council on Foreign Relations (July 21, 2011) Online at: http://blogs.cfr.org/campbell/2011/07/21/boko-haram-splits/.

7.   For a discussion of this, please see James J.F. Forest, "Terrorism as a Product of Choices and Perceptions," in *Terrorizing Ourselves*, edited by Benjamin H. Friedman, Jim Harper, and Christopher A. Preble (Washington, DC: Cato Institute, 2010), pp. 23-44.

8.   Ibid.

9.   Alex Thurston, "Threat of Militancy in Nigeria," Commentary for Carnegie Endowment for International Peace, September 1, 2011. Online at: http://carnegieendowment.org/2011/09/01/threat-of-militancy-in-nigeria/4yk8.

10.   John E. Mack, "Deeper Causes: Exploring the Role of Consciousness in Terrorism," *Ions Noetic Sciences Review*, June-August 2003, p. 13.

11.   Bruce Hoffman, *Inside Terrorism* (Revised Edition) (New York: Columbia University Press, 2006), pp. 40-41.

12.   Lydia Khalil, "Authoritarian and Corrupt Governments," in *Countering Terrorism and Insurgency in the 21st Century (Vol. 2: Combating the Sources and Facilitators)*, edited by James J.F. Forest (Westport, CT: Praeger, 2007).

13.   Peter W. Singer, "Corporate Warriors: The Rise of the Privatized Military Industry and its Ramifications for International Security," *International Security* 26(3) (Winter 2001/2002), p. 196. Also, an excellent example is found in Jane's Intelligence Review, "African Struggle over Smuggled Weapons," November 23, 1999.

14.   Christopher Carr, "Combating the International Proliferation of Small Arms and Light Weapons," in *Countering Terrorism and Insurgency in the 21st Century (Vol.*

2: Combating the Sources and Facilitators), edited by James J.F. Forest (Westport, CT: Praeger, 2007).

15. Shahdad Naghshpour, Joseph J. St. Marie and Samuel S. Stanton, Jr. "The Shadow Economy and Terrorist Infrastructure, in *Countering Terrorism and Insurgency in the 21st Century (Vol. 2: Combating the Sources and Facilitators)*, edited by James J.F. Forest (Westport, CT: Praeger, 2007).

16. Recent examples of triggering events include the films of Theo Van Gogh, which precipitated a violent response among Islamist radicals and eventually led to his murder; the publication of cartoons portraying the prophet Mohammed, producing a wave of violent protests and actions worldwide; and Israel's military actions against Lebanese and Palestinian militants, which have mobilized protests among Muslims as far away as Indonesia.

17. Paul R. Ehrlich and Jianguo Liu. "Socioeconomic and Demographic Roots of Terrorism," in *The Making of a Terrorist, Vol. 3: Root Causes*, edited by James J.F. Forest (Westport, CT: Praeger, 2005).

18. Directorate of National Intelligence, *Global Trends 2025: A Transformed World* (Report of the National Intelligence Council's 2025 Project, November 2008), p. 43. Online at: http://www.dni.gov/nic/NIC_2025_project.html. Also, see Colleen McCue and Kathryn Haahr, "The Impact of Global Youth Bulges on Islamist Radicalization and Violence," *CTC Sentinel*, Vol. 1, Issue 1 (October 2008) pp. 12-14.

19. See James J.F. Forest, "The Final Act: Ideologies of Catastrophic Terror," published by the Fund for Peace Expert Series, online at: http://www.fundforpeace.org/web/images/pdf/forest.pdf.

20. Assaf Moghadam, "The Salafi-Jihad as a Religious Ideology." *CTC Sentinel* 1, no. 3 (February 2008): 14-16.

21. According to Andrew Kydd and Barbara Walter, "of the forty-two groups currently designated as foreign terrorist organizations by the U.S. state department, thirty-one seek regime change, nineteen seek territorial change, four seek policy change, and one seeks to maintain the status quo." Andrew Kydd and Barbara Walter, "The Strategies of Terrorism," *International Security* 31(1), (Summer 2006): 49-80 (p. 52).

22. The Islamic Movement of Uzbekistan (IMU), also known as Islamic Party of Turkestan, is made up of militant Islamist extremists mostly from Uzbekistan, but includes other Central Asian nationalities and ethnic groups as well. The group has mainly conducted small-scale armed attacks, including car bombings and taking hostages in Kyrgyzstan, Uzbekistan, and Tajikistan.

23. John Horgan, "The Social and Psychological Characteristics of Terrorism and Terrorists," in *Root Causes of Terrorism: Myths, Realities and Ways Forward*, edited by Tore Bjorgo (London: Routledge, 2005), p. 45.

24. Andrew Silke, "An Introduction to Terrorism Research," in *Research on Terrorism: Trends, Achievements and Failures*, edited by Andrew Silke (London: Frank Cass, 2004), p. 20.

25. John Horgan, "The Social and Psychological Characteristics of Terrorism and Terrorists," in *Root Causes of Terrorism: Myths, Realities and Ways Forward*, edited by Tore Bjorgo (London: Routledge, 2005), p. 49.

26. Clark McCauley, "Psychological Issues in Understanding Terrorism and Response to Terrorism," in *Psychology of Terrorism: Coping with the Continuing Threat* (Condensed Edition), edited by Chris Stout (Westport, CT: Praeger, 2004), p. 35.

27. Marc Sageman, *Understanding Terror Networks* (Philadelphia: University of Pennsylvania Press, 2004), p. 91.

28. Chris Stout, "Introduction," in *Psychology of Terrorism: Coping with the Continuing Threat* (Condensed Edition), edited by Chris Stout (Westport, CT: Praeger, 2004), p. xiv. See also: Rex A. Hudson, *Who Becomes a Terrorist and Why: The 1999 Government Report on Profiling Terrorists* (Guilford, CT: The Lyons Press, 2001); and Robert A. Pape, "The Strategic Logic of Suicide Terrorism," American Political Science Review 97, no. 3 (August 2003), pp. 343-361.

29. For more on this, please see John Horgan, "The Search for the Terrorist Personality," in *Terrorists, Victims and Society: Psychological Perspectives on Terrorism and its Consequences*, edited by Andrew Silke (Chichester, England: John Wiley and Sons, 2003); and Andrew Silke, "Cheshire-Cat Logic: The Recurring Theme of Terrorist Abnormality in Psychological Research," *Psychology, Crime and Law* 4 (1998), pp. 51-69.

30. For example, see Michael E. Leiter, Testimony (Statement for the Record) before the Senate Committee on Homeland Security and Governmental Affairs, July 10, 2008; Moghaddam, Fathali M. "The Staircase to Terrorism: A Psychological Exploration," *American Psychologist* 60 (2005), pp. 161-169; and Clark McCauley, "Pathways Towards Radicalization," START Research Brief, October 2008. National Consortium for the Study of Terrorism and Responses to Terrorism.

31. Max Taylor and John Horgan, "A Conceptual Framework for Addressing Psychological Process in the Development of the Terrorist," *Terrorism and Political Violence* 18, no. 4 (2006), p. 2.

32. Ibid.

33. Ibid, 13.

34. Leiter, Testimony, July 10, 2008.

35. Marc Sageman, *Understanding Terror Networks* (Philadelphia: University of Pennsylvania Press, 2004), p. 178.

36. John E. Mack, "Deeper Causes: Exploring the Role of Consciousness in Terrorism," *Ions Noetic Sciences Review*, June-August 2003, p. 14.

37. Jessica Stern, *Terror in the Name of God* (New York: HarperCollins, 2003. Ecco Trade Paperback Edition, 2004), p. 282.

38. Ibid.

39. Ahmad Salkida, "Sect Leader Vows Revenge," *Daily Trust* July 27, 2009. Online at: http://wwrn.org/articles/31419/?&place=nigeria.

40. See Last 2008, p. 9.

41. Farourk Chothia, "Who are Nigeria's Boko Haram?" *BBC News* (August 26, 2011), online at: http://www.bbc.co.uk/news/world-africa-13809501.

42. 2011 CIA Factbook, https://www.cia.gov/library/publications/the-world-factbook/geos/ni.html.

43. Ibid.

44. See Onigu Otite, *Ethnic Pluralism and Ethnicity in Nigeria* (Shaneson, Ibadan, 1990), pp. 44-57 (cited in Mustapha, 2005, Page 6, Table 2).

45. Abdul Raufu Mustapha, "Ethnic Structure, Inequality and Governance of the Public Sector in Nigeria," CRISE Working Paper No. 18 (May 2005), Center for Research on Inequality, Human Security and Ethnicity (Queen Elizabeth House, Oxford University), p. 5. Online at: http://www.crise.ox.ac.uk/pubs/workingpaper18.pdf .

46. 2011 CIA Factbook.

47. Ibid.

48. "A Man and a Morass," *The Economist*, (May 28, 2011), p. 26.

49. For a more extensive history of West Africa, and of Nigeria specifically, please see Basil Davidson, *A History of West Africa, 1000-1800: The Growth of African Civilization* (London: Longman, 1967); Toyin Falola and Matthew M. Heaton, A History of Nigeria (Cambridge University Press, 2008); and John Campbell, *Nigeria: Dancing on the Brink* (Plymouth, UK: Rowman & Littlefield, 2011).

50. Some parts of the following discussion originally appeared in James Forest and Matt Sousa, *Oil and Terrorism in the New Gulf* (Boulder, CO: Lexington Press), pp. 82-94.

51. See Karl Maier, *This House Has Fallen: Crisis in Nigeria* (London: Penguin, 2000).

52. Scott Pegg, "Globalization and Natural Resource Conflicts," *Naval War College Review* 61(4), (Autumn 2003), p. 89.

53. Ed Blanche, "Africa's Teetering Giant," *Jane's Islamic Affairs Analyst*, December 1, 2004.

54. Five Charged with Planning to Shoot Down Obasanjo's Helicopter," *IRIN News*, October 22, 2004.

55. However, it must be noted that his attempt in 2007 to change the constitution in order to allow him to seek a third term in office is widely viewed as a blemish on his democratic record.

56. See electoral results map on p. 27 of "A Man and a Morass," *The Economist*, (May 28, 2011).

57. Alex Thurston, "Threat of Militancy in Nigeria," Commentary for Carnegie Endowment for International Peace, September 1, 2011. Online at: http://carnegieendowment.org/2011/09/01/threat-of-militancy-in-nigeria/4yk8.

58. John Campbell and Asch Harwood, Nigeria's Challenge, The Atlantic (June 24, 2011), online at: http://www.theatlantic.com/international/archive/2011/06/nigerias-challenge/240961/1/.

59. Ibid.

60. Ibid.

61. Ibid.

62. Ibid.

63. J. Kayode Fayemi and Fummi Olonisakin, "Nigeria," in *Challenges of Security Sector Governance in West Africa*, Alan Bryden, Boubacar N'Diaye and 'Funmi Olonisakin (eds.). Geneva Centre for the Democratic Control of Armed Forces (June 2008), p. 244.

64. Peter Chalk, Islam in West Africa: The Case of Nigeria, in *The Muslim World after 9/11*, edited by Angel Rabasa, Cheryl Benard, et al. (Santa Monica, CA: RAND, 2004), p. 417.

65. Notes from meeting with Nigerian interviewee #4.

66. William Reno, "Clandestine Economies, Violence, and States in Africa," *Journal of International Affairs*, 53(2), Spring 2000: pp. 433-459.

67. Notes from meeting with Nigerian interviewee #12.

68. John Alexander, *Africa: Irregular Warfare on the Dark Continent*, JSOU Report 09-5 (May 2009), Tampa, FL: JSOU Press, p. 49.

69. John Campbell and Asch Harwood, "Nigeria's Challenge," *The Atlantic* (June 24, 2011), online at: http://www.theatlantic.com/international/archive/2011/06/nigerias-challenge/240961/1/.

70. Hisham Sharabi, *Neopatriarchy: A Theory of Distorted Change in Arab Society* (London: Oxford University Press, 1988), p. 45-48. Cited in Roby C. Barret, *Yemen: A Different Political Paradigm in Context* (Tampa, FL: JSOU Press, 2011).

71. "A Man and a Morass," *The Economist*, (May 28, 2011), p. 27.

72. Murray Last, "Muslims and Christians in Nigeria: An Economy of Panic," *The Round Table: The Commonwealth Journal of International Affairs* (2007), p. 609.

73. Philip Ostien, "Jonah Jang and the Jasawa: Ethno-Religious Conflict in Jos, Nigeria," *Muslim-Christian Relations in Africa* (August 2009), p. 3.

74. Human Rights Watch, "Corruption on Trial: The Record of Nigeria's Economic and Financial Crimes Commission (August 25, 2011), p. 2. Available online at: http://www.hrw.org/reports/2011/08/25/corruption-trial.

75. "A Man and a Morass," *The Economist*, (May 28, 2011), p. 26.

76. Ibid.

77. Ibid.

78. Notes from meeting with Nigerian interviewee #7.

79. Notes from meeting with Nigerian interviewee #2.

80. "A Man and a Morass," *The Economist*, (May 28, 2011), p. 27.

81. Notes from meeting with Nigerian interviewee #11.

82. Notes from meeting with Nigerian interviewee #12.

83. Notes from meeting with Nigerian interviewee #11.

84. Abdel-Fatau Musah, *West Africa: Governance and Security in a Changing Region*, (International Peace Institute, February 2009), p. 7.

85. Ibid.

86. Joe Brock, "Nigerian poverty rising despite economic growth," *Reuters*, February 13, 2010. Online at: http://www.reuters.com/article/2012/02/13/us-nigeria-poverty-idUSTRE81C0KR20120213?feedType=RSS&feedName=worldNews.

87. "A Man and a Morass," *The Economist*, (May 28, 2011), p. 27.

88. Notes from meeting with Nigerian interviewee #2.

89. This is a conservative estimate, while others have suggested much higher numbers. See, for example, "1.2 Million Miss Out in Varsity Admissions", *Business Day* (July 6, 2009), online at: http://www.businessdayonline.com/index.php?option=com_content&view=article&id=3624:12-million-miss-out-in-varsity-admissions&catid=89:learning&Itemid=347 and "1 Million Candidates Miss University Admissions Annually," *Leadership Nigeria* (November 16, 2009), online at: http://www.leadershipnigeria.com/index.php/news/headlines/8430-1m-candidates-miss-university-admission-annually--nuc.

90. CIA Factbook, 2011. Online at: https://www.cia.gov/library/publications/the-world-factbook/rankorder/2066rank.html?countryName=Nigeria&countryCode=ni&regionCode=afr&rank=4#ni.

91. "A Man and a Morass," *The Economist*, (May 28, 2011), p. 27.

92. Notes from meeting with Nigerian interviewee #1; Also, "A Man and a Morass," *The Economist*, (May 28, 2011), p. 27.

93. "Groping Forward: Nigeria's New Government," *The Economist* (November 12, 2011), p. 56

94. "A Man and a Morass," *The Economist*, (May 28, 2011), p. 27.

95. "Let them have fuel," *The Economist*, January 21, 2012. Online at: http://www.economist.com/node/21543199.

96. Heather Murdock, "Nigeria finds $4 billion in fuel corruption," *Global Post* (UK), January 20, 2012. Online at: http://www.globalpost.com/dispatch/news/regions/africa/nigeria/120119/nigeria-oil-fuel-corruption.

97. Abdel-Fatau Musah, *West Africa: Governance and Security in a Changing Region*, (International Peace Institute, February 2009), p. 7.

98. For example, see Peter Nwilo's writings on oil pollution and mangrove destruction in the Niger Delta.

99. The Environmental Assessment of Ogoniland report (released August 9, 2011) is available online at: http://www.unep.org/nigeria, and also at: http://postconflict.unep.ch/publications/OEA/UNEP_OEA.pdf.

100. I. Samuel Ibaba, Terrorism in Liberation Struggles: Interrogating the Engagement Tactics of Movement for the Emancipation of the Niger Delta" *Perspectives on Terrorism*, (Fall 2011).

101. Philip Ostien, "Jonah Jang and the Jasawa: Ethno-Religious Conflict in Jos, Nigeria," *Muslim-Christian Relations in Africa* (August 2009), p. 3.

102. Ibid.

103. Based on the per capita representation in parliament which gave the North half of the seats, half of the cabinet now came from the North. See Eghosa Osaghae, 'The Federal Cabinet, 1951-1984', in Peter P. Ekeh & Eghosa E. Osaghae (eds.), *Federal Character and Federalism in Nigeria* (Heinemann, Ibadan, 1989), p. 138.

104. Abdel-Fatau Musah, *West Africa: Governance and Security in a Changing Region*, (International Peace Institute, February 2009), p. 16.

105. I. Samuel Ibaba, "Terrorism in Liberation Struggles: Interrogating the Engagement Tactics of Movement for the Emancipation of the Niger Delta" *Perspectives on Terrorism*, (Fall 2011).

106. Ibid.

107. Ibid.

108. Michael Watts, Ike Okonta, and Dimieari Von Kemedi, "Economies of Violence: Petroleum, Politics and Community Conflict in the Niger Delta, Nigeria," (Washington, DC: U.S. Institute of Peace, 2004), p. 2.

109. The Kaima Declaration, Resolutions of all the Youths Conference held at Kaima, Bayelsa State, to Explore Strategies for the Survival of The Ijaw Nation in Nigeria, December 11, 1998.

110. Ibaba Samuel Ibaba & Augustine Ikelegbe, "Militias and Pirates in the Niger Delta," paper presented at Institute of Security Studies (ISS), work Shop on Militia and Rebel Movements: Human Insecurity and State Crisis in Africa, Pretoria South Africa, April 20-21, 2009, p.13.

111. Osmond Chidi, "9 Foreign Oil Workers Seized in Nigeria," *Associated Press* (February 19, 2006); "Nine Hostages are Human Shields: Militants," *Reuters* (February 19, 2006); and "Nigerian Militants Assault Oil Industry, Abducting 9 Foreigners," *New York Times* (February 19, 2006), online at: http://www.nytimes.com/2006/02/19/international/africa/19nigeria.html.

112. Notes from Nigeria interview #4.

113. For a more detailed account, see I. Samuel Ibaba "Terrorism in Liberation Struggles" in *Perspectives on Terrorism*.

114. See BP Statistical Review of World Energy (June 2009); available online at http://bp.com/statisticalreview. Also, see Chris Ajaero, Nigeria's Lost Trillions, *Newswatch Magazine*, May 4, 2009, p. 21. Notably, in February 2011 President Goodluck Jonathan announced that Nigeria's crude oil production had increased to 2.6 million barrels per day. See http://allafrica.com/stories/201102221027.html.

115. Issaka K. Souare, "A Critical Assessment of Security Challenges in West Africa," ISS Situation Report 18 October 2010.

116. See, for example, James Cockayne and Phil Williams, *The Invisible Tide: Towards an International Strategy to Deal with Drug Trafficking Through West Africa* (New York: The International Peace Institute, October 2009); and Joseph Kirschke, "The Coke Coast: Cocaine and Failed States in Africa," *World Politics Review*, September 9, 2008.

117. Vanda Felbab-Brown and James J.F. Forest, "Political Violence and Illicit Economies of West Africa," *Terrorism and Political Violence* 24(1).

118. Ibid.

119. See, for example, Stephen Ellis, "West Africa's International Drug Trade," *African Affairs*, 108(431), 2009: 171-196. Elsewhere in Africa, the drug trade has long routes as well, be it cannabis cultivation in Morocco, qat cultivation in East Africa, or the production of methamphetamines and other synthetic drugs, such as mandrax, in South Africa.

120. United Nations Office on Drugs and Crime, *Transnational Trafficking and the Rule of Law in West Africa: A Threat Assessment* (Vienna: UNODC, July 2009). See also the UNODC website on drug trafficking in Nigeria, at: http://www.unodc. org/nigeria/en/drug-prevention.html.

121. Ibid., 4.

122. UNODC (July 2009), p. 19

123. Ibid., 20

124. See, for example, Geoffrey Wood, "Business and Politics in a Criminal State: The Case of Equatorial Guinea," *African Affairs*, 103(413), 2004: 547-567.

125. UNODC (July 2009), 75.

126. Abdel-Fatau Musah, *West Africa: Governance and Security in a Changing Region*, (International Peace Institute, February 2009), p. 8; Also, see James J.F. Forest and Matthew V. Sousa. *Oil and Terrorism in the New Gulf: Framing U.S. Energy and Security Policies for the Gulf of Guinea* (New York: Lexington Press, 2006), pp. 27-30, 52-59, 62-68, 75-108, and 110-125.

127. See the UNODC website on Human Trafficking and the Smuggling of Migrants, at: http://www.unodc.org/nigeria/en/human-trafficking-and-smuggling-of-migrants.html.

128. UNODC (July 2009), p. 6.

129. Abimbola O. Adesoji, "Between Maitatsine and Boko Haram: Islamic Fundamenalism and the Response of the Nigerian State," *Africa Today* 57(4) (Summer 2011), p. 113.

130. Shahdad Naghshpour, Joseph J. St. Marie, and Samuel S. Stanton, Jr., "The Shadow Economy and Terrorist Infrastructure," in *Countering Terrorism and Insurgency in the 21st Century*, edited by James J.F. Forest (Westport, CT: Praeger, 2007).

131. Portions of this discussion have appeared previously in Vanda Felbab-Brown and James Forest, "Political Violence and the Illicit Economies of West Africa," *Terrorism and Political Violence*, 24(1) (Winter 2012).

132. Zuwaqhu A. Bonat, "Economic Deregulation, the Peasantry and Agricultural Development in Nigeria: A Kaduna State Case Study," in *The Political Economy of Nigeria Under Military Rule: 1984-1993*, edited by Said A. Adejumobi and Abubakar Momoh (Harare: Sapes, 1995), p. 209.

133. Rotimi T. Suberu, *Ethnic Minority Conflicts and Governance in Nigeria* (Ibadan: Spectrum Books Limited, 1996), p. 54.

134. Joe Brock, "Several Killed in Central Nigeria Religious Violence," Reuters (Nov. 24, 2011).

135. Philip Ostien, "Jonah Jang and the Jasawa: Ethno-Religious Conflict in Jos, Nigeria," *Muslim-Christian Relations in Africa* (August 2009), p. 2.

136. Ibid.

137. Ostien, p. 14-15. See §23(1)(a) and FCC Act §17(2)(k).

138. Murray Last, p. 609.

139. For a detailed account, please see Hugh Johnston, *Fulani Empire of Sokoto* (Oxford University Press, 1967).

140. Peter Chalk, "Islam in West Africa: The Case of Nigeria," In *The Muslim World after 9/11*, edited by Angel Rabasa, Cheryl Benard, et al. (Santa Monica, CA: RAND, 2004), p. 416. See also, Matt Steinglass, "Why is Nigerian Islam so Radical?" *New York Times* (December 1, 200).

141. See Chapter 6 for a description of the Qadiriyya and Tijaniyya brotherhoods, the two main Islamic organizations in West Africa.

142. John N. Paden, "The Sokoto Caliphate and its Legacies (1804-2004)," online at: http://www.dawodu.com/paden1.htm.

143. John Esposito, *The Oxford Encyclopedia of the Modern Islamic World*, 4th Ed. (Oxford University Press, 1995), p. 105. Cited in Jonathan Hill, p. 16.

144. Jonathan Hill, p. 16.

145. Karl Maier, "Obituary: Sheikh Abubakar Mahmud Gumi," *The Independent* (UK) (September 16, 1992). Online at: http://www.independent.co.uk/news/people/obituary-sheikh-abubakar-mahmud-gumi-1551628.html.

146. Matt Steinglass, "Why is Nigerian Islam so Radical?" *New York Times* (December 1, 200).

147. See Loimeier, (1997), pp. 16-28.

148. Karl Maier, "Obituary: Sheikh Abubakar Mahmud Gumi," (September 16, 1992).

149. Benjamin Barber, "Terrorism, Interdependence and Democracy," in The Making of a Terrorist, Volume 3: Root Causes, edited by James J.F. Forest (Westport, CT: Praeger, 2005), p. 210. See also, Benjamin R. Barber, *Jihad vs. McWorld* (New York: Times Books, 1995).

150. Murray Last, "Muslims and Christians in Nigeria: An Economy of Panic," *The Round Table: The Commonwealth Journal of International Affairs* (2007), pp. 605-616.

151. Last, p. 607.

152. Philip Ostien, "Jonah Jang and the Jasawa: Ethno-Religious Conflict in Jos, Nigeria," *Muslim-Christian Relations in Africa* (August 2009), p. 3.

153. For details, see, for example, Bruce Baker, "Protection from Crime: What is on Offer for Africans?" *Journal of Contemporary African Studies*, 22(2), 2004: 165-188; Bruce Baker, *Taking the Law into Their Own Hands* (Aldershot: Ashgate, 2002); and Rasheed Olaniyi, "*Hisba* and the *Sharia* Law Enforcement in Metropolitan Kano," http://www.ifra-nigeria.org/IMG/pdf/Rasheed_Olaniyi_-_Hisba_and_ the_Sharia_Law_Enforcement_in_Metropolitan_Kano.pdf.

154. This description of Hisba is from the National Consortium for the Study of Terrorism and Responses to Terrorism (START) database, online at: http://www.start. umd.edu/start/data_collections/tops/terrorist_organizations_by_country.asp.

155. Bestman Wellington, "Nigeria and the Threat of Al-Qaeda Terrorism," Terrorism Monitor Vol. 6, No. 12 (June 12, 2008). See also Nicolas Florquin and Eric G. Berman (ed.s), *Armed and Aimless; Armed Groups, Guns, and Human Security in the ECOWAS region*, Geneva, 2005.

156. Ibid.

157. In addition to the Hisba gangs of the north, another prominent Nigerian example is the Oodua People's Congress (OPC), which operates mainly in Yoruba territory. They are a combination of vigilantism with crime-fighting; members pursue armed robbers into zones that policemen are scared to enter (but whether they systematically hand over the suspects to the official police is debatable). See Yvan Guichaoua, "The Making of an Ethnic Militia: The Oodua People's Congress in Nigeria," CRISE Working Paper No. 26 (November 2006), Center for Research on Inequality, Human Security and Ethnicity, Queen Elizabeth House, Oxford University. Online at: http://www.crise.ox.ac.uk/pubs/workingpaper26.pdf.

158. See, for example, David Killingray, "The Maintenance of Law and Order in British Colonial Africa," *African Affairs*, 85 (340): pp. 411-437; and David Pratten, "Introduction to the Politics of Protection: Perspectives on Vigilantism in Nigeria," *Africa* 78(1), 2008: pp. 1-15.

159. Zachary Devlin-Foltz, "Africa's Fragile States: Empowering Extremists, Exporting Terrorism," *Africa Security Brief* no. 6 (August 2010), p. 4.

160. J. Kayode Fayemi and Fummi Olonisakin, "Nigeria," in *Challenges of Security Sector Governance in West Africa*, Alan Bryden, Boubacar N'Diaye and 'Funmi Olonisakin (eds.). Geneva Centre for the Democratic Control of Armed Forces (June 2008), p. 246.

161. Muhammed Kabir Isa, "Militant Islamist Groups in northern Nigeria," in *Militias, Rebels and Islamist Militants: Human Insecurity and State Crises in Africa*,

edited by Wafula Okumu and Augustine Ikelegbe (Pretoria: Institute for Security Studies, 2010), p. 313.

162. International Crisis Group, "Northern Nigeria: Background to the Conflict," *Africa Report no. 168* (Brussels: December 20, 2010), p. 18.

163. For a detailed description, see Abimbola O. Adesoji, "Between Maitatsine and Boko Haram: Islamic Fundamenalism and the Response of the Nigerian State," *Africa Today* 57(4) (Summer 2011), pp. 99-119.

164. International Crisis Group, "Northern Nigeria" (December 20, 2010), p. 18.

165. Bestman Wellington, "Nigeria and the Threat of Al-Qaeda Terrorism," (June 12, 2008). See also Nicolas Florquin and Eric G. Berman (ed.s), *Armed and Aimless; Armed Groups, Guns, and Human Security in the ECOWAS region*, Geneva, 2005.

166. For more details of these events, see "New 'Taleban' clashes in Nigeria," BBC News (January 7, 2004). Online at: http://news.bbc.co.uk/2/hi/africa/3376979.stm; and "Nigerians 'crush' Islamic uprising," BBC News (January 5, 2004). Online at: http://news.bbc.co.uk/2/hi/africa/3368627.stm.

167. "Nigerians 'crush' Islamic uprising," *BBC News* (January 5, 2004). Online at: http://news.bbc.co.uk/2/hi/africa/3368627.stm.

168. "Nigeria police kill 27 Taleban," BBC News (Sept. 24, 2004), online at: http://news.bbc.co.uk/2/hi/africa/3685280.stm.

169. Muhammed Kabir Isa, "Militant Islamist Groups in northern Nigeria," in *Militias, Rebels and Islamist Militants: Human Insecurity and State Crises in Africa*, edited by Wafula Okumu and Augustine Ikelegbe (Pretoria: Institute for Security Studies, 2010), p. 328.

170. This paragraph of analysis appeared previously in Vanda Felbab-Brown and James J.F. Forest, "Political Violence and Illicit Economies of West Africa," *Terrorism and Political Violence* 24(1).

171. See, for example, David Keen, *Conflict and Collusion in Sierra Leone* (Palgrave Macmillan, 2005); and Jimmy D. Kandeh, "The Criminalization of the RUF Insurgency in Sierra Leone," in *Rethinking the Economics of War: The Intersection of Need, Creed, and Greed*, Cynthia A. Arnson and I. William Zartman, eds., (Washington, DC: Woodrow Wilson Center, 2005): pp. 84-107.

172. Abdel-Fatau Musah, *West Africa: Governance and Security in a Changing Region*, (International Peace Institute, February 2009), p. 8.

173. John Carpenter, Nigeria's Challenge, The Atlantic (June 24, 2011), online at: http://www.theatlantic.com/international/archive/2011/06/nigerias-challenge/240961/1/.

174. For example, see Isa Umar Gusau, "Boko Haram: How It All Began," *Daily Trust*, 02 August 2009. Online at: http://sundaytrust.com.ng/index.php?option=com_content&view=article&id=825:boko-haram-how-it-all-began-&catid=3:people-in-the-news&Itemid=110.

175. Freedom C. Onuoha, "The Islamist Challenge: Nigeria's Boko Haram Crisis Explained," *African Security Review* 19(2), p. 55.

176. Isioma Madike, "Boko Haram: Rise of a deadly sect," *National Mirror* (June 19, 2011). Online at: http://nationalmirroronline.net/sunday-mirror/big_read/14548. html; this claim is also made in Emma Ujah, Emeka Mamah, Kingsley Omonobi, Chioma Obinna & Daniel Idonor, 'Yar'Adua Orders Probe of Boko Haram's Leaders' Killing', *Vanguard* (online edition), 4 August 2009. Online at: http://www.van-guardngr.com/2009/08/yaradua-orders-probe-of-boko-haram-leaders-killing/.

177. For example, see Isa Umar Gusau, "Boko Haram: How It All Began," *Daily Trust*, 02 August 2009. Online at: http://sundaytrust.com.ng/index.php?option=com_ content&view=article&id=825:boko-haram-how-it-all-began-&catid=3:people-in-the-news&Itemid=110.

178. Farourk Chothia, "Who are Nigeria's Boko Haram?" *BBC News* (August 26, 2011), online at: http://www.bbc.co.uk/news/world-africa-13809501.

179. Adam Nossiter, "Killings Signal Violent Revival of Nigeria Sect," *New York Times* (October 19, 2010).

180. For more, see Suleiman Saidu, "Almajiri and Matters Arising," *Leadership* (October 19, 2011), online at: http://allafrica.com/stories/201110191031.html; and Christian Purefoy, "Nigeria's Almajiri children learning a life of poverty and violence" CNN (January 7, 2010). Online at: http://articles.cnn.com/2010-01-07/world/nigeria.children.radicalization_1_religious-violence-religious-clashes-kano?_s=PM:WORLD.

181. Adam Nossiter, "Killings Signal Violent Revival of Nigeria Sect," *New York Times* (October 19, 2010).

182. Toni Johnson, "Boko Haram," Council on Foreign Relations (November 7, 2011), online at: http://www.cfr.org/africa/boko-haram/p25739.

183. N.D. Danjibo, "Islamic Fundamentalism and Sectarian Violence: The "Maitatsine" and "Boko Haram" Crises in Northern Nigeria," *Proceedings of the IFRA Conference on Conflict and Violence in Nigeria*, edited by Clement Boutillier (Ibadan: Institute for Research on Africa, 2009); and Saleh Dan Galadima, "The Metamorphosis of Boko Haram," *Leadership* (24 July 2011), online at: http://allafrica. com/stories/201107240006.html. Also, for more on the comparison and linkages between the Maitatsine and Boko Haram, see Abimbola O. Adesoji, "Between Maitatsine and Boko Haram: Islamic Fundamenalism and the Response of the Nigerian State," *Africa Today* 57(4), (Summer 2011), pp. 99-119.

184. Toni Johnson, "Boko Haram," Council on Foreign Relations (November 7, 2011), online at: http://www.cfr.org/africa/boko-haram/p25739.

185. Freedom Onuoha article, p. 58.

186. Isioma Madike, "Boko Haram: Rise of a Deadly Sect," National Mirror (June 19, 2011). Online at: http://nationalmirroronline.net/sunday-mirror/big_ read/14548.html; and Isa Umar Gusau, "Boko Haram: How it All Began," *Sunday Trust*, (August 2, 2009), online at: http://sundaytrust.com.ng/index.

php?option=com_content&view=article&id=825:boko-haram-how-it-all-began-&catid=3:people-in-the-news&Itemid=110.

187.   Toni Johnson, "Boko Haram," Council on Foreign Relations (November 7, 2011), online at: http://www.cfr.org/africa/boko-haram/p25739.

188.   Freedom Onuoh, p. 58.

189.   For detailed descriptions of these incidents, see the Global Terrorism Database, 1970-2010 (National Consortium for the Study of Terrorism and Response to Terrorism, University of Maryland); and Freedom C. Onuoha, "The Islamist Challenge: Nigeria's Boko Haram crisis explained," *African Security Review 19*, no. 2 (June 2010), p. 7.

190.   Ademola Adedeji, "1000 Boko Haram Members in Prison, Awaiting Trial" *The Punch (Lagos)*, October 14, 2009.

191.   Ikechukwu Nnochiri, "Boko Haram: Yusuf had only 4,000 followers in 2009, Army tells court." *Vanguard* (Abuja), December 8, 2011. Online at: http://www.vanguardngr.com/2011/12/boko-haram-yusuf-had-only-1000-followers-in-2009-army-tells-court/.

192.   Col. Benjamin Ahanotu, the commander of the task force that arrested Yusuf on July 30, 2009, testified at the trial that the Boko Haram leader had been handed over to the police alive. See http://www.thenationonlineng.net/2011/index.php/news/29044-how-boko-haram-leader-yusuf-was-arrested-by-army-chief.html and http://www.vanguardngr.com/2011/12/boko-haram-yusuf-had-only-4000-followers-in-2009-army-tells-court/.

193.   As described later in this chapter, Boko Haram leader Shaykh Muhammed Abu Bakr Bin Muhammed al Shakwa pledged his allegiance to AQIM in October 2010 using AQIM's media outlet al Andalus.

194.   Muhammad Isa chapter in book, p. 329.

195.   For a review of how Boko Haram's tactical capabilities have evolved, see Scott Stewart, "Boko Haram Militants Remain a Regional Threat, *STRATFOR* January 26, 2012.

196.   "Boko Haram Jailbreak: The Morning After," This Day (September 20, 2010), online at: http://allafrica.com/stories/201009220395.html.

197.   197 BBC News, "'Boko Haram' gunmen kill Nigerian Muslim cleric Birkuti" (June 7, 2011), online at: http://www.bbc.co.uk/news/world-africa-13679234.

198.   "The Rise of Boko Haram in Nigeria," David Cook, *CTC Sentinel* (September 2011), p. 3.

199.   See Appendix A for details on this and several other attacks against Muslim leaders by Boko Haram.

200.   Ahmad Salkida, "Sect Leader Vows Revenge," *Daily Trust* July 27, 2009. Online at: http://wwrn.org/articles/31419/?&place=nigeria.

201.   "Nigeria's Boko Haram Islamists bombed Abuja Police Headquarters," *BBC* (June 17, 2011). Online at: http://www.bbc.co.uk/news/world-africa-13805688:

and John Campbell and Asch Harwood, "Nigeria's Challenge," *The Atlantic* (June 24, 2011).

202. Misbahu Bashir, Abubakar Yakubu and Ronald Mutum, "8 Killed in Force Headquarters Blast." *Daily Trust* (June 17, 2011). Online at: http://dailytrust.com.ng/index.php?option=com_content&view=article&id=21286:8-killed-in-force-hqtrs-blasts&catid=2:lead-stories&Itemid=8.

203. Scott Stewart, "The Rising Threat from Nigeria's Boko Haram Militant Group," STRATFOR Global Intelligence, (November 10, 2011). Available at: http://www.stratfor.com/weekly/20111109-rising-threatnigerias-boko-haram-militant-group.

204. Ibid.

205. Karen Leigh, "Nigeria's Boko Haram: Al Qaeda's New Friend in Africa?" Time (August 31, 2011). Online at: http://www.time.com/time/world/article/0,8599,2091137,00.html#ixzz1g0144UvU.

206. Lawal Ibrahim, "Nigeria: Bank Robbery Suspects Boko Haram Members" *Daily Trust*, (February 4, 2010), online at: http://wwrn.org/articles/32601/?&place=nigeria.

207. Njadvara Musa, "Police: 6 Die When Town Attacked in North Nigeria," *ABC News* and *Associated Press* (December 4, 2011), online at: http://abcnews.go.com/International/wireStory/police-die-town-attacked-north-nigeria-15083057#.TuU5KPLNkqM.

208. Hafiz Ringim, "Boko Haram, Armed Robbers Attack 100 Bank Branches," *This Day Live*, (December 10, 2011), online at: http://www.thisdaylive.com/articles/boko-haram-armed-robbers-attack-100-bank-branches/104715/.

209. A video of his killing was posted online at: http://www.youtube.com/watch?v=N_m4PBSzU7Y.

210. Ndahi Maram, "Boko Haram Financier Arrested in Maiduguri," *Vanguard* (January 4, 2011). Online at: http://www.vanguardngr.com/2011/01/boko-haram-financier-arrested-in-maiduguri/; and Hamza Idris, "Boko Haram Financier, 91 Others in Police Net," *Weekly Trust* (January 1, 2011). Online at: http://weeklytrust.com.ng/index.php?option=com_content&view=article&id=5013:boko-haram-financier-91-others-in-police-net&catid=41:news&Itemid=30.

211. "Nigeria Police Kill Islamist Sect Financier," *The Telegraph* (February 27, 2011). Online at: http://www.telegraph.co.uk/news/worldnews/africaandindianocean/nigeria/8350635/Nigeria-police-kill-Islamist-sect-financier.html.

212. Bayo Oladeji, Uchenna Awom, and Chizoba Ogbeche, "Alleged Boko Haram Sponsorship - Senator Ali Ndume Arrested," *Leadership* (Abuja), November 22, 2011. Online at: http://allafrica.com/stories/201111220273.html.

213. "Nigeria Police Kill Islamist Sect Financier," *The Telegraph* (February 27, 2011). Online at: http://www.telegraph.co.uk/news/worldnews/africaandindianocean/nigeria/8350635/Nigeria-police-kill-Islamist-sect-financier.html.

214. Atika Balal, "Police Sergeant Says, 'We Shot Boko Haram Leader'" Daily Trust (August 2, 2011), online at: http://allafrica.com/stories/201108020226.html.

215. "Nigeria Police Kill Islamist Sect Financier," *The Telegraph* (February 27, 2011). Online at: http://www.telegraph.co.uk/news/worldnews/africaandindianocean/ nigeria/8350635/Nigeria-police-kill-Islamist-sect-financier.html.

216. Ikechukwu Nnochiri, "Boko Haram - Ndume Fails to Get Bail," *Vanguard* (December 6, 2011), online at: http://allafrica.com/stories/201112060534.html.

217. Laide Akinboade, "Boko Haram Spokesman Fingers Senator, Ambassador as Sponsors," *Vanguard* (November 22, 2011), online at: http://allafrica.com/sto-ries/201111220352.html.

218. "Some Senators & Ambassadors are Boko Haram Funders: Arrested Boko Haram Spokesman," *Eagle News Network* (November 22, 2011), online at: http://eagle-newsnigeria.net/display.php?newsid=678.

219. Dauda Mbaya, "Boko Haram Financier Arrested in Maiduguri," *Leadership* (January 5, 2011), online at: http://allafrica.com/stories/201101050631.html.

220. "Media, Govt, Donor Agencies Unite on Education for Orphans," *Vanguard* (July 6, 2011). Online at: http://www.vanguardngr.com/2011/07/media-govt-donor-agencies-unite-on-education-for-orphans/.

221. Muhammad Kabir Isa, "Militant Islamist Groups in Northern Nigeria," in *Militias, Rebels and Islamist Militants: Human Insecurity and State Crises in Africa*, edited by Wafulu Okumu and Augustine Ikelegbe (Pretoria: Institute for Security Studies, 2010), p. 332.

222. Ibid.

223. Ibid.

224. IRIN report (November 24, 2011).

225. Muhammad Kabir Isa, "Militant Islamist Groups in Northern Nigeria," p. 332.

226. Ibid.

227. Zuwaqhu A. Bonat, "Economic Deregulation, the Peasantry and Agricultural Development in Nigeria: A Kaduna State Case Study," in *The Political Economy of Nigeria Under Military Rule: 1984-1993*, edited by Said A. Adejumobi and Abuba-kar Momoh (Harare: Sapes, 1995), p. 195.

228. Andrew Kydd and Barbara Walter, "The Strategies of Terrorism," *International Security* 31(1), (Summer 2006): 49-80 (p. 52).

229. Roy J. Eidelson and Judy I. Eidelson, "Dangerous Ideas: Five Beliefs that Propel Groups Toward Conflict," *American Psychologist* 58, no. 3 (March 2003), pp. 182-192.

230. Alex Thurston, "Threat of Militancy in Nigeria," Commentary for Carnegie Endowment for International Peace, September 1, 2011. Online at: http://carn-egieendowment.org/2011/09/01/threat-of-militancy-in-nigeria/4yk8.

231. Ahmad Salkida, "Sect Leader Vows Revenge," *Daily Trust* July 27, 2009. Online at: http://wwrn.org/articles/31419/?&place=nigeria.

232. See Last 2008, p. 9.

233. Peter Chalk, "Islam in West Africa: The Case of Nigeria," *The Muslim World After 9/11*, edited by Angel M. Rabasa, Cheryl Benard, Peter Chalk et al. (Santa Monica, CA: RAND Corporation, 2004), p. 419.

234. Peter Chalk, "Islam in West Africa," p. 419.

235. Peter Chalk, "Islam in West Africa," p. 421.

236. Farourk Chothia, "Who are Nigeria's Boko Haram?" *BBC News* (August 26, 2011), online at: http://www.bbc.co.uk/news/world-africa-13809501.

237. Toni Johnson, "Boko Haram," Council on Foreign Relations (November 7, 2011), citing the original source, which is: http://www.examiner.com/conservative-in-yakima/never-before-has-nigeria-experienced-such-violence-by-muslims-pt-ii.

238. Muhammad Kabir Isa, "Militant Islamist Groups in Northern Nigeria," p. 332.

239. Charlie Szrom and Chris Harnisch, *Al Qaeda's Operating Environments: A New Approach to the War on Terror* (Washington DC: The American Enterprise Institute, March 2011), p. 10.

240. See James J.F. Forest, "Al Qaeda's Inconvenience Truths: A Study of Influence Warfare," *Perspectives on Terrorism*, 8(1) January 2012.

241. "Is al-Qaeda working in Nigeria?" BBC News (Aug 4 2009), online at: http://news.bbc.co.uk/2/hi/africa/8182289.stm.

242. Paul Ohia, Michael Olugbode and Shola Oyeyipo, "UK Security Agents: Al Qaeda Plans to Operate from Country," *This Day* (4 July 2011), online at: http://allafrica.com/stories/201107061022.html.

243. "Experts warn of alliance between Al-Qa'idah, Nigeria's Boko Haram," *BBC Monitoring International Reports* 15 June 2010. *Academic OneFile*. Web. 20 Nov. 2011.

244. "Boko Haram Releases Eid Al-Fitr Address Via Al Qaeda in North Africa's Media Division Calling on Muslims to Wage Jihad," Arabic Media Monitor, October 2, 2010. And, see "Nigeria: Boko Haram in AQIM's Inner Circle," *The Africa Report*, October 14, 2011. Online at http://www.theafricareport.com/index.php/201110145175378/west-africa/nigeria-boko-haram-in-aqim percentE2 percent80 percent99s-inner-circle-5175378.html.

245. James R. Clapper, "Statement for the Record on the Worldwide Threat Assessment for the U.S. Intelligence Community," Statement of the Director of National Intelligence, February 10, 2011, pg. 18. Available at: http://www.dni.gov/testimonies/20110210_testimony_clapper.pdf.

246. See "Al Qaeda training reaches Nigerian Islamists," *IPT News*, June 16, 2011. However, other sources indicate it may only be speculation that Boko Haram has established links with al-Shabaab. See UN Office for the Coordination of Humanitarian Affairs, "Understanding Boko Haram Radicals," *IRIN News* (July 21, 2011), online at: http://www.irinnews.org/report.aspx?reportid=93250.

247. Ibid.

248. Paul Ohia, Michael Olugbode and Shola Oyeyipo, "UK Security Agents: Al Qaeda Plans to Operate from Country," *This Day* (4 July 2011), online at: http://allafrica.com/stories/201107061022.html.

249. See Alex Thurston, "Nigeria's Terrorism Problem," Foreign Policy (August 26, 2011), online at: http://www.foreignpolicy.com/articles/2011/08/26/nigerias_terrorism_problem; and the BBC news coverage of the attack against the UN building in Abuja, at: http://www.bbc.co.uk/news/world-africa-14677957.

250. Karen Leigh, "Nigeria's Boko Haram: Al-Qaeda's New Friend in Africa?" *TIME Magazine* (August 17, 2011). Online at: http://www.time.com/time/world/article/0,8599,2091137,00.html.

251. "Nigerian security service links Boko Haram extremist to Al Qaeda." *BBC Monitoring International Reports* 2 Sept. 2011. Academic OneFile. Web. 20 Nov. 2011. Also, see "Algiers anti-terrorism forum expresses concern over AQLIM-Boko Haram ties." *BBC Monitoring International Reports* 18 Nov. 2011. *Academic OneFile.* Web. 20 Nov. 2011.

252. David Alexander, "African Islamist group seen as U.S. threat – general," *Reuters* (September 15, 2011). Online at: http://www.reuters.com/article/2011/09/15/us-usa-defense-africa-idUSTRE78E13920110915.

253. Jorge Benitez, "EU official warns of spreading al Qaeda offshoot," NATO Source Alliance News Blog, The Atlantic Council, September 9, 2011. Available at: http://www.acus.org/natosource/eu-official-warnsspreading-al Qaeda-offshoot. Cited in Patrick Meehand and Jackie Speier, *Boko Haram: Emerging Threat to the U.S. Homeland*, U.S. House of Representatives Committee on Homeland Security, Subcommittee on Counterterrorism and Intelligence (November 30, 2011).

254. See Patrick Meehan and Jackie Speier, *Boko Haram: Emerging Threat to the U.S. Homeland*, U.S. House of Representatives Committee on Homeland Security, Subcommittee on Counterterrorism and Intelligence (November 30, 2011), p. 15; and Ezra Ijioma and George Agba, "Boko Haram has Ties with Al Qaeda: Algeria Intelligence," *Leadership* (Abuja), November 14, 2011.

255. U.S. Diplomatic Mission to Nigeria, "Emergency Message for American Citizens" (November 5, 2011), online at: http://nigeria.usembassy.gov/emac_11052011.html. One of the possible hotel targets, the Transcorp Hilton (where I stayed during a week's visit to Abuja) is near the Louis Edet House, the Police Headquarters building where the June 2011 car bomb attack occurred. Also, see "Nigeria: Boko Haram threatens more attacks." *BBC Monitoring International Reports* 9 Nov. 2011. *Academic OneFile.* Web. 20 Nov. 2011.

256. "Boko Haram claims al-Qaeda links," News24, November 24, 2011. Available at:http://m.news24.com/news24/Africa/News/Boko-Haram-claims-al-Qaeda-links-20111124.

257. Patrick Meehan and Jackie Speier, *Boko Haram: Emerging Threat to the U.S. Homeland*, U.S. House of Representatives Committee on Homeland Security, Subcommittee on Counterterrorism and Intelligence (November 30, 2011), p. 13.

258. James R. Clapper, "Unclassified Statement for the Record on the Worldwide Threat Assessment of the U.S. Intelligence Community for the House Permanent Select Committee on Intelligence" (February 2, 2012).

259. Patrick Meehan and Jackie Speier, *Boko Haram: Emerging Threat to the U.S. Homeland*, U.S. House of Representatives Committee on Homeland Security, Subcommittee on Counterterrorism and Intelligence (November 30, 2011), p. 13.

260. Jon Gambrell, "Nigeria: Radical Muslim Sect Grows More Dangerous," Associate Press, November 4, 2011. Online at: http://www.breitbart.com/article.php?id=D9QQ3V200&show_article=1.

261. See John Campbell, "Boko Haram Splits?" Council on Foreign Relations (July 21, 2011) Online at: http://blogs.cfr.org/campbell/2011/07/21/boko-haram-splits/.

262. Jon Gambrell, "Nigeria: Radical Muslim Sect Grows More Dangerous," Associate Press, November 4, 2011. Online at: http://www.breitbart.com/article.php?id=D9QQ3V200&show_article=1.

263. Samuel Aruwan and Dauda Mbaya, "Boko Haram Kills Yusuf's Family Head," *Leadership* (September 18, 2011). Online at: http://www.leadership.ng/nga/articles/5316/2011/09/18/boko_haram_kills_yusuf percentE2 percent80 percent99s_family_head.html; and Samuel Aruwan, "Babakura's Last Word Before His Death," *Leadership* (September 20, 2011). Online at: http://allafrica.com/stories/201109200518.html.

264. Patrick Meehan and Jackie Speier, *Boko Haram* (November 30, 2011), p. 13.

265. Notes from Interviewee #1.

266. Notes from Interviewee #6.

267. John Campbell, "To Battle Nigeria's Boko Haram, Put Down Your Guns: How to Undermine the Growing Islamist Threat, *Foreign Affairs* (September 9, 2011). Online at http://www.foreignaffairs.com/articles/68249/john-campbell/to-battle-nigerias-boko-haram-put-down-your-guns.

268. UN Office for Coordination of Humanitarian Affairs, "Analysis: What Will Follow Boko Haram?" *IRIN News* (November 24, 2011).

269. Jennifer Cooke, Statement before the U.S. House of Representatives, Subcommittee on Counterterrorism and Intelligence, "Hearing on Boko Haram – Emerging Threat to the U.S. Homeland" (November 30, 2011), online at: http://homeland.house.gov/hearing/subcommittee-hearing-boko-haram-emerging-threat-us-homeland.

270. See National Bureau of Statistics, as reported online by the information service Trading Economics (accessed February 29, 2012). http://www.tradingeconomics.com/nigeria/gdp-growth-annual.

271. See Tobi Soniyi, "Nigiera: Boko Haram – Why Security Agencies Have Failed," *This Day* (July 20, 2011), online at: http://allafrica.com/stories/201107201234.html.

272. Jonah Fisher, "Are Nigeria's Boko Haram getting foreign backing?" *BBC* June 21, 2011. http://www.bbc.co.uk/news/world-africa-13843967.

273. UN Office for Coordination of Humanitarian Affairs, "Analysis: What Will Follow Boko Haram?" *IRIN News* (November 24, 2011).

274. Amnesty International, *Killing At Will: Extrajudicial Executions and other Unlawful Killings by the Police in Nigeria* (London: Amnesty International, 2009). Online at: http://www.amnesty.org/en/library/asset/AFR44/038/2009/en/f09b1c15-77b4-40aa-a608-b3b01bde0fc5/afr440382009en.pdf.

275. Stephanie Schwartz, "Is Nigeria a Hotbed of Islamic Extremism?" *USIP Peace Brief* 27 (Washington, DC: U.S. Institute of Peace, May 4, 2010).

276. Human Rights Watch, "Nigeria: Arbitrary Killings by Security Forces in Jos" (December 19, 2008), p. 1, online at: http://www.hrw.org/news/2008/12/19/nigeria-arbitrary-killings-security-forces-jos, as cited in Jonathan Hill, *Sufism in Northern Nigeria* (2010), p. 35.

277. "Understanding Nigeria's Boko Haram Radicals," *IRIN News* (July 18, 2011). Online at: http://www.irinnews.org/report.aspx?reportid=93250.

278. "Nigeria plans talks with Islamist group Boko Haram" *BBC News* (July 30, 2011). Online at: http://www.bbc.co.uk/news/world-africa-14356349.

279. "Understanding Nigeria's Boko Haram Radicals," *IRIN News* (July 18, 2011). Online at: http://www.irinnews.org/report.aspx?reportid=93250.

280. Jonah Fisher, "Are Nigeria's Boko Haram getting foreign backing?" *BBC* (June 21, 2011). http://www.bbc.co.uk/news/world-africa-13843967.

281. Notes from interviewee #3.

282. John Campbell, "To Battle Nigeria's Boko Haram" (September 9, 2011).

283. See Tedd Robert Gurr, *Why Men Rebel* (Princeton, NJ: Princeton University Press, 1970); and Jurgen Habermas, *Legitimation Crisis* (Boston: Beacon Press, 1975).

284. Suleiman M. Bisalla, "Brig-Gen. Raji, the Road to Court Marshal," *Daily Trust* (August 25, 2011). Online at: http://allafrica.com/stories/201108250762.html.

285. For more on this, please see James Forest (ed.), *Influence Warfare: How States and Terrorist Struggle to Shape Perceptions* (Westport, CT: Praeger, 2009).

286. Magali Rheault and Bob Tortora, "Northern Nigerians' Views Not in Line with Boko Haram's," Gallup (February 20, 2012), online at: http://www.gallup.com/poll/152780/northern-nigerians-views-not-line-boko-haram.aspx.

287. For example, see James B. Love, *Hezbollah: Social Services as a Source of Power*, JSOU Report 10-5 (June 2010), Tampa, FL: JSOU Press.

288. BBC News, "'Boko Haram' gunmen kill Nigerian Muslim cleric Birkuti" (June 7, 2011), online at: http://www.bbc.co.uk/news/world-africa-13679234.

289. Abdel-Fatau Musah, *West Africa: Governance and Security in a Changing Region*, (International Peace Institute, February 2009), p. 14.

290. Ibid.

291. Eric Rosand, Alistair Millar and Jason Ipe, *Civil Society and the UN Global Counter-Terrorism Strategy: Opportunities and Challenges* (Washington, DC: Center on Global Counterterrorism Cooperation, September 2008), p. 3.

292. Jonathan Hill, *Sufism in Northern Nigeria: Force for Counter-Radicalization?* (Carlisle, PA: Strategic Studies Institute, 2010), p. 4.

293. Roman Loimeier, Islamic Reform and Political Change in Northern Nigeria (Evanston, IL: Northwestern University Press, 1996), pp. 19-20.

294. Jonathan Hill, *Sufism in Northern Nigeria:* p. 17.

295. Jonathan Hill, *Sufism in Northern Nigeria:* p. 17.

296. This paragraph summarizes Roger Blench, Selbut Longtau, Umar Hassan and Martin Walsh, *The Role of Traditional Rulers in Conflict Prevention and Mediation in Nigeria* (DFID Nigeria, September 2006), p. 24.

297. Jonathan Hill, *Sufism in Northern Nigeria:* p. 15.

298. Muhammad Kabir Isa, "Militant Islamist Groups in Northern Nigeria," in *Militias, Rebels and Islamist Militants: Human Insecurity and State Crises in Africa*, edited by Wafulu Okumu and Augustine Ikelegbe (Pretoria: Institute for Security Studies, 2010), p. 329.

299. For example, see Roman Loimeier, *Islamic Reform and Political Change in Northern Nigeria* (Evanston, IL: Northwestern University Press, 1996).

300. Jonathan Hill, *Sufism as a Force* (2010), p. 18.

301. Peter Chalk, "Islam in West Africa: The Case of Nigeria," *The Muslim World After 9/11*, edited by Angel M. Rabasa, Cheryl Benard, Peter Chalk et al. (Santa Monica, CA: RAND Corporation, 2004), p. 419.

302. Ibid, 419.

303. Li Alkali, Samuel Aruwan and Abdulrahaman Tonga, "Sheikh Gumi Released" Leadership (Abuja), Sept. 5, 2010. Online at: http://allafrica.com/stories/201009060437.html.

304. As noted earlier, 12 northern states—including Zamfara, Sokoto, Kano, Katsina and Niger—have passed into law the criminal law sections of the Islamic Shari'a, with punishments ranging from flogging for imbibing alcohol to stoning in cases of proven adultery.

305. Charlie Szrom and Chris Harnisch, *Al Qaeda's Operating Environments: A New Approach to the War on Terror* (Washington DC: The American Enterprise Institute, March 2011), p. 10.

306. 306 Jonah Fisher, "Are Nigeria's Boko Haram getting foreign backing?" BBC June 21, 2011. http://www.bbc.co.uk/news/world-africa-13843967.

307. Jonathan Hill, *Sufism in Northern Nigeria:* p. 13.

308. Jonathan Hill, *Sufism in Northern Nigeria:* p. 13.

309. Stephanie Schwartz, "Is Nigeria a Hotbed of Islamic Extremism?" USIP Peace Brief 27 (Washington, DC: U.S. Institute of Peace, May 4, 2010).

310. Ibid.

311. See LibForAll Foundation, http://www.libforall.org/home.html as cited in Rosand, et al. *Civil Society and the UN Global Counter-Terrorism Strategy* (2008), p. 9.

312. Eric Rosand, Alistair Millar and Jason Ipe, *Civil Society and the UN Global Counter-Terrorism Strategy: Opportunities and Challenges* (Washington, DC: Center on Global Counterterrorism Cooperation, September 2008), p. 9.

313. For descriptions and photos of recent traditional and political leaders of Nigeria, please see the website: http://www.kingdomsofnigeria.com/.

314. For a detailed account of Nigeria's pre-colonial and colonial history, please see: Toyin Falola and Matthew Heaton, *A History of Nigeria* (Cambridge University Press, 2008); David Northrup, *Trade Without Rulers: Pre-Colonial Economic Development in South-Eastern Nigeria* (Oxford University Press, 1978); and Oma Djebah, et al., "Royal Fathers: Their Power, Influence, Relevance," *BNW News* (2003-08-31), available online at: http://news.biafranigeriaworld.com/archive/2003/aug/31/028.html.

315. Roger Blench, Selbut Longtau, Umar Hassan and Martin Walsh, *The Role of Traditional Rulers in Conflict Prevention and Mediation in Nigeria* (DFID Nigeria, September 2006), p. 11.

316. Blench, et. al., p. 1.

317. Sklar, Richard L. "The Premise of Mixed Government in African Political Studies," in O. Vaughan (ed.) *Indigenous Political Structures and Governance in Africa* (Ibadan: Sefer Books Ltd, 2003), pp. 3-25.

318. William F. S. Miles, "Traditional rulers and development administration: Chieftaincy in Niger, Nigeria, and Vanuatu," *Studies in Comparative International Development, Volume 28, Number 3*, (Fall 1993), pp. 31-50.

319. Blench, et al., p. 24.

320. For example of community decision-makers, see F.A. Kuponiyi, "Community Power Structure: The Role of Local Leaders in Community Development Decision Making in Ajaawa, Oyo State, Nigeria," *Anthropologist* 10(4), (2008) pp. 239-243.

321. See Ali D. Yahaya, "Traditional leadership and institutions" in *Northern Nigeria: A Century of Transformation, 1903-2003*, edited by Alhaji M. Yakuba, Ibrahim M. Jumane, Asmain G. Saeed (2005: Arewa House, Ahmadu Bello University, Kaduna, Nigeria), p. 242.

322. Blench, et. al., p. 126.

323. Information on most of the organizations listed here can be found online through various search engines, though in several cases an organization is very small and does not have its own web presence.

324. Lauren Ploch, "Nigeria: Elections and Issues for Congress," Congressional Research Service (May 17, 2011), p. 1. Online at: http://assets.opencrs.com/rpts/RL33964_20110401.pdf.

325. "France to help Nigeria with Boko Haram militants," defenceWeb, November 14, 2011. Online at: http://www.defenceweb.co.za/index.php?option=com_content&view=article&id=21097:france-to-helpnigeria-with-boko-haram-militants&catid=56:diplomacy-a-peace&Itemid=111.

326. U.S. House of Representatives, 2011, p. 24.

327. Lauren Ploch, "Nigeria: Elections and Issues for Congress," Congressional Research Service (May 17, 2011), p. 29. Online at: http://assets.opencrs.com/rpts/RL33964_20110401.pdf.

328. See James J.F. Forest, "Terrorism as a Product of Choices and Perceptions," in *Terrorizing Ourselves*, edited by Benjamin H. Friedman, Jim Harper, and Christopher A. Preble (Washington, DC: Cato Institute, 2010), pp. 23-44; and James Forest (ed.), *Influence Warfare: How States and Terrorist Struggle to Shape Perceptions* (Westport, CT: Praeger, 2009).

329. Niger Delta Technical Committee Report, 2008.

330. Ibrahim Mshelizza, "Nigerian Islamist Sect Rejects Amnesty Deal," *Reuters* (May 10, 2011). Online at: http://af.reuters.com/article/topNews/idAF-JOE74902620110510; and Alex Thurston, "Nigeria's Islamist Rebel Group Rejects Amnesty Deal," *Christian Science Monitor* (May 16, 2011). Online at: http://www.csmonitor.com/World/Africa/Africa-Monitor/2011/0516/Nigeria-s-Islamist-rebel-group-rejects-amnesty-deal.

331. Department of Defense, *Irregular Warfare (IW) Joint Operating Concept (JOC)*, September 11, 2007, p. 6. Online at: http://www.fas.org/irp/doddir/dod/iw-joc.pdf.

332. Cindy R. Jebb and Madelfia A. Abb, "Human Security and Good Governance: A Living Systems Approach to Understanding and Combating Terrorism," in *The Making of a Terrorist, Volume 3: Root Causes*, edited by James J.F. Forest (Westport, CT: Praeger, 2005).

333. Patrick Meehan and Jackie Speier, *Boko Haram: Emerging Threat to the U.S. Homeland*, U.S. House of Representatives Committee on Homeland Security, Subcommittee on Counterterrorism and Intelligence (November 30, 2011), p. 26.

334. For details, see Robert J. Pauly, Jr. and Robert W. Redding, Denying Terrorists Sanctuary Through Civil Military Operations," in *Countering Terrorism and Insurgency in the 21st Century (Volume 1: Strategic and Tactical Considerations)*, edited by James J.F. Forest (Westport, CT: Praeger Security International, 2007), pp. 273-297.

335. U.S. House of Representatives, 2011, p. 24.

336. Greg Miller, "U.S. officials believe al-Qaeda on brink of collapse," *Washington Post* July 26, 2011). Online at: http://www.washingtonpost.com/world/national-security/al-qaeda-could-collapse-us-officials-say/2011/07/21/gIQAFu2pbI_story_1.html . Also, see Roby C. Barrett, Yemen: *A Different Political Paradigm in Context*, JSOU Report 11-3 (May 2011), Tampa, FL: JSOU Press.

337. Russell D. Howard, *Intelligence in Denied Areas*, JSOU Report 07-10 (December 2007) Tampa, FL: JSOU Press, pp. 25-32, 29.

338. Ibid., 27.

339. Jessica Glicken Turnley, *Cross-Cultural Competence and Small Groups: Why SOF are the Way SOF are*, JSOU Report 11-1 (March 2011) Tampa, FL: JSOU Press, pp. 10-11.

340. Jonah Fisher, "Are Nigeria's Boko Haram getting foreign backing?" *BBC* June 21, 2011. http://www.bbc.co.uk/news/world-africa-13843967.

341. Jack Marr, John Cushing, Brandon Garner and Richard Thompson, "Human Terrain Mapping: A Critical First Step to Winning the COIN Fight, *Military Review* 88 (March/April 2008), p. 37-51; Todd J. Hamill, Richard F. Drecko, James W. Chrissis, and Robert F. Mills, "Analysis of Layered Social Networks," *IO Sphere* (Winter 2008); and Montgomery McFate, "The Military Utility of Understanding Adversary Culture." *Joint Forces Quarterly* 38 (Third Quarter 2005), pp. 42-48.

342. Admiral Eric T. Olson, USSOCOM Posture Statement (June 4, 2009), p. 3. Also, the United States Special Operations Command (USSOCOM) *Strategic Plan, Focus Area 1: The Operator* notes that "The Operator needs to be prepared to excel across the myriad of defense, diplomacy, and development activities..." DOD USSOCOM Strategic Plan (December 18, 2009), p. 8.

343. For example, Christopher Jasparro recently argued that countering an ideology requires determining where a message originates from, along what paths it has diffused, and how the conditions by which it resonates vary from place to place. [0]See Christopher Jasparro, "Sociocultural, Economic and Demographic Aspects of Counterterrorism," in *Countering Terrorism and Insurgency in the 21st Century (Vol. 2: Combating the Sources and Facilitators)*, edited by James J.F. Forest (Westport, CT: Praeger, 2007).

344. Kim Cragin and Scott Gerwehr, *Dissuading Terror: Strategic Influence and the Struggle Against Terrorism* (Santa Monica, CA: RAND Corporation, 2005); and Kim Cragin and Peter Chalk, *Terrorism and Development: Using Social and Economic Development to Inhibit a Resurgence of Terrorism.* (Santa Monica, CA: RAND Corporation, 2003).

345. For example, Anthony Cordesman recently argued that Saudi security is best protected through social, religious and economic reforms, and not by their current security-only approach. Anthony H. Cordesman, "Saudi Security and the War on Terrorism: International Security Operations, Law Enforcement, Internal Threats, and the Need for Change." Center for Strategic and International Studies (March 2002). Online at: http://www.csis.org/media/csis/pubs/saudiwarterr030302.pdf. Sherifa Zuhur recommends that the United States encourage the Saudi government to increase political participation, improve the intelligence services, urge responsiveness to human rights, and increase multilateral discussions relating to anti-terrorism. Sherifa Zuhur, "Saudi Arabia: Islamic Threat, Political Reform, and the Global War on Terror." Strategic Studies Institute (March 2005), p. 1-65. Online at http://www.strategicstudiesinstitute.army.mil/Pubs/display.cfm?pubID=598.

346. Adam Nossiter, "Western Officials Seek Softer Approach to Militants in Nigeria," *New York Times* (August 31, 2011), p. A9. Online at: http://www.nytimes.com/2011/08/31/world/africa/31nigeria.html?_r=1&ref=global-home.

347. Lauren Ploch, "Nigeria: Elections and Issues for Congress," Congressional Research Service (May 17, 2011), p. 30. Online at: http://assets.opencrs.com/rpts/RL33964_20110401.pdf.

348. Lauren Ploch, "Nigeria: Elections and Issues for Congress," Congressional Research Service (May 17, 2011), p. 30. Online at: http://assets.opencrs.com/rpts/RL33964_20110401.pdf.

349. Unless otherwise indicated by separate citations, the sources for the incidents listed here include the Global Terrorism Database, 1970-2010 (National Consortium for the Study of Terrorism and Response to Terrorism, University of Maryland); Freedom C. Onuoha, "The Islamist Challenge: Nigeria's Boko Haram crisis explained," *African Security Review* 19, no. 2 (June 2010), p. 7; and John Campbell, Nigeria Security Tracker (filter: Boko Haram), a crowdmap resource online at: https://nigeriasecuritytracker.crowdmap.com/main. To read more about John Campbell's work, visit http://blogs.cfr.org/campbell.

350. "Boko Haram Jailbreak: The Morning After," This Day (September 20, 2010), online at: http://allafrica.com/stories/201009220395.html.

351. see Imam, I., and Adinoyi, S. (2010) "Jos Bombings: Group Claims Responsibility" This day, 27 December, http://www.thisdayonline.info/nview.php?id=190764.

352. See "Nigerian police: Gubernatorial candidate assassinated," CNN (January 28, 2011). Online at: http://edition.cnn.com/2011/WORLD/africa/01/28/nigeria.violence/; and "Six killed in Nigerian political massacre," *The Daily* (January 28, 2011). Online at: http://www.telegraph.co.uk/news/worldnews/africaandindianocean/nigeria/8289512/Six-killed-in-Nigerian-political-massacre.html.

353. See Boko Haram and Nigeria's Elections, http://sahelblog.wordpress.com/2011/04/25/boko-haram-and-nigerias-elections.

354. Joe Brock, "Nigerian Islamist sect claims bomb attack: paper." *Reuters*. (June 17, 2011), online at: http://af.reuters.com/article/topNews/idAFJOE75G0BF20110617?sp=true; "Army Barracks Attack Ahead of Goodluck Jonathan's Inauguration," http://www.reuters.com/article/2011/05/30/us-nigeria-explosion-idUSTRE74S2O220110530; and http://www.vanguardngr.com/2011/06/boko-haram-claims-responsibility-for-bomb-blasts-in-bauchi-maiduguri/; and "Evening Attack in Zaria," Weekly Trust (May 29, 2011), online at: http://weeklytrust.com.ng/?option=com_content&view=article&id=6234:inauguration-day-blastshow-bombs-affected-our-lives-by-victims&catid=40:coverstories&Itemid=26.

355. "Shehu of Borno's Brother Killed," (May 30, 2011) online at: http://allafrica.com/stories/201106010765.html.

356. "David Usman Shot Dead," *BBC News* (June 7, 2011), online at: http://www.bbc.co.uk/news/world-africa-13724349; and "Militants Kill Muslim Cleric Ibrahim Burkuti", BBC News (June 6, 2011), online at: http://www.bbc.co.uk/news/world-

africa-13724349; and http://www.iol.co.za/news/africa/radical-cleric-gunned-down-in-nigeria-1.1079878.

357. Ahmed Mari, "Five Killed in Fresh Bomb Explosions in Maiduguri," *Daily Champion* (June 7, 2011), online at: http://allafrica.com/stories/201106080755.html; See also "11 killed in multiple bombings in Nigerian city," Panapress (June 7, 2011), online at: http://www.panapress.com/11-killed-in-multiple-bombings-in-Nigerian-city--12-777249-30-lang2-index.html; and Hamza Idris and Yahaya Ibrahim, "Three Blasts Kill 10 in Bono," *Daily Trust* (8 June 2011), online at: http://allafrica.com/stories/201106080424.html.

358. Ndahi Marama, "Another Bomb Explosion Kills 4 in Borno - as Boko Haram Claims Responsibility for Abuja Blast," Vanguard (16 June 2011). Online at: http://allafrica.com/stories/201106170218.html; and "Explosion kills four children in Borno," *Reuters* (June 17, 2011), online at: http://234next.com/csp/cms/sites/Next/News/Metro/Politics/5717053-147/explosion_kills_four_children_in_borno.csp.

359. Misbahu Bashir, Abubakar Yakubu & Ronald Mutum, 8 killed in Force Hqtrs blasts," *Daily Trust* (June 17, 2011). Online at: http://dailytrust.com.ng/index.php?option=com_content&view=article&id=21286:8-killed-in-force-hqtrs-blasts&catid=2:lead-stories&Itemid=8.

360. "Death toll in Boko Haram attack rises to five," *Next* (June 20, 2011), online at: http://234next.com/csp/cms/sites/Next/News/5719549147/death_toll_in_boko_haram_attack.csp; and Ndahi Marama, "Boko Haram Strikes Again, Kill Two in Maiduguri," *Vanguard* (20 June 2011), online at: http://allafrica.com/stories/201106201962.html.

361. Muawiyya Garba Funtua, "Nigeria Police: 8 Killed in Sect-Style Killings," *ABC News* (June 21, 2011). Online at: http://abcnews.go.com/International/wireStory?id=13892080.

362. "Nigerian bank and police station attacked in Katsina," *BBC News* (June 21, 2011), online at: http://www.bbc.co.uk/news/world-africa-13861739.

363. Will Connors, "Nigeria Struggles Against Militant Upsurge," *Wall Street Journal* (June 29, 2011), online at: http://online.wsj.com/article/SB10001424052702303627104576413954141322660.html.

364. Hamza Idris and Yahaya Ibrahim, "LG Boss Killed, Bomb Blast in Maiduguri," *Daily Trust*, (July 4, 2011). Online at: http://allafrica.com/stories/201107041536.html; "Blast kills five at northeast Nigeria bar," *Reuters* (July 3, 2011), online at: http://allafrica.com/stories/201107041536.html; and "Boko Haram kills LG boss, 4 others in Borno" (July 4, 2011). Online at: http://www.vanguardngr.com/2011/07/boko-haram-kills-lg-boss-4-others-in-borno/.

365. Daniel Kanu, Andrew Utulu, Rotimi Akinwumi And Abdulkareem Haruna, "Boko Haram Kills Four, Steals N21.5 Million LG Salaries in Borno," Daily Independent (July 4, 2011). Online at: http://allafrica.com/stories/201107050865.html; and Yahaya Ibrahim, "Robbers kill four, snatch local govt salary in Borno," *Daily Trust* (July 5, 2011). Online at: http://dailytrust.com.ng/index.php?option=com_c

ontent&view=article&id=22369:robbers-kill-four-snatch-local-govt-salary-in-borno&catid=1:news&Itemid=2.

366. Abdulkareem Haruna and Patience Ogbodo, "Boko Haram Overruns Bauchi Police Armoury," Daily Independent (July 6, 2011), online at: http://allafrica.com/stories/201107070671.html.

367. Hamza Idris, "Six Killed As JTF Patrol Team Escapes Blast in Borno," *Daily Trust* (July 6, 2011), online at: http://allafrica.com/stories/201107071059.html.

368. "Several injured by explosion in north Nigeria town," *Reuters Africa*, (July 10, 2011), online at: http://af.reuters.com/article/nigeriaNews/idAFLDE76A0ZF20110711.

369. "Teacher Gunned Down in Maiduguri" *Leadership* (August 8, 2011).

370. "Attack on Maiduguri Police Station" *This Day* (August 9, 2011).

371. "Muslim Cleric Assassinated in Ngala" *AFP* (August 12, 2011).

372. "Suicide Bomber Dies in Unsuccessful Maiduguri Attack," *Reuters* (August 15, 2011).

373. "Suspected Boko Haram Members Kill Policemen" *Reuters* (August 19, 2011).

374. "Police, Bank Attacks in Gombi," *AFP* (August 25, 2011).

375. "Attack on UN Headquarters in Abuja" STRATFOR (August 26, 2011), online at: http://www.stratfor.com/analysis/20110826-nigeria-boko-haram-demonstrates-improved-capability-un-bombing.

376. "Gunmen Shot Muslim Cleric Dead in Maiduguri" *Ascology News* (September 4, 2011).

377. "Seven Die in Misau," *Vanguard* (September 12, 2011).

378. Four Dead in Maiduguri Shooting, *Reuters* (September 13, 2011).

379. "Bombing and Shootout in Maiduguri," *AFP* (October 1, 2011).

380. "Gunmen Murder Three in Maiduguri," *AFP* (October 3, 2011).

381. "Bomb Blast, Shooting Rock Nigerian City," *AFP* (October 9, 2011). Online at: http://beegeagle.wordpress.com/2011/10/09/bomb-blast-shooting-rock-nigerian-city-police/.

382. "Boko Haram Muslim Sect Attacks Nigerian Bank," *Huffington Post* (October 12, 2011). Online at: http://www.huffingtonpost.com/2011/10/12/boko-haram-muslim-sect_n_1007111.html.

383. "Prison Guard Killed by Suspected Militants in Maiduguri" *Associated Press* (October 13, 2011).

384. "Borno Vigilante Head Killed," *Daily Trust* (October 15, 2011).

385. "Nigerian lawmaker shot dead, police suspect sect," *Reuters* (October 17, 2011). Online at: http://af.reuters.com/article/topNews/idAFJOE79G09E20111017.

386. "Gombe Police Station Blast Kills Three," Reuters (October 16, 2011).

387. "Muslim Cleric and His Student Killed in Maiduguri," *Daily Trust* (October 19, 2011).

388. "Nigerian sect says killed journalist for spying." *Reuters*. (October 25, 2011). Online at: http://af.reuters.com/article/nigeriaNews/idAFL5E7LP1WQ20111025.

389. "Gunmen Murder Borno Cleric," *Daily Trust* (October 29, 2011).

390. "Explosion Rocks Maiduguri," *ANP/AFP* (October 30, 2011).

391. "Suicide Bombers Hit Military HQ in Maiduguri," *AFP* (November 4, 2011); and "Gunmen Kill Soldier in Maiduguri," *Daily Trust* (November 4, 2011).

392. "Nigeria Boko Haram attack 'kills 63' in Damaturu." *BBC News*. (November 5, 2011). Online at: http://www.bbc.co.uk/news/world-africa-15605041; and Jon Gambrell, "Nigeria: Boko Haram Suicide Attack Killed Dozens." *Huffington Post World*. (November 5, 2011). Online at: http://www.huffingtonpost.com/2011/11/05/nigeria-boko-haram-suicide-attack_n_1077595.html.

393. "Attack on Police Station in Mainok," *Leadership* (November 9, 2011).

394. "Boko Haram Kills Village Head's Brother," *The Nation* (November 11, 2011). Online at: http://issuu.com/thenation/docs/november_11__2011.

395. "Two Wounded in Bomb Blast," Radio Netherlands Worldwide (November 13, 2011).

396. "Man Gunned Down Near Shehu of Borno's Palace," *Leadership* (November 13, 2011).

397. "Gunmen Kill Student," *Guardian*, (November 14, 2011).

398. "Attack on Maiduguri Police Station," *Leadership* (November 21, 2011). Online at: http://allafrica.com/stories/201111230178.html.

399. "Protocol Officer and Herbalist Gunned Down," *Daily Trust* (November 21, 2011). Online at: http://allafrica.com/stories/201111280351.html.

400. "Boko Haram Claims Responsibility for Nigeria Attacks," *The Telegraph* (December 25, 2011), online at: http://www.telegraph.co.uk/news/worldnews/africaandindianocean/nigeria/8977493/Boko-Haram-claims-responsibility-for-Nigeria-attacks.html; and "Nigeria's Boko Haram Blamed for Maiduguri attack," *BBC News* (December 30, 2011), online at: http://www.bbc.co.uk/news/world-16366477.

401. "Nigerian death toll from Boko Haram attacks 'nears 1,000'," *Reuters*, January 24, 2012. Online at: http://www.guardian.co.uk/world/2012/jan/24/boko-haram-killed-nearly-1000.

402. "Nigeria's Boko Haram suspected in Kano police attack," *BBC News*, January 30, 2012. Online at: http://www.bbc.co.uk/news/world-africa-16786025.

403. Job Gambrell, "Sect Gunmen Free 119 in Nigeria Prison, Kill Guard," *Associated Press*, February 16, 2012. Online at: http://abcnews.go.com/topics/news/world/boko-haram.htm.

404. Women, children killed as Boko Haram attack market," *Vanguard* (Nigeria), February 20, 2012. Online at: http://www.vanguardngr.com/2012/02/30-killed-as-boko-haram-attack-market/.

405.   Ahmed Saka and Job Gambrell, "Suicide car bomber kills 3 outside Nigeria church," *Associated Press*, February 26, 2012. Online at: http://abcnews.go.com/topics/news/world/boko-haram.htm.

406.   "Boko Haram attacks police state in Adamawa State." *Sahara Reporters*, February 28, 2012. Online at: http://saharareporters.com/news-page/boko-haram-attacks-police-station-adamawa-state.

407.   Haruna Umar and Shehu Saulawa, "Police station, schools attacked in North Nigeria," *Associated Press*, February 28, 2012. Online at: http://abcnews.go.com/topics/news/world/boko-haram.htm.

GPO U.S. GOVERNMENT PRINTING OFFICE: 2012—530–020/60010